The T

This volume is dedicated to

Ehsan Yarshater (1920–2018)
Gilbert Lazard (1920–2018)

Already available in *The Idea of Iran* series

Birth of the Persian Empire, Vol. 1
Edited by Vesta Sarkhosh Curtis (British Museum) and Sarah Stewart (SOAS, London).
ISBN: 978-1-84511-062-5

The Age of the Parthians, Vol. 2
Edited by Vesta Sarkhosh Curtis (British Museum) and Sarah Stewart (SOAS, London).
ISBN: 978-1-84511-406-0

The Sasanian Era, Vol. 3
Edited by Vesta Sarkhosh Curtis (British Museum) and Sarah Stewart (SOAS, London).
ISBN: 978-1-84511-690-3

The Rise of Islam, Vol. 4
Edited by Vesta Sarkhosh Curtis (British Museum) and Sarah Stewart (SOAS, London).
ISBN: 978-1-84511-691-0

Early Islamic Iran, Vol. 5
Edited by Edmund Herzig (University of Oxford) and Sarah Stewart (SOAS, London).
ISBN: 978-1-78076-061-2

The Age of the Seljuqs, Vol. 6
Edited by Edmund Herzig (University of Oxford) and Sarah Stewart (SOAS, London).
ISBN: 978-1-78076-947-9

The Coming of Mongols, Vol. 7
Edited by David O. Morgan (University Wisconsin-Madison) and Sarah Stewart (SOAS, London).
ISBN: 978 1 78831 285 1

Iran After the Mongols, Vol. 8
Edited by Sussan Babaie (The Courtauld Institute of Art, University of London).
ISBN: 978-1-7883-1528-9

The Timurid Century

The Idea of Iran

Volume IX

Edited By

Charles Melville

(University of Cambridge)

in association with The London Middle East Institute at SOAS

Supported by the Soudavar Memorial Foundation

SOUDAVAR
MEMORIAL FOUNDATION

I.B.TAURIS

LONDON • NEW YORK • OXFORD • NEW DELHI • SYDNEY

I.B.TAURIS
Bloomsbury Publishing Plc
50 Bedford Square, London, WC1B 3DP, UK
1385 Broadway, New York, NY 10018, USA

BLOOMSBURY, I.B. TAURIS and the I.B. TAURIS logo are trademarks of Bloomsbury Publishing Plc

First published in Great Britain 2020

Cover image: Arthur M. Sackler Gallery, Smithsonian Institution, Washington, D.C.: The Art and History Collection, LTS1995.2.27

A catalogue record for this book is available from the British Library.
A catalog record for this book is available from the Library of Congress.

ISBN: HB: 978-1-8386-0613-8
PB: 978-1-8386-0688-6
ePDF: 978-1-8386-0615-2
eBook: 978-1-8386-0614-5

Series: The Idea of Iran, volume 9

Typeset by P. Fozooni

Printed and bound in Great Britain

To find out more about our authors and books visit www.bloomsbury.com and sign up for our newsletters.

Contents

Illustrations

Acknowledgements

The first volume of the *Idea of Iran* was published in 2005 and the current volume, number 9, is testimony to the continuing success of the annual Symposia and the appeal of the topic to which they are devoted; both the conferences and publications have become a popular contribution to academic work on Iran.

The publication of the Series is due to the generosity of the Soudavar Memorial Foundation and its continued support year after year. We are particularly grateful to Mrs Fatema Soudavar-Farmanfarmaian for her interest and advice and for helping to ensure the success of the Series. As always, the publication would not have been possible without the skill and meticulous eye for detail of Parvis Fozooni, who formats and typesets the papers. We also thank Andy Platts for her invaluable copy-editing and Judith Acevedo for preparing the Index.

Although her name no longer appears on the cover, I would like to acknowledge the continuing vital role played by my colleague, Dr Sarah Stewart from SOAS, who has shepherded both the Symposia and the resulting publications through their evolution from the very outset. Her experience and support have been crucial in getting yet another volume into the light of day.

This volume is dedicated to the memory and outstanding achievements in the field of Persian studies of Ehsan Yarshater, himself an embodiment of the Idea of Iran, and of Gilbert Lazard, who gave so much to the study of Persian language and linguistics: both passed away in September 2018.

We would like to thank Joanna Godfrey and Rory Gormley and the staff at I.B. Tauris/Bloomsbury for their help in producing the publication.

Introduction

Charles Melville
(University of Cambridge)

The 'Timurid' symposium, sponsored by the Soudavar Memorial Foundation, took place on 18–19 November 2017, under the somewhat provocative title, 'The Turko-Timurid Intermezzo'. The notion behind this was that, in the period between the collapse of the 'Abbasid Caliphate in 1258 and the advent of the Safavids in 1501, the nature of the state was more ostensibly secular than it had been under the Sunni–Islamic hegemony of the caliphs and those claiming their delegated authority that preceded the Mongol invasions, and was again under the charismatic Shi'i–Sufi rule introduced by the Safavids that followed the fall of the Timurids. Religion, of course, did not disappear. The Mongols' conversion to Islam after 1295 provided government with one plank of its legitimacy, but the rulers themselves claimed no spiritual authority and relied, apart from their military powers of coercion, on their Chinggisid descent or primacy within the essentially nomadic structures imported from the Inner Asian steppes.

Whatever the value of such a perspective on the nature of rule in the Mongol and Timurid periods, the concept of an 'intermezzo' did not find favour; for a start, 250 years is too long for an interval and perhaps the Timurid century likewise, though Vladimir Minorsky's celebrated 'Iranian intermezzo', identifying the brief period between the Arab and Turkish monopoly of rule on the Iranian plateau, lasted 110 years.[1] Hans Roemer's proposal of a 'Turkmen intermezzo'[2] is now considered to be rather dated. More importantly, recent work has shown how a significant element of the fusion of Perso-Islamic and Mongol traditions that emerged in the Ilkhanid and Timurid era was the formulation of a sacral kingship that endowed the rulers with a universal heaven-derived kingship, starting with Ghazan Khan, which allowed 'divinized forms of kingship to inhabit the Islamic monotheistic world'.[3] And indeed, there are much greater continuities in this and other aspects of the times between and within the pre-Mongol and post-Mongol periods than are generally acknowledged.

Beatrice Manz's chapter in this volume highlights many recurring patterns of succession practices, of interactions between rulers and their bureaucracies, the military contributions of the Iranians alongside the warlike Turks, centre–periphery relations and the geographical delineations of power, not to mention a shared 'mythical' past of very long-term encounters across the Oxus as expressed in the *Shahnama*. These can be found equally in the Safavid period that followed. Daniel Zakrzewski's examination of the role of Tabriz as a capital, perceived as bestowing power over the whole kingdom of Iran on whoever controlled the city, regardless of the actual extent of territorial control, also focuses on one specific aspect of this question. At the same time, he nicely links the patronage of religious complexes and monuments with the projection of royal splendour: again, hardly something novel or unique to the Timurid era.

It is perhaps easier to imagine Persian history as a slowly evolving continuum, cut up into 'dynastic periods' or centuries for convenience, and the 'Idea of Iran' likewise. A thematic, rather than a chronological, framework would no doubt stimulate many refreshing insights into the essence of Persian government, religion, economy, art, language and literature as cultivated in Iran's diverse landscapes over the centuries. Nevertheless, in the current scheme of things, we are starting to leave the Mongols and the turbulent, blood-soaked fourteenth century behind and to contemplate a new era, often regarded as marking a high point of artistic achievements. Were there distinctive elements about the Timurid century and were they apparent to its contemporaries?

The fifteenth century saw the slow disintegration of the empire roughly assembled through the military conquests of Timur (d. 1405), ultimately dividing Iran (as so often in the past) into independent realms to the East and West of the central *kavir*. While the Timurids retained their hold on Khorasan and Transoxiana, the west was lost to the Qara Qoyunlu and Aq Qoyunlu Turkmen regimes. Both polities were the heirs of the Chinggisid dispensation and, despite their political rivalries, grappled with the same questions of legitimacy and exemplify the same process of combining the 'steppe' notions of rule with Perso-Islamic concepts and a centralized bureaucracy with powerful autonomous apanage holders. The period also witnessed popular challenges to Sunni religious orthodoxy and a renewed emphasis on the scholarly achievements of the past. In the meantime, a great cultural florescence, partly born of the rivalry of competing courts, notably at Herat, Samarqand, Tabriz, Shiraz and Baghdad, make the fifteenth century a byword for great artistic, literary and scientific activity.

What does the Idea of Iran mean at this period? Can we discern the ways that contemporaries viewed their traditions and their environment (natural or built); what was the view of outsiders, and how does modern scholarship define the distinctive aspects of the period? These are some of the questions explored in the symposium dedicated to this rich and highly productive interval that was the springboard for the formation of new imperial Ottoman, Safavid, Mughal and Ozbek orders of succeeding centuries.

Historiographers carry a heavy load in recording their era, in their choice of material and the way it is reported. Many of them were bureaucrats and literati, usually attached to a court and importantly, therefore, writing for a patron.

They are, naturally, among the main sources for our own ideas of Iran at the time they were writing. Shahzad Bashir reviews two history books, written at either end of the Timurid century: Taj-e Salmani's history of ca. 1410, covering the five turbulent years after the death of Timur, and Fazlollah Khonj-Esfahani's *Mehman-nama-ye Bokhara*, written a century later, concerning his sojourn in Ozbek Transoxiana. Although both are works of history, recording events of the time through a particular lens – a highly personal one in the case of Khonji-Esfahani, writing far from home – what is striking is their literary quality, their use of language to emphasize moral, religious or political precepts and the highly selective nature of their narrative of events.

The Persian language is indeed a crucial ingredient of Iran's cultural identity – how could it be otherwise? The awareness of the works of past masters and the deeply felt need to be embedded in the same strong literary, artistic and scientific traditions, through emulation, translation or expropriation, can be found in vigorous existence throughout the Timurid century. It is expressed in the production of 'universal' histories and biographical dictionaries of poets and saints, the compilation of albums of painting and calligraphy and production of scientific texts in Persian. Admiration for the *ghazal*s of Hafez of Shiraz and their mystical richness, developed in the Sufi-infused context of the court of Soltan-Hoseyn-e Bayqara in Herat, was articulated in emulations of his poetry in both Persian and Turkish, as Marc Toutant reveals in connection with the famous opening ghazal of Hafez's *Divan*. Maria Subtelny's chapter examines how the same court environment witnessed the sustained effort of Hoseyn Va'ez Kashefi in translating into Persian and rewriting the works of his predecessors across a range of religious, literary, ethical and esoteric subjects, to the point of what would now be considered plagiarism but at the time could be viewed as a legitimate attempt to absorb and surpass them, preserving them in a form appropriate for new late-Timurid audiences. At the same time, as shown by Elaheh Kheirandish, an effort of translation of a classic Arabic work on practical geometry also speaks of the continuing vitality of Iranian contributions to this field of scientific investigation, as well as the desire to make it accessible to Persianate scholarship.

As in science and literature, so in the arts of the book, and particularly the illumination and beautification of poetic and literary texts: that is, awareness of a tradition – relatively recent, with antecedents in the previous century – taken forward and developed to an extraordinary pitch of refinement under the impetus of Timurid patronage. Eleanor Sims' chapter identifies the scale and proportions as one distinctive element of Timurid manuscript production. Her dissection of the celebrated single-page painting of Homay meeting Homayun in a beautiful (and 'typical') Persian garden notes its timeless qualities, enhanced indeed by the lack of certainty as to when and where it was actually created. Elements and models from across the Persianate cultural zone are drawn together into a fortunate synthesis that could itself be taken as one of the hallmarks of the Timurid century.

While the majority of chapters in the volume to hand speak of the Iranians' engagement with their own unfolding history, operating within the broad confines of the Persian-speaking Eastern Islamic world, there are a few hints of interactions beyond this already wide region. In the case of the sciences, there is evidence of an awareness of developments in the European West, specifically in mechanical clock making. Western appreciation of the contributions of Ologh Beg's observatory and team of astronomers at Samarqand lay well in the future, but some exchange of knowledge and a recognition of technical skills enjoyed by Iranian scholars certainly existed. We have few other indications of the perception of Iranian society at this time in the eyes of contemporaries, but two Iranian travel narratives discussed by John Woods give us a brief insight into encounters with the wider world beyond Iran's territorial borders. Both journeys were essentially pilgrimages and took the authors to the Arab lands and the Ottoman Empire, where one of them, Sayyed Mir 'Ali Tusi (a native of Mashhad) remained. Sayyed Kamal al-Din Abivardi, on the other hand, returned to Herat after his travels had taken him to the other capital cities, Constantinople, Cairo and Tabriz. His journey seems to have been as much in pursuit of love as for any more formal reason, and his anecdotes reflect something of how the Iranians (the *'Ajamis*) were perceived by those he encountered in what turned out, it seems, to be an unsuccessful quest.

Regrettably, Michele Bernardini's contribution to the symposium, 'The exaltation of Iran by others: The Turks as promoters of the Idea of Iran', and Elena Paskaleva's presentation of her fresh archival discoveries relating to the architecture of Timurid Samarqand, are not included in this volume. The eight remaining chapters nevertheless reflect the richness of the period and scope of topics discussed, justifying the unprecedented extension of the symposium into a second day, though some gaps remain to be filled, notably connections with India at this period.

I am grateful to the authors for addressing the issues set out at the start, where possible, concerning the Idea of Iran, which I felt had been lost sight of in some earlier volumes in the series: this is not just another conference on the Timurids, so much as an aim to get below the surface of events in an attempt to understand the nature of the age as seen and lived by its contemporaries. The book departs from previous volumes in other small ways, such as a modified transliteration scheme and format for the chapters, and the inclusion of an Index, which I hope will set a pattern for the future explorations of the Idea of Iran as we approach more modern times.

Notes:

1. V. Minorsky, 'Persia: Religion and history', in *Iranica. Twenty Articles* (Tehran: University of Tehran, 1964), pp. 242–59 (at p. 245).
2. Hans R. Roemer, 'Das turkmenische Intermezzo – Persische Geschichte zwischen Mongolen und Safawiden', *Archäologische Mitteilungen aus Iran* 9 (1976), pp. 263–97.
3. Jonathan Brack, 'Theologies of auspicious kingship: The Islamization of Chinggisid sacral kingship in the Islamic world', *Comparative Studies in Society and History* 60, no. 4 (2018), pp. 1143–71 (quotation at p. 1170), building on recent ground-breaking work by A. Azfar Moin, *The Millennial Sovereign. Sacred Kingship & Sainthood in Islam* (New York: Columbia University Press, 2012), see chap. 1 on Timur; also Evrim Binbaş, *Intellectual Networks in Timurid Iran: Sharaf al-Dīn 'Alī Yazdī and the Islamicate Republic of Letters* (Cambridge: Cambridge University Press, 2016), on the development of this theme under Shāhrokh.

1

Arbiters of Iran: Chroniclers and Patrons in an Age of Literary Bounty

Shahzad Bashir
(Brown University)

To reconstruct how people alive in circumstances vastly different from our own may have understood their surrounding world is a complicated matter. We must begin the task by examining available verbal and pictorial descriptions, but any interpretations we can provide must also account for the invisible but crucial framework that led to the production of the surviving artefacts. And we have also to imagine the producers as having complex lives that went beyond the bits of evidence they have left for us. Although the authors were embedded within societal structures, their personal predilections and stakes must remain opaque to us to one degree or another. What significance, if any, did the idea of Iran hold for those from the past whose work we scrutinize today to address our interests? I believe it is best to regard this as an open question. The suspense created by such a posture allows us to examine evidence without overdetermining its meanings based solely on our present-day valorizations.

In as much as the subject is Iran as an idea – and not a territory or a people – the viewpoint must be that of hindsight. Iran is always a place and time located in the past, whose continuously changing narration in the ephemeral present makes it into an idea. And the past is conditioned by anticipation of the future, which determines, in great part, what is deemed worth recounting. I venture that these observations are true universally when considering a complex notion such as Iran, although in this chapter I will explore the suggestion by concentrating on the specific period that is the subject of this volume. The Turko-Timurid era provides abundant materials regarding the idea of Iran, which we must approach with mild mistrust for our interpretive instincts, if we wish to accord the material its due. The vast volume of texts and paintings at our disposal exhibits great internal diversity. There are surely many different, even contradictory, ideas about Iran to be found here, enmeshed with much besides. Scholarship over the past few decades has generated numerous authoritative studies from these materials, many by colleagues who are contributors to this volume. As is often the case in historiography, the abundance of sources is no guarantee of certainty of information or interpretation. Indeed, stories we can tell become ever more complicated as sources increase in number and are treated comparatively.

Through these overarching comments I wish to emphasize the specific approach to sources that I am adopting for this chapter. Instead of processing information in such a way that we would be led to a synthesis, I am inclined to privilege unknowability as a productive analytical stance.[1] What we do not, or cannot, know is not a detriment to analysis but a valuable datum. It tells of what our interlocutors from the past did not care to record, due to immediate political expediency, or because it was not of interest or was quotidian enough not to deserve comment. Moreover, what we may consider missing indicates our presumptions, revealed when different cosmologies are juxtaposed with our own. The task of critical historiography is to create accounts that bridge the gap between the obvious and the unknowable by employing intuition, comparison and plausibility. Texts and other materials from the Turko-Timurid era are ripe for such an approach because excellent baseline histories of the period have already been produced over the past few decades.

In the discussion below, I move through a series of topics that I see operating in understandings of the past in materials produced during the Turko-Timurid period. Ideas about Iran run through these topics since the producers of the material wrote in literary Persian and had origins in Iran and Central Asia. While my view derives from reading widely across genres and sources, I have decided to exemplify the topics through reference to only two works, to avoid making this short treatment a litany of citations. The sources I highlight are relatively well known, although they are also decidedly atypical. I see them as signposts for broader patterns due to the richness of expression found in them.[2]

The *Tarikhnama* of Taj-e Salmani (d. after 1411) was composed around 1410 and claims to report on political events connected to Timurid courts in Samarqand and Herat during the short period 1404–9. Written in high literary style and teeming with poetic citations in Persian and Arabic, this extended work pertains to the beginning of the Timurid era. It speaks of the tumultuous time after Timur's death in 1405 and, I argue, is an attempt at controlling the past in the interests of its sponsor. The author was employed initially by Timur's grandson Khalil Soltan (d. 1409), Timur's immediate successor in Samarqand, but wrote his work under the patronage of Mirza Shahrokh (d. 1447) and his son Ologh Beg (d. 1449). At the time the work was written, Shahrokh and Ologh Beg were parties in an uncertain and highly contested political field, although their lineage eventually came to dominate Timurid dynastic politics during the first half of the fifteenth century. The *Tarikhnama* allows us to think about relationships between elite patrons and the scholars and secretaries who formed the administrative backbone of Iranian political structures throughout the medieval period. It indicates also how literary narratives about the past were deployed as components of socio-political legitimacy.

The *Mehman-nama-ye Bokhara* of Fazlollah b. Ruzbehan Khonji-Esfahani (d. 1521) was composed around 1510 and thus comes from the end of the Turko-Timurid era. This lengthy work reports on a period of about 14 months over the years 1509 and 1510, during which the author was a scholar and advisor at the court of Shibani Khan Ozbek (d. 1510). As an erstwhile chronicler to the Aq Qoyunlu Turkomans, Khonji-Esfahani forms a link between the Turko-Timurid period and the age of Safavid–Ozbek rivalry during the early sixteenth century in Iran and Central Asia. His reports on travels through parts of this region in the company of Ozbeks create a picture of the world that is tied to his understanding of his present time as a tragedy. Behind the topsy-turvy world he describes stands the sense of an idealized past where scholars such as him occupied positions worthy of their talents. By Khonji-Esfahani's time, the chaotic world described in Salmani's work had become a desirable stable past. I utilize this work to understand notions of order and disorder contemporary with it. Because the work is an account of travels, it provides us with a sense of the lay of the land in the Iranian world during this period.

Although mined on occasion for details of events and for observations on groups and persons, the two works I utilize have not been the subject of sustained analysis.[3] I have chosen to concentrate on them for a mix of reasons: they bookend the period and are connected to a variety of interests important for the topic covered by this volume; both authors were renowned and multi-talented intellectuals of their times and their cultural and ideological investments give us glimpses into the milieu of classes that produced all the materials we possess; and the narratives contained in the texts are idiosyncratic, transgressing customary genres. The authors narrate their immediate circumstances under the shadow of idealized pasts and with an eye to the future. Understood as artefacts of their contexts, their representations can be seen to telegraph ideas pertaining to Iranian senses of history and society as experienced in the Turko-Timurid period.

History's Two Voices

Taj-e Salmani was a learned court secretary compelled to become a chronicler due to the force of circumstances. This is as viable a way as any other to understand his surviving work and the other meagre information available to us. He recounts moving from Shiraz to Samarqand in the year 800/1397–98, probably as a part of the process by which scholars from regions conquered by Timur were directed to head to the imperial capital.[4] His name appears in lists of court officials and we also have evidence that he crafted letters and decrees as a secretary and was a renowned calligrapher.[5] He composed his only major work, the *Tarikhnama*, in 813/1410, and his account of the request that led to it is interesting for its details. He recounts that one day, as he sat on the sidelines in Shahrokh's court, the discussion turned to the 'qualities and benefits of knowing truth and loyalty, and the damage and harm owing to disloyalty and maliciousness'. The king then turned to the author to say that:

> continuation of the history of the era of rule of Hazrat-e Khaqan [Timur] … has become a constricting knot due to the ravages of time and the march of events, turning [the matter] into distracting shackles. You must write it up in pleasant and illuminating expression, in correct and wise words that are easy to understand, entirely free of odd similes, artificialities, and strange diversions — [hemistich] this work is yours and of no one else.[6]

Salmani says that he resisted taking up the task, citing lack of ability, but Shahrokh persisted by praising his literary capabilities. He then launched the excuse that he was not aware of the relevant events in detail and did not know who to ask to get reliable information. Shahrokh responded that this was not a problem: he himself had an excellent memory and knew all details of what had come to pass. He would provide the correct information while Salmani's job would be to turn this into eloquent narrative.[7]

A patron's request followed by an author's initial protestation and eventual acceptance of the commission are familiar topoi in Persian literature. Salmani's purported dialogue with the king adds particulars that illuminate the relationship between rulers and scholars. The initial request attributed to Shahrokh draws a direct connection between historical narration and the socio-political order. He is saying that the troubled political situation of the time – rife with internal warfare between various claimants to Timur's throne – is coterminous with the fact that the recent past has not been made the subject of a veracious narrative. The writing of history is thus being presented as the same thing as the passage of the events themselves, leading to the contention that a truthful telling of the story would rectify the circumstances. This is obviously not an innocent request to be taken at face value. Shahrokh was a major contender in the struggles of the time and he is asking for the creation of a historiographical narrative that would support his claims. As things came to pass, Salmani's work is the most detailed source to provide information about the years it covers. But all its contents are refracted through the patronage signalled in the story about the narrative's origins.[8]

Salmani's report makes Shahrokh stand as the ultimate guarantor of the information conveyed in his work. This is a relatively rare direct instantiation of the fact that narratives such as the *Tarikhnama* contain the braiding of two mutually interdependent agencies. The rulers are the narratives' subjects and sponsors, while the words belong to authors who can produce the complex literary prose and poetry that was synonymous with the notion of history in this context. Complexity caused by the fact that 'history' refers to both events from the past and narratives about such events creates a productive ambiguity that continues to mark our work as modern historians. The dialogue between Salmani and Shahrokh cited in the *Tarikhnama* is an iteration of this issue particular to premodern Persian historiography. The encounter also emblematizes the highly contested political circumstances that characterize the whole Turko-Timurid era.

The period saw a boom in the production of narratives about the past – chronicles, prosopographical narratives such as genealogies and *tazkera*s, hagiographies, and so on – because of an abundance of patrons who needed narratives that would legitimize them in the face of competitors. The socio-political imperative expanded the ranks of classes that would meet the demand, with the eventual works exhibiting ever greater literary showmanship due to the contested circumstances. The patrons required that authors process the past with an eye towards the futures they desired as sponsors. Shahrokh's complaint that things had not gone right since Timur's death is simultaneously wistful and aspirational. The narrative he seeks from Salmani is expected to portray Shahrokh in the image of his incontestable father. Salmani's telling of the story acquiesces to the request since the work is clearly biased towards Shahrokh's faction among the Timurids. But, by casting Shahrokh as the guarantor of the details, Salmani also takes a step away from the work's contents. I think he is asking to be judged for the quality of his language rather than the veracity of reports on events, which he knows can be narrated from many perspectives. The result is an eminently complex account in which two voices – those of the author and the sponsor – are intimately intertwined without either one subsuming the other in its entirety.

In the beginning of this section I suggested that we think of Salmani as an accidental historian. This is warranted based on the way he describes the genesis of the *Tarikhnama*, the only historical work attributed to him that is, moreover, concerned with a very short period of recent memory. As in most Persian historiography of this period, the account progresses without overt chronological tethering to a calendar or a clear genealogical order. The narrative moves from one incident to the next on the basis of loosely implied causality, and lengths of sections tally the ideological import of the matter being conveyed. The longest section in the work (running to 78 pages in print) is devoted to Timur's death. Salmani's representation of this event, the narrative's clear centrepiece, is kaleidoscopic in its colourfulness and complexity. The information provided here is not simply that Timur had died, something conveyed in a sentence that is preceded by a relatively small section on his illness. The vast majority of the section consists of expressions of regret in poetry and prose attributed to the author himself and many others. The point then is the emotional and material disorder unleashed on the world as a result of the death.[9] Salmani's description of Timur stands apart from that of his descendants quite starkly. While he is portrayed as a world conqueror – his dominions stretching from the borders of China to Byzantium[10] – all the coverage of the activities of his sons and grandsons are limited to events in Iran and Central Asia over the course of four years (1405–9). The narrative's geographical scope is inflected in favour of the major cities, the centres of power and literary activity. This includes encomiastic poetry on Samarqand, Turkestan, Shiraz, Isfahan, Yazd and Herat.[11] While Shahrokh had requested a work that would seamlessly continue the story from Timur's time, the account Salmani produced contains a qualitative break. The conqueror's death changes the historiographical scope from an account of his perpetually expanding Eurasian empire to skirmishes between his descendants limited to Iran and Central Asia.

The Magic of Language

In his survey of Timurid historiography, John Woods describes Salmani's work as a grandiloquent account, overstuffed with Qur'anic and verse quotations, and characterized by an 'almost gossipy undertone' that includes 'remarks on the social roots, family backgrounds, and character traits of various opponents of Shahrukh's policies'.[12] If my understanding of the functions of the work is correct, the capacity for literary flourish that strikes us as superfluous in a chronicle today may have been the very reason why Shahrokh chose Salmani as the historiographical mouthpiece for his political ambitions. The work's purpose was not to preserve information for posterity but to give the recent past a colouring suited to the patron's imminent aims. The force of the prose was, in turn, expected to inspire loyalty among power holders in a highly contentious situation. The task needed a wordsmith rather than a forensically inclined historian, a suggestion that can be corroborated from Salmani's general views on the capacities of language and those who can best manipulate it.

In one section towards the work's end, Salmani describes the political interplay between Shahrokh and his nephew 'Omar (d. 1407), a son of Shahrokh's older brother Miranshah who seems to have been favoured by Timur in his lifetime. At various points, he was left in charge of the imperial capital, Samarqand, and was the governor of Azerbaijan and adjacent lands at the time of Timur's death. As a prominent member of the dynasty, he was a vigorous participant in the internecine struggle after the conqueror's death. His career indicates occasional coalition with his father and his brother Khalil Soltan, but he also changed his allegiance to Shahrokh, their main opponent, at one point. Salmani states that, during the time 'Omar accepted Shahrokh's overlordship, he was shown great consideration. Made the governor of Mazandaran, he went from a state of indigence to affluence and power. But this treatment did not garner Shahrokh his long-term loyalty and he rebelled soon after finding his footing. Shahrokh's first instinct was to send him conciliatory messengers who extolled the virtues of family filiation. This tactic having failed, Shahrokh eventually confronted him in battle, which 'Omar lost handily. Compelled to flee the scene, he was gravely injured in an altercation with another group. He was brought to Shahrokh's camp in a sorry state and was again treated with kindness and mercy. But he died while on the way to Herat, having been dispatched there to recuperate on Shahrokh's orders.[13]

Salmani's account of 'Omar's story contains an extended digression at the point where he mentions that Shahrokh decided to send a skilled ambassador to him to bring him to reason. He extols the qualities of such an emissary as someone:

Who vanquishes the arrow by (the strike of) his tongue,
with craft and trickery, leads the demon (to be captured) in the bottle.
When his speech reaches land and sea,
a great cry rises from fowl and fish.[14]

Further, the efficacious ambassador's extraordinary power to affect the world is described as being predicated on the art of arranging words into speech:

To assemble words, honing their meanings through intellect
is a magic, no exaggeration—without doubt, a matter revealed.
It's a jewel-filled treasure, a pearl-laden sea;
secrets you will find in its every subtlety.
A sea, for whose grace, and in whose envy,
the ocean dissipates away, mouth dribbling, skirts drenched in tears.
Sequestered bashfully within it is a key,
the pearl under the sea's chest, the gem in the mine's veins.
Its fine points are young girls (behind) the veil of the unseen:
fortifying, fairy faced, heart's desires—tucked away.
Each feature of theirs contains an enticing charm,
in the bends of their curly hair dwells eternal life.[15]

These verses encapsulate an ideology of language in which its ablest producers can act upon those who hear them in magical ways. Their ability to craft language is akin to the manufacture of spells that beguile. Here this language's extraordinary operational capacity is put to the service of inculcating truths, such as Shahrokh's purportedly sincere appeal to 'Omar in the name of family amity. The verses also imply that a messenger who would say something to an audience in plain fashion is likely to fail in conveying the message irrespective of it being true. What is needed is language that, first, ensnares based on its outer form, and then leads to the truth by inviting rumination. In the verses' extended metaphors, words made into speech are the surfaces of land and sea, and their meanings are pearls and gems that are extracted through cogitative effort. Effective language becomes personified into beautiful bodies, its pleasures being akin to erotic dalliance.

The verses I have translated match the overall tenor of Salmani's narrative in the *Tarikhnama*. On the side of production, this is the work of someone with extensive training, a prodigious memory, and a knack for versification and ornate prose. But importantly, it is also a chronicle reporting on events and not a narrative allowed creative licence beyond what the work's patrons would find acceptable. The work also makes demands on its reader in the form of familiarity with conventions and prior literature, and patience to piece the message together on the basis of hints. Shahrokh's capacity to employ someone to produce language like this was a part of his royal claim, an aspect of his bid to become Timur's successor. In this reading, Shahrokh's request that Salmani write in a plain way would have to be treated as disingenuous. But we have to remember that Salmani is the one who tells us what Shahrokh said, and this in a narrative dedicated to conveying the message through allusions. The fact is, we cannot fully resolve the seeming contradiction. His attribution of the statement to Shahrokh may be the continuation of a convention governing the way kings make requests to scholars. Or it could be Salmani upending the king's intentions, writing in a way that fitted the occasion in his view as a learned scholar and secretary. The contradiction could be a wry jest, transmitting ironies of Salmani's profession to us centuries later. It seems to me that, for our usage of Salmani's work, leaving all these (and other possibilities) open as options makes the source a richer ground for our efforts at reconstructing the Turko-Timurid period.

Order in a Dissonant World

Advancing a century from Salmani's time, we find central Iranian lands in turmoil. But the principals locked in confrontation now are different from Timur's successors. Shahrokh has, by this time, become regarded as Timur's primary successor, his long reign (which ended in 1447) including sponsorship of other historiographical works that eclipsed Taj-e Salmani's endeavours.[16] Iran and Central Asia have few Timurids left as overlords, the dynasty acquiring a new lease of life only a few years later in India when Babor (d. 1529) conquered Delhi in 1526. Herat and Samarqand, earlier ruling seats of Shahrokh and his son Ologh Beg, are in the hands of Shibani Khan Ozbek (d. 1510) who is locked in a struggle for power with Shah Esma'il (d. 1524), the self-declared king of Iran who defeated the Aq Qoyunlu Turkomans in 1501. And to understand aspects of the Turko-Timurid cultural world, we can turn to the work of another man from Shiraz.

Fazlollah b. Ruzbehan Khonji-Esfahani (d. ca. 1521) was born into a family of scholars and secretaries and travelled to the Hejaz, the Levant and Egypt as a youth in the company of his Sufi master Pir Jamal al-Din Ardestani (d. 1474–75). He received the commission to write a chronicle of the reign of Soltan Ya'qub Aq Qoyunlu (d. 1490) as a young man, completing the work in 1491. His affiliation with the Aq Qoyunlu and the strident Sunni identity visible throughout his works, made it inopportune for him to remain in western Iran after the rise of the Safavids in 1501. This led to, first, a stint at the Timurid court of Soltan-Hoseyn-e Bayqara (d. 1506) in Herat. Shibani Khan Ozbek conquered Herat in 1507, leading local scholars like Khonji-Esfahani to shift to his retinue. He composed the *Mehman-nama-ye Bokhara* in this capacity, while shadowing Shibani Khan's movements across various regions of Iran and Central Asia during the period 1509–10. This ruler was defeated and killed by Shah Esma'il in 1510 but Khonji-Esfahani stayed with the Ozbeks in the areas they controlled in Central Asia. He composed a Mirror for Princes entitled *Soluk al-moluk* for the later Ozbek ruler 'Obeydollah Khan (d. 1539) in 1514. His activities towards the end of his life are unclear and the date of his death is placed variously between 1519 and 1521.[17]

As in other chronicles, Khonji-Esfahani's *Mehman-nama-ye Bokhara* is predicated on the dual authority of a king and a scholar. But unlike Salmani's work, the balance of power in this instance is quite equal between the two parties. In his introduction, the author remarks that he had originally intended to name the work the *Travelogue of Bukhara* (*Safarnama-ye Bokhara*), signifying his own travel in the company of the city's ruler. However, when his intention to write became known to the king, he requested that the name be changed to the *Guest Narrative of Bukhara* (*Mehman-nama-ye Bokhara*).[18] While both names are centred on the author himself (he is the traveller or the guest), only the second one has the king, as the presumptive host, acknowledged in the title. The work has a decidedly autobiographical tone, although its stated purpose is to describe and celebrate the king's activities. Overall, the narrative comes across as a chronicle of the interactions between the scholar and the king, the two being able to assert themselves independently. The pair also stand above everyone else since, among people alive at the time, the work's remarks of praise are limited entirely to members of the Ozbek dynasty. Other scholars with whom the author interacts are presented invariably as simpletons or prone to error. The likely audience of the work were not scholars but the political elite, since whenever Khonji-Esfahani cites a religious text in Arabic he provides the Persian translation prior to using it for an argument. This would be superfluous for the scholarly classes in Central Asia but was a necessity for the rulers.[19]

The *Mehman-nama-ye Bokhara* proceeds by describing life at the court as the king makes political decisions, engages in intellectual debates, and travels to confront enemies at the edges of his domains. The ostensible basis for this is the passage of time, the narrative reporting on approximately 14 months of the court's activities without following a chronological order. But a consideration of the matters Khonji-Esfahani chooses to discuss suggests that more than description is at stake. The narrative is imbued with a moral urgency directed at the ruler that can be pinned to the author's circumstances. Although describing himself as part of a glittering court, he is riven with anxiety regarding the present and future of what he holds dear in terms of land, society and normative principles.

From the very beginning, Khonji-Esfahani's references to Shibani Khan are especially grandiose: the Imam of the age, God's caliph, reviver of the ways of the rightly-guided caliphs, and religious renewer of the ninth (Islamic) century.[20] In a number of places, he endows the king with miraculous abilities that are said to have been the source of his military victories, inexplicable by other means.[21] He discusses at length a well-known *hadith* report according to which Mohammad predicted that a man named Haris b. Harras would rise from Transoxiana and would set the world aright by his dedication to Islam and the protection of Mohammad's descendants. The followers of this man were expected to have small eyes and round faces, which had led some in earlier periods to identify him as Hülegü Khan, the Mongol conqueror of Baghdad. Khonji-Esfahani opines that this could not be correct since Hülegü had no care for Islam and Muslims. The prediction was meant to refer to a Muslim ruler who would start in Transoxiana and then make his way westward. The prophecy then matched Shibani Khan due to his own and his followers' Turkic facial features and his political trajectory. The crucial thing about this identification was that it pushed Shibani Khan to carry out the as yet unfulfilled part of the prophecy over the rest of his career. Once recognized as a messianic deliverer, he was expected to root out religious deviants, such as the Kazakhs and Shah Esma'il and his followers. Khonji-Esfahani's dedication to Shibani Khan was thus connected to his hopes for the king's expected role as a restorer of the proper order.[22]

As with the desire for religio-political correction at the level of rulers, the *Mehman-nama-ye Bokhara* contains numerous discussions where the author depicts himself clarifying matters of Islamic law and theology for his host. This includes the insistence that *shari'a* rules on inheritance have precedence over those of the Mongol *yasa*, despite Shibani Khan's view, backed up by some local scholars, that the latter seemed more logical.[23] As the author himself remarks at the end, the mixture of historical description, religious arguments, political incitation and expression of personal sentiment contained in *Mehman-nama-ye Bokhara* makes it a unique work.[24]

Taken in totality, Khonji-Esfahani's drive to instruct his audience may be seen as a symptom of the grudge he bore his circumstances. The world in which he lived had not accorded him the due of the type of learned man and able administrator he understood himself to be. Within his disappointment with the cosmic disorder is encoded a sense of the proper order. Here Sunni rulers would be in charge of Muslim polities and would heed advice from scholars like him in the process of ruling by the injunctions of the shari'a. Khonji-Esfahani made his vision in this regard explicit a few years after the composition of the *Mehman-nama-ye Bokhara* when he wrote a Mirror for Princes for a successor to Shibani Khan.[25] But a desire for the proper order that would correct the fact of present disorder is pervasive in the eclectic work in which he pinned his aspirations on Shibani Khan.

Places that Speak

Although identified with Bokhara alone in the title, Khonji-Esfahani's narrative meanders extensively over the landscape of Iran and Central Asia. His intention to call it a travelogue was quite apt in this regard. The work's geographical content has both spatial and temporal dimensions, each inflected in multiple ways. Regarding space, he exemplifies what someone from his background would have seen as familiar versus alien. His references to major cities such as Bukhara, Samarqand, Herat and Mashhad consist of praises in verse and contain little in the way of physical description. The mention of these places required no introduction for the presumed audience. In contrast, the river Jaxartes (Syr Darya) and lands beyond it controlled by the Kazakhs are explained topographically. The river marked a limit of greater Iran, the land within which Khonji-Esfahani felt at home.[26] His descriptions of sunrise and morning light containing verses he composed for the occasion also convey a sense of wonder at new landscapes.[27] Some culinary habits of Central Asians similarly get an extended treatment: he describes the deliciousness and great nourishing power of fermented mare's milk (kumis), insisting that it is legal to drink according to Shafe'i views. In contrast, while he assures Shibani Khan that it is lawful to eat fox meat, he claims himself averse to it on the basis of instinct and lack of habit.[28] Both kumis and fox meat deserve description due to their unfamiliarity to the author himself and his presumed audience.

Senses of belonging and alienation with respect to land projected in the work relate to Khonji-Esfahani's knowledge of time in the form of past events. Space deemed familiar is so because of his knowledge about past peoples. This is evident from his citing historical details about places, such as who lived or was buried where, and what major events had come to pass there in the past. Among places well known to him, the longest section contains his account of travelling with Shibani Khan to Mashhad. This was a part of the king's stay in Khorasan, sandwiched between travel to Marv and Tus. Khonji-Esfahani begins the account of the region with his own side trip to the mausoleum of the famous Sufi master Sheykh Abu Sa'id Abu'l-Kheyr (d. 1049) in Mehneh. The narrative then proceeds to a lengthy theoretical justification for the benefits of visiting the graves of eminent persons, followed by a further dilation on the same topic with specific reference to the grave of Imam Reza (d. 819) in Mashhad. He reports on Shibani Khan's visit to the mausoleum, also providing the text of a poem that the king had composed in Turkish in praise of the Imam. Mashhad as it appears here is a place enveloped in memory. The Imam's body buried there imparts to it a force that attracts visitors and then affects them powerfully when they are present on site. The correct working of this process requires guidance from a scholar such as Khonji-Esfahani, who can cite both history and true doctrine to make the visit efficacious.[29]

While the *Mehman-nama-ye Bokhara* contains ample expression of the author's personal opinions throughout, his references to a grievous illness he suffered while accompanying Shibani Khan on the campaign against the Kazakhs stands out for its sentimentality. His first mention of the illness states that he insisted on continuing his advisory duties despite the onset of extreme discomfort.[30] When the illness persisted, the king advised that it would be better that he leave the army camp and, instead, become the caretaker of gifts being sent to the shrine of the great Central Asian Sufi master Ahmad Yasavi (d. 1166) in Turkestan. He initially resisted, seeing it as a mark of cowardliness, and felt himself highly energized upon eating some rabbit meat. But this seemingly fortifying meal led to severe bloody diarrhoea that eventually forced him to accept the fate of departing for the shrine where the illness continued to progress.[31]

The matter eventually reached a point where he felt that he was certain to die in the near future. In this state, he was overcome with the desire to see the Prophet Mohammad, which he had known was a common occurrence for people nearing the end of their earthly lives. A vision of indescribable beauty ensued, which led him to compose a poem in praise of the Prophet. He then fell into unconsciousness such that his companions felt that perhaps he had already died. In his own recollection, although he first felt completely oblivious to his surroundings, it occurred to him that he could see clearly, and think, while all the other senses seemed to have been nullified. He then understood that a dervish present there asked a companion to recite the Ya-Sin chapter of the Qur'an. As soon as this began, his senses returned and he was able to lift his hand to his forehead and feel it swimming in sweat.[32]

In this detailed narrative – which has the character of a partial death and resurrection – Khonji-Esfahani describes that he wrote a will at the moment when he felt that he had little time to live. This included the instructions that were an epitaph to be put on his grave, it should let passers-by know that he had died a martyr in circumstances of exile. Verses in Arabic were to be inscribed to convey this:

While alive, I was not one to plead carnal passion.
    Killed by love, I must have the type [of love] within a martyr.
Endless tears poured forth from my eyelids.
    Overwhelmed by them, I drown a martyr.
Fire of passion set my sides aflame.
    Consumed by it, I burn a martyr.

He then adds that it should also be arranged that vessels full of water be placed near the grave because quenching thirst is one of the greatest acts of charity. To reflect this, the epitaph was also to include the following quatrain in Persian:

To the world's causeway we came—and stayed a while.
Many a wonder we saw—and became.
Our lifetime was a mouthful of water.
Decanted from the jug of heaven we flowed—and then were done.[33]

Khonji-Esfahani's instinct to write his own obituary through these verses shows a man with a strong desire to control the message. The verses he wanted put on the epitaph project existential humility combined with a passion for seeing the world run in what he deemed to be the correct way. Geographical and historiographical descriptions in his work are attuned to similar readings of the places he went to, seeing them as topography overlaid with morality tales of past lives. Accustomed to curating the past, he wanted to modulate how people in the future would see him. The ultimate venue to effect such a vision was his grave, the piece of land that was to become identical to him through the placement of his name over it. Through this, his own life would be turned into a tale of the past, with lessons. Perhaps my approximate translations of his verses into English above answer a desire to be remembered, expressed in the throes of a terrible illness on the Central Asian steppe more than half a millennium ago.

Conclusion

The idea of Iran runs through all the themes I have highlighted in this chapter. It pertains to questions of political and intellectual authority, the nature and flavour of language used to describe the past, senses of normative order and the chaos unleashed in its absence, and the inclination to understand landscapes and other aspects of the physical environment as venues imbued with human presence. None of these themes are exclusive to the Turko-Timurid period; they can be said to apply to all historical contexts, in Iran and elsewhere. This context's specificity lies in the way the themes play out in the light of socio-historical contingencies particular to the era.

The relationship between chroniclers and patrons that I have highlighted contains a productive tension that is part of the richness of the period's historiographical production. The interdependence of the two parties involved here reflects a formal distinction between roles rather than being a matter of radically different capacities. The sources indicate that numerous Timurid and Turkoman princes were highly learned and could readily compose complex literary works. And chroniclers doubling as bureaucrats could hold power beyond that of the royal persons who were their putative masters. But the distinction between the subject and the storyteller – the patron and the author – was a persistent principle of the socio-political cosmos. As I have shown elsewhere, a similar pattern obtains in the case of the great Sufi masters of the age and their hagiographers.[34] And the same can be traced in literary patterns concerned with other social groups, such as poets, painters, calligraphers, and so on. All these cases suggest that the social order correlated with literary invention through specific conventions. But conventional rules condition articulation rather than restricting expression. The imperative for us is to be especially mindful of the frames that surround the information given in sources from this period.

Intricate language, filled with poetry and rhyming prose, is a pervasive feature of the period's literature. Its utilization in the historiographical field can be traced earlier, to the work of authors such as Vassaf (fl. 1328) who was regarded as a great exemplar of the genre in the fifteenth century and after.[35] On the extreme end of this trend lies the popularity of the science of puzzles (*'elm-e mo'amma*), regarded as an ultimate marker of intelligence and erudition.[36] Based on paying attention to self-conscious discussion about language, I suggest that, for authors from the period, investment in linguistic complexity was meant to mimic the conundrum of the observed world. An intricate world required language to match, and those who could create and decipher such language held the key to knowledge and understanding. This fact applied as much to narratives about the past as it might to theology and philosophy. The elaborate language of authors such as Salmani and Khonji-Esfahani was underpinned by epistemological and aesthetic commitments rather than being a mere convention or a fleeting fashion.

Even the brief glimpses of the Turko-Timurid world I have provided in this chapter should have conveyed the sense of political turbulence that pervades the period. The enduring political competition had social and intellectual concomitants, making the fifteenth century the incubator of novel ideas and practices that cast a long shadow over subsequent times. We should understand the political and socio-intellectual scenes as being connected through a dialectic of inversion. As in the example of Khonji-Esfahani, the political disorder acted as an imperative to propose ways of ordering. These could both hearken to the idealized past and propose new dawns led by messianic deliverers. Their sophistication notwithstanding, no propositions for new orders were able to win the day. Instead, they fed into a competitive field, leading to ever greater experimentation. The immense volume of literature and art we know to have been created under Turko-Timurid auspices had as its engine the disorder–order dialectic that characterizes the period.

When telling the story of ideas, it can be easy to forget that ideas always exist only in conjunction with the minds and circumstances of living human subjects. This is especially the case with an idea with a remit as expansive as Iran. In abstract terms, we can chart Iran over millennia and across a vast and varying geography. But ultimately, there is no Iran that exists outside the historically locatable circumstances of living human beings. Views of Iran we have from the Turko-Timurid periods are anchored in the voices of literary masters such as Salmani and Khonji-Esfahani, who belonged to particular classes and expressed themselves in ways that must have seemed natural in their circumstances. When reading their works, we must look for matters such as ideology, commitments and interests. But it pays also to attend to the personal, the voice that conveys its unique experience to us across the centuries. By acknowledging Irans of the past different from ours, we keep Iran alive as an idea for the future.

Notes:

1. For a theoretical account of historiographical practice akin to my view see Ethan Kleinberg, *Haunting History*.
2. For an overarching assessment of the characteristics and development of historiography during the period see Charles Melville, 'The Mongol and Timurid periods'.
3. The lengthiest recent treatments of the works are: Evrim Binbaş's use of the *Tarikhnāma* while reconstructing the genealogy of Sharaf al-Din Yazdi's *Zafarnāma*, see *Intellectual Networks in Timurid Iran*, pp. 224–32; and Ali Anooshahr's reading of *Mehmān-nāma-ye Bokhārā* while assessing the role assigned to Central Asia in discourses of imperial legitimacy, *Turkestan and the Rise of Eurasian Empires*, pp. 84–113.
4. Tāj-e Salmāni, *Tārikhnāma*, p. 87. The recent edition of this work takes into account Hans Robert Roemer's earlier edition and German translation, *Šams al-husn: Eine Chronik vom Tode Timurs bis zum Jahre 1409* and the facsimile of a manuscript in Istanbul published by İsmail Aka, *Tarihnâme*. As Saburi explains in his introduction, Roemer misidentified the work's title as *Shams al-hosn* based on a later marginal note on a manuscript (pp. xxiv–xxvi).
5. Salmāni, *Tārikhnāma*, pp. xx–xxiv. For some further details, see Fetemeh Rostami, 'Tārikhnegāri-ye *Shams ol-hosn*', pp. 55–74. The most consequential decree attributed to Salmāni's composition is Ologh Beg's order dated 25 August 1411 that Muslim scholars brought to Samarqand by Timur were free to return to their homelands. This may have been a source of satisfaction given that Salmāni may have come from Shiraz to Samarqand as a part of the conscription. Some sources attribute to Salmāni the invention of the *nasta'liq* calligraphic style. This is a hyperbole since the script is attested before his lifetime.
6. Salmāni, *Tārikhnāma*, pp. 29–30.
7. Ibid., pp. 33–34. For a nice parallel, see Charles Melville, 'Between Firdausī and Rashīd al-Dīn', pp. 52–55.
8. I am not suggesting that we should read all the contents of Salmāni's work as dictated by Shāhrokh. The point is only that the rhetorical representation of the division of labour should be taken seriously as a reflection of the conditions in which the work was produced.
9. Salmāni, *Tārikhnāma*, pp. 94–172.
10. Ibid., p. 23.
11. Ibid., pp. 37–38, 87–89, 356–60, 419. A later work attributes to Salmāni verses in praise of Herat that are not included in the *Tārikhnāma*, Mo'in al-Din Zamchi Esfezāri, *Rowzāt al-jannāt fi owsāf madinat Harāt*, vol. I, pp. 21–22.
12. John Woods, 'The rise of Tīmūrid historiography', p. 89.
13. Salmāni, *Tārikhnāma*, pp. 360–85, 548–49 (n. 92).
14. Ibid., p. 373.
15. Ibid., p. 374.
16. For reviews of the relevant sources see Binbaş, *Intellectual Networks*, pp. 169–250, and Beatrice Forbes Manz, *Power, Religion and Politics in Timurid Iran*, pp. 49–78.

17. For further biographical details, see the review of sources in the introduction to the edition of Khonji-Esfahāni's history of Soltān Ya'qub Aq Qoyunlu, *Tārikh-e 'ālam ārā-ye Amini*, ed. M.A. 'Āsheq, pp. xv–xxxvi. The *nesba* Esfahāni in this author's name is a reference to the family's origins rather than the place of his birth.
18. Fazlollāh b. Ruzbehān Khonji-Esfahāni, *Mehmān-nāma-ye Bokhārā*, p. 6.
19. The translation from Arabic to Persian is pervasive throughout the text.
20. Khonji-Esfahāni, *Mehmān-nāma*, p. 1.
21. Ibid., pp. 1–2, 128, 215–17, 276–78.
22. Ibid., pp. 95–99. Messianic claims were a major feature of the Iranian religious world during the fifteenth century. For details see Shahzad Bashir, *Messianic Hopes and Mystical Visions*, pp. 29–75.
23. Khonji-Esfahāni, *Mehmān-nāma*, pp. 22–28.
24. Ibid., pp. 354–55.
25. Fazlollāh b. Ruzbehān Khonji-Esfahāni, *Soluk al-moluk*.
26. Khonji-Esfahāni, *Mehmān-nāma*, pp. 85–86, 116–20, 264–65.
27. Ibid., pp. 74–75, 77, 92–93, 111, 237, 304.
28. Ibid., pp. 174–79.
29. Ibid., pp. 327–47. In addition to Mashhad and its environs, the work includes less extensive but qualitatively similar encounters with the burial places of the Central Asian Sufi masters Bahā' al-Din Naqshband (pp. 47–48, 53), 'Abd al-Khāleq Ghejdovāni (pp. 60–70), and Ahmad Yasavi (pp. 129–32, 168–69, 255–62).
30. Ibid., pp. 93–94.
31. Ibid., pp. 128–40.
32. Ibid., pp. 248–53.
33. Ibid., p. 249.
34. Cf. Shahzad Bashir, *Sufi Bodies*, pp. 197–213.
35. Cf. Judith Pfeiffer, 'A turgid history of the Mongol Empire in Persia', pp. 107–29.
36. Cf. Binbaş, *Intellectual Networks*, pp. 81–89.

Bibliography:

Aka, İsmail, *Tarihnâme* (Ankara: Türk Tarih Kurumu Basımevi, 1988).

Anooshahr, Ali, *Turkestan and the Rise of Eurasian Empires: A Study of Politics and Invented Traditions* (New York: Oxford University Press, 2018).

Bashir, Shahzad, *Messianic Hopes and Mystical Visions: The Nūrbakhshīya between Medieval and Modern Islam* (Columbia: University of South Carolina Press, 2003).

— *Sufi Bodies: Religion and Society in Medieval Islam* (New York: Columbia University Press, 2011).

Binbaş, Evrim, *Intellectual Networks in Timurid Iran: Sharaf al-Dīn 'Alī Yazdī and the Islamicate Republic of Letters* (Cambridge: Cambridge University Press, 2016).

Esfezāri, Mo'in al-Din Zamchi, *Rowzāt al-jannāt fi owsāf madinat Harāt*, ed. Sayyed Mohammad Kāzem Emām, 2 vols (Tehran: Enteshārāt-e Dāneshgāh-e Tehrān, 1959).

Khonji-Esfahāni, Fazlollāh b. Ruzbehān, *Soluk al-moluk*, ed. Mohammad 'Ali Movahhed (Tehran: Khvārazmi, 1984).

— *Tārikh-e 'ālam ārā-ye Amini*, ed. Mohammad Akbar 'Āsheq (Tehran: Mirās-e Maktub, 2003).

— *Mehmān-nāma-ye Bokhārā*, ed. Manuchehr Sotudeh (Enteshārāt-e 'elmi va farhangi, 2006).

Kleinberg, Ethan, *Haunting History: For a Deconstructive Approach to the Past* (Stanford: Stanford University Press, 2017).

Manz, Beatrice Forbes, *Power, Religion and Politics in Timurid Iran* (Cambridge: Cambridge University Press, 2007).

Melville, Charles, 'Between Firdausī and Rashīd al-Dīn', *Studia Islamica* 104/105 (2007), pp. 45–65.

— 'The Mongol and Timurid periods', in *Persian Historiography*, ed. Charles Melville (London: I.B. Tauris, 2012), pp. 155–208.

Pfeiffer, Judith, 'A turgid history of the Mongol Empire in Persia: Epistemological reflections concerning a critical edition of Vaṣṣāf's *Tajziyat al-amṣār va tazjiyat al a'ṣār*', in *Theoretical Approaches to the Transmission and Edition of Oriental Manuscripts*, ed. Judith Pfeiffer and Manfred Kropp (Wurzburg: Ergon Verlag, 2007), pp. 107–29.

Roemer, Hans Robert, *Šams al-husn: Eine Chronik vom Tode Timurs bis zum Jahre 1409* (Wiesbaden: Steiner, 1956).

Rostami, Fetemeh, 'Tārikhnegāri-ye *Shams ol-hosn* va vojuh-e eshterāk-e ān bā do āsār-e mota'ākher khud (*Zafarnāma-ye* Yazdi va *Jāme' al-tavārikh-e* Hasani)', *Tārikhnegari va Tārikhnegāri* 10 (Autumn and Winter 1391/2013), pp. 55–74, online at https://www.noormags.ir/view/fa/articlepage/1060355/ [accessed 15 March 2019].

Salmāni, Tāj-e, *Tārikhnāma (Shams al-hosn)*, ed. Akbar Saburi (Tehran: Enteshārāt-e Doktor Mahmud Afshār, 2015).

Woods, John, 'The rise of Tīmūrid historiography', *Journal of Near Eastern Studies* 46, no. 2 (1987), pp. 81–108.

2

The Local and the Universal in Turko-Iranian Ideology

Beatrice Forbes Manz*
(Tufts University)

We frequently see the pairing of Iran and Turan in Iranian texts of the post-Mongol period, just as we see the pairing of Turk and Tajik. These pairings suggest at once opposition and complementarity; the first in territory and history, the second in culture. Both refer to imperial traditions – the one Persian and Perso-Islamic, and the other based in the steppe empires of the Turks and Mongols. When put together they present the image of two known and relatively homogeneous entities, the distinction between them more important than differences within. After the eleventh century, in Iran and indeed most of the Middle East, almost all the large states were ruled by dynasties of Turko-Mongolian origin whose legitimation still depended on their connection to past empires of the steppe. The bureaucrats, scholars and ulema who made up the intellectual elite were educated in the Perso-Islamic tradition, which ensured them a distinct and prestigious place within the Turko-Mongolian state. Thus, the separateness and the universality of these two identities was constantly reiterated. Nonetheless, we must recognize that the two imperial traditions overlapped significantly in territory and that they shared centuries of historical experience.

By the fifteenth century the Islamic caliphate in Baghdad and the unified Mongol Empire had been gone for more than 150 years and regional rule had taken over in both the steppe and the central Islamic lands. Over that time, the practice of government and the ideologies behind it had adjusted to a new and more fractured world. In this chapter I want to investigate the ways in which the two universalist ideologies overlapped with each other and how each accommodated sub-imperial identities and regional claims.

Common Practices and Ideologies

If we are to understand the relationship between the Turko-Mongolian and Iranian traditions I believe we must broaden our conception of the holders of Iranian culture. We often regard the Persian bureaucrats and scholarly classes as those who defined Perso-Islamic statecraft and identity; these are the people

* I want to thank Louise Marlow for reading the draft of this chapter and for her useful comments.

who produced most of the texts we read and who have shaped our perception both of Iranian society and of its Turko-Mongolian rulers. I want here to go beyond the central court and chancellery and attempt also to understand the Iranian regional rulers and landed elites, including military actors, who made up the governing stratum below that of the Turko-Mongolian rulers. Instead of relying on textual discussions of habits of rule, I will emphasize the actions of rulers and their servitors. When we do this, we achieve a more comprehensive view of Perso-Islamic political practice and one that differs less starkly from that of the steppe.

Let us first look at the issue of military activity. In the distinctions drawn between Turks and Tajiks, one of the most standard characterizations is that of the superior military capability of the Turks, in contrast to the more cultured Tajiks, who lacked warrior skills. This characterization is clearly expressed in the histories written by Iranian bureaucrats for Turko-Mongolian rulers. One can take as an example Mo'in al-Din Zamchi Esfezari's account of the leader of the Ulus Chaghatay, Amir Qazaghan, attacking the Iranian Malek Mo'ezz al-Din Kart of Herat in 752/1351–52. First of all, as a Tajik, the malek had no right to claim sovereignty, which was reserved for the descendants of Chinggis Khan. Second, as a Tajik, the malek could not understand war and would soon be defeated.[1]

However, scholars are increasingly questioning how fully we should accept the bureaucrats' portrayal of society and are recognizing the possibility that Iranian rulers and their servitors might have been active and even skilled in war.[2] To understand the role of Iranian elites we have to expand our sources and read with particular care. When we try to look below the top level of leadership in medieval Iran, we begin to recognize how very little our sources tell us about the social structure of town and countryside. The dynastic histories concentrate on campaigns and on events in the major cities – usually the provincial capitals, in which a regional governor kept his *divan* and a garrison of soldiers. Other cities are mentioned primarily in accounts of campaigns or rebellions. Medieval histories, moreover, are shaped by conventions that assign different roles to each population and often ignore events and practices which do not fully conform to the dominant paradigm.

When we look at local histories, we see very active politics, and here sometimes we can discover the actions not just of local rulers, but of some of the people who served under them. These men led armies of Iranian soldiers, sometimes on their own and sometimes within larger states. When they were not campaigning for others, they were often fighting rivals within their own territories. The Caspian regions of Gilan and Mazandaran produced several local histories, one written in the fifteenth century by a member of a ruling family, Zahir al-Din Mar'ashi (ca. 1412–89), which gives a detailed account of innumerable struggles over local thrones.[3] The southeastern regions of Farah and Sistan also had traditions of independent regional rule and the history of

Sistan is recorded in two regional chronicles, from the fourteenth and sixteenth centuries.[4] The Caspian regions and Sistan remained separate from the centre for centuries, under sometimes long-lasting dynasties. One can argue that such areas were atypical and set apart geographically by desert or mountain, and thus able to preserve military and political traditions lost elsewhere. However, they were nonetheless strategic regions, important in politics beyond their borders; the Caspian regions stretched across the northern east–west route constantly travelled by caravans and military expeditions, and their local rulers served within the armies of successive larger powers. Sistan and Farah likewise were connected to both Khorasan and Kerman. We must furthermore recognize that there is an element of chance in the production and preservation of historical sources. We are well informed about these regions not only because they were important, but also because they produced local histories which have survived to the present.

For regions covered only in more general histories we are given much less information on local military elites during times of strong rule, but in periods of disorder we can find them playing a part in politics and thus appearing in the histories. The historian Gheyas al-Din ‘Ali Faryumadi, writing at the close of the fourteenth century, described the situation at the end of the Ilkhanate and mentioned local rulers asserting power in Kashan, Sava, Qom and Kerman.[5] The Timurid histories make it clear that there were still local Iranian military elites active and powerful in Qom, Sava and Kashan into the period of Shahrokh.[6] We also find Iranian soldiers in the Timurid armies, some under their own commanders; Iranians were not in the top positions but were definitely active.[7] While Iranian troops are less frequently mentioned than Turko-Mongolian ones, they participated in most campaigns and could make a significant difference in the outcome of succession struggles and regional contests. Turks and Tajiks interacted not only within the *divan* and the palace, but also in the army.

While the Turks have been considered superior in the military sphere, they have often been portrayed as inferior in statecraft, needing to be instructed by their Persian bureaucrats. In particular, centralization and decentralization have been described as a major fault line between Iranian and Turkic traditions. Two particular practices are ascribed to the Turkic heritage: shared rule among family members, with inheritance moving first within a generation before passing to the next, and the granting of large appanages to family and followers. According to this formulation, Turko-Mongolian states are distinguished by the fact that power is seen to belong to the entire ruling dynasty, with the senior member becoming khan as *primus inter pares*.[8] This system led to the possibility of several candidates for the throne and thus to armed struggle, which can be seen as a form of election and has been called ‘bloody tanistry’.[9]

In discussing Perso-Islamic administrative ideals, scholars – and the histories they read – often portray the Persian administrators supporting a centralized bureaucratic state, in opposition to the centrifugal tendencies of Turko-Mongolian tradition. There are well-known examples of Persian bureaucrats promoting fiscal centralization as a return to correct Islamic government, while at the same time enhancing the position of the central ruler at the expense of subordinate members of the dynasty and powerful tribal leaders. Two attempted reforms are often cited for the fifteenth century. One is the attempt in 894/1489 by Qazi 'Isa Savaji under Uzun Hasan Aq Qoyunlu to abolish the trade tax (*tamgha*) and the system of land grants with tax immunities (*soyurghals*) in the name of a return to Islamic practice.[10] The other example is the reforms of the Timurid Soltan-Hoseyn-e Bayqara's chief administrator, Majd al-Din Mohammad, aimed against both the *soyurghal* holdings of the sultan's close servitors and the fiscal improprieties of members of the chancellery. This action was again presented as a return to Islamic statecraft, and was accompanied by a publicized Islamic reform by Soltan-Hoseyn himself.[11] Both these movements ended in failure, due partly to resistance from the powerful Turko-Mongolian elite, but also because of opposition from other Iranians serving the dynasty, many of whom united against the monopolizing of administrative power by these two bureaucrats. In the case of the Aq Qoyunlu, the proposed reforms also threatened some of the Iranian ulema, who benefited from tax-exempt land grants. Thus these 'Islamizing reforms' had much to do with personal power, both for rulers and for bureaucrats, and threatened not only Turks, but also Iranians. Not all Iranians favoured centralized imperial rule.

In comparing Turkic and Iranian practices of rule, we should not limit ourselves to contrasting the actions of Turkic dynasties with the ideals and practices of their Iranian bureaucrats. It is more appropriate to examine the actions of Turkic rulers in relation to the actual practice of Iranian dynasties who controlled parts of Iran during the Islamic period. Did the Iranians create unified, centralized states? We should recognize first of all that most Iranian dynasties, like others in the Middle East, did not practise primogeniture. We do sometimes see power passing from father to son, but inheritance by brothers was also common, as were lengthy succession struggles. One can take as an example the Buyid dynasty of the tenth century, which was founded by three brothers originally from Deylam, each of whom controlled a different region. While there seems sometimes to have been a pre-eminent member of the dynasty, only rarely were the Buyid realms united. Nonetheless their politics remained closely connected and subject to interference from relatives. Despite the title 'Shahanshah' adopted by several Buyid rulers, power continued to be contested among the members of the dynasty through the whole period of their rule. The Buyids did often pass power to their sons, but surviving brothers were likely to contest the succession.[12]

The two dynasties that sprang up in southern and central Iran after the fall of the Ilkhans, the Injuids and Mozaffarids, were founded by members of the military elite of Iran who had risen in the service of the Ilkhans. They both show a pattern similar to that of the Buyids and a sense of common ownership of a divided realm. The Injuid founder, Sharaf al-Din Mahmud, claimed descent from Khvaja ‘Abdollah Ansari of Herat. On gaining control of southern Iran, he put three of his sons in control of its provinces. In the succession struggle after the death of the last Ilkhan Abu Sa‘id, Sharaf al-Din soon lost his life but his sons managed to achieve intermittent control over Fars, Esfahan, Kerman and Lorestan, centring their rule in Shiraz and fighting for control with outside dynasties and with each other. The 12 years of unitary rule under the last Injuid, Abu Ishaq, was due largely to the death of all his brothers.[13]

The Mozaffarids, who succeeded the Injuids as rulers of southern Iran, came from an originally Arab family in Khvaf, and had served the Mongol *atabeg* of Yazd. The founder of the dynasty, Mobarez al-Din Mohammad, achieved the governorship of Yazd under Abu Sa‘id, and after his death achieved control over Bam, Shiraz, Esfahan and Yazd, which he parcelled out as appanages among his sons. After his deposition and death, his sons spent their lives disputing each others' territory. When Timur arrived in the region, he initially kept the dynasty intact, appointing its members to the various regions; most were willing, but one brother remained inimical. Thus here again we see a sense of common ownership of territory, along with constant rivalry to achieve pre-eminence.[14] It seems clear that neither corporate sovereignty nor bloody tanistry was limited to the Turkic tradition. Thus, when we consider Iranians along with Turks as military and political actors, we see that their habits of rule were not entirely different: both Turks and Iranians had political practices which encouraged fragmentation.

Regionalism in Iran and Turan

It is clear that the concept of Iran/Turan as an opposing and complementary pair was shared by Turks and Iranians and that from early times the boundary was seen as the Oxus.[15] However, although the north/south boundary had important symbolic value, rule frequently extended across it,[16] and in practice it was often less significant than the divisions between eastern and western regions of the Middle East. This was true within both traditions. It has been noted that Iran was often divided between east and west, with Khorasan on one side and central Iran on the other. We see this in the ‘Abbasid period, with Buyid power extending as far east as Rayy, while the Ghaznavids controlled Ghazna and Khorasan, sometimes extending their control into central Iran. Although the Seljuqs brought both regions into their realm, as David Durand-Guédy has shown, the consciousness of difference remained active. The eastern and western sections of Iran were separated by history and even language. When the Seljuqs brought Khorasanian servitors with them to Esfahan and made them pre-eminent in the city, the previous elites, who came from western Iran, were bitterly resentful. Esfahan was part of western Iran, attached to the culture of Baghdad. We have been accustomed to see the vizier Nezam al-Molk as the representative of Iranian culture instructing the Turkic Seljuqs in the political traditions of his homeland, but to some Esfahanis he was the outsider from Khorasan, achieving domination over the life of a city which belonged to a different part of Iran, 'Eraq-e 'Ajam.[17] The east–west division of Iran remains visible in the Mongol period, due in part to the fact that the two major pasture regions were Khorasan in the east and Azerbaijan in the west, each serving as a centre for Mongol rule.

In the late thirteenth and fourteenth centuries, Khorasan became a battleground between the Ilkhans and the more conservative Chaghatayid Khanate, with the Iranian Kartid kings, as vassals of the Ilkhans, ruling the central regions from Herat. The politics at the fall of the Ilkhanate show fault lines in Turko-Mongolian culture which coincided with the regional traditions of the central Islamic lands. Now we see three areas developing different forms of legitimation within the steppe tradition. In Anatolia, the tribal confederations of the Qara Qoyunlu and Aq Qoyunlu – and briefly also the Ottomans – harked back to the Turkic Oghuz tradition, claiming descent from the mythical figure of Oghuz Khan connected to the Turkic Tü-Chüeh Empire, which had controlled much of the steppe from the sixth to the eighth century. This provided a useful Islamic identity, since the infant Oghuz Khan was said to have refused his mother's milk until she converted to Islam or at least monotheism.[18]

In Azerbaijan and central Iran, legitimation derived from the Mongol Empire, but primarily through the Ilkhans. The two Turko-Mongolian dynasties that established states in the central Ilkhanid territories, the Chupanids and the Jalayerids, both belonged to lineages which had intermarried with the Ilkhans and they enthroned Chinggisid puppet khans to legitimize their rule. In coinage, administration and artistic styles, the Jalayerids in particular followed the Ilkhanid example.[19] In this region, despite the continuing prestige of the Ilkhans, the Chinggisid monopoly on sovereign power had begun to weaken. The Chupanids began to claim Iranian descent for some of their puppet khans and, in the 1350s, the Jalayerids abandoned the fiction of a puppet khan and began to rule in their own name.[20]

Khorasan, on the other hand, was under the influence of the Chaghatayid Khanate and had a more conservative ideology. Here, throughout the fourteenth century, the Chinggisid house remained the only dynasty that could legitimately claim sovereign power. When the non-Chinggisid Qara'unas emirs took power over the western part of the Chaghatayid Khanate in 1346–47 and formed the Ulus Chaghatay, they ruled through a Chinggisid puppet, and Timur continued the practice when he seized power in 1370. In western Khorasan, which had remained within the Ilkhanate, Mongol powers descended from the commanders appointed to Khorasan by the Ilkhans, together with Iranian viziers and Sufi sheykhs, gathered together in 1336 to elect as khan Toghay Timur, a descendant of Chinggis Khan's brother.[21] Toghay Timur attempted to expand his power to the west, and apparently did, for some time, win the loyalty of the Mongol governor Eretna in Anatolia, but he was ultimately unable to achieve any success outside the eastern provinces.[22]

Although the Timurids did succeed in uniting Iran, the division between east and west remained visible during their rule, as it had under the Seljuqs and Ilkhans. It is notable that among the Iranian commanders in Timurid armies, those of Khorasan and Sistan, and to a lesser extent those of Mazandaran, appear to have achieved the greatest power and respect. The Sarbedarid emirs of Sabzavar, for example, continued to be favoured after their overthrow and were installed as governors of several smaller regions.[23] The political division between east and west reappeared with the weakening of Timurid central government. As Shahrokh declined during his final illness, his grandson Soltan-Mohammad, made governor of Qom, Soltaniya, Ray and Qazvin in 845/1441–42, soon began to expand his power and attract local rulers. He received delegations with tribute or gifts from a large number of regions, including Kashan, Sari, Esfahan, Firuzkuh and Azerbaijan. Thus, he threatened to create a separate and potentially independent power in central Iran. He appears, moreover, to have had ambitions in Fars, and Shahrokh ordered preparations to be made for the defence of Yazd, Shiraz and Abarquh.[24] Shahrokh died of illness while campaigning against Soltan-Mohammad in 850/1447. After his grandfather's death, Soltan-Mohammad moved quickly to re-establish his hold over central Iran and to annex Fars, while Khorasan and Transoxiana also emerged as separate centres of power. All struggled to control the capital at Herat. Soltan-Mohammad was eventually defeated and killed by his brother Abu'l-Qasem Babor, centred in Khorasan, but Abu'l-Qasem was not able to retake central and western Iran, which fell to the Qara Qoyunlu. Khorasan remained Timurid, despite several attempts at conquest by the Qara Qoyunlu and Aq Qoyunlu.[25] Thus we see a persistent division in Iran, both cultural and political, which endured even when Iran was unified under the Seljuqs, Mongols and Timurids.

As I have shown, the political and cultural divisions among the Turks and Mongols in the Middle East came to correspond to the east–west territorial division of Iran. There were also other divisions among the steppe peoples, which reflected not only the original divisions of the Mongol Empire, but also both earlier and later historical experience. The best known distinction was that between the Turkmen, who were of Oghuz descent and well established within the Middle East from the eleventh century, and the Turko-Mongolians, who had participated in the enterprise of the Mongol Empire. This has been touched on above, in the use of the Oghuz myth by the Turkmen dynasties of Anatolia, who now found it useful to assert a source of steppe prestige separate from that of the Mongols. To the Turks of the Mongol Empire, however, the Turkmen remained solidly inferior, a sentiment strongly expressed by Timur in writing to his Ottoman rival, Soltan Bayezid. Bayezid had written to Timur boasting that his ancestor Ertoghrul had defeated a large army of Mongols and Tatars.[26] Timur, for his part, wrote that Bayezid was giving himself airs beyond his station, since he was known to be the descendant of a Turkmen boatman, and Turkmen were famously without judgement.[27]

Within the Mongolian heritage itself there were also divisions by this time. The Timurids called themselves Chaghatay; members first of the Chaghatayid Khanate and then of the Ulus Chaghatay. Now the people of the eastern Chaghatayid Khanate, still loyal to their Chinggisid Khans but less adept in the Perso-Islamic tradition, were considered different and inferior. They were called Moghul or, more disdainfully, Chete, meaning robbers. The eastern Chaghatayids considered the Chaghatay less fully within the Mongol and Chinggisid tradition and called them all Qara'unas – mixed or mongrel.[28] The term Ozbek, used for the nomads of the eastern Qepchaq steppe, could also be a derogatory term for Turko-Mongolian groups considered uncultured.

In constructing ideas of loyalty and legitimation Turko-Mongolian and Iranian rulers looked not only to their own traditions, but also to the recent history of regions within the Middle East, much of it shared by the two groups. When Timur began to campaign in Iran, he challenged the Jalayerids' claim to be heirs to the Ilkhanid legacy. The province of Azerbaijan, over which Timur appointed his son Miranshah as governor, is referred to as the Kingdom of Hülegü.[29] Timur's son and successor, Shahrokh, referred in actions and in titles to the Ilkhanids, continuing Ilkhanid works and styles, and imitating the great Islamizing Ilkhan Ghazan.[30] In Khorasan and Transoxiana, which were the centres of their rule, the Timurids attached themselves to the general Chinggisid legacy, but also to that of the Chaghatayid Khanate which had controlled the region more recently. The service of their Barlas ancestor Qarachar Noyan to Chinggis Khan's second son Chaghatay, followed by the service of his descendants to successive Chaghatayid khans, became the subject of an elaborate myth fostered first by Timur and then by Shahrokh.[31] The Ottoman sultan Bayezid, turning east against Timur and aiming at the annexation of eastern Anatolia, wrote to the Mamluk sultan requesting that the shadow ʻAbbasid caliph declare him heir to the Seljuq Sultanate of Rum, which had controlled central Anatolia from the late Seljuq through most of the Mongol period.[32] The southeastern province of the Timurid realm – the region of Kabul and Ghazna, was remembered as the realm of Mahmud of Ghazna.[33] In Sistan, the memory of the Saffarid dynasty founded by Yaʻqub b. Leyth al-Saffar in the ninth century remained compelling; despite numerous conquests and periods of outside rule, successive dynasties claimed descent from them. The author of the sixteenth-century continuation of the *Tarikh-e Sistan*, Malek Shah Hoseyn, claimed descent from the Saffarids and presented the founding moment of the new Mehrabanid dynasty in 1233 as a convocation of descendants of Ya'qub from around Sistan, gathering to acclaim Malek Shams al-Din as ruler.[34] Thus rulers attached themselves not only to imperial myth, but also to the history of individual regions.

Varied Uses of the Shahnama and Iranian Myth

Just as the memory of recent kingdoms served to legitimize new dynasties, often commemorating a shared Turkic and Iranian history, the history and legend of ancient Iran served dynasties of various origins This trend began early, with the 'Abbasid dynasty's use of Iranian structures and royal symbolism. The interest of both the Ilkhans and the Timurids in the *Shahnama* is well known, shown in famous cultural artifacts from the thirteenth-century palace at Takht-e Soleyman to the magnificent illustrated *Shahnama* manuscripts commissioned by Mongol and Timurid royal patrons.[35] The affinity of the steppe rulers for the *Shahnama* could be explained as an attempt to assimilate the culture of their Iranian subjects while laying claim to their imperial tradition, but there were other causes for the attraction. They could also claim connection to the traditions preserved in the *Shahnama* through their association with the legendary Turanian king Afrasiyab, commonly connected to the Turks in the medieval period, and identified with the Turkic hero Er Alp Tonga.

Although Ferdowsi glorifies pure Iranian descent and depicts Afrasiyab and the Turanians as enemies of the Iranians, Dick Davis has pointed out that some of the greatest heroes of the *Shahnama* were related to the famous enemies of Iran: the Turanian Afrasiyab and the Arab Zahhak. The exemplary Kayanian king Kay Khosrow traced his ancestry back to Kay Kavus through Siyavosh, but also to Turan, on both sides of the family. His paternal grandmother was from Turan, related to Afrasiyab, and his mother was Afrasiyab's daughter. Thus he was at least half Turanian. The hero Rostam, son of Zal, traced his maternal ancestry back to the demon king Zahhak, king of the Arabs.[36] Therefore Turks and Arabs could claim connection not only to the villains, but also to the heroes of Iranian legend.

It is interesting to note that for some Iranians likewise the figures of Zahhak and Afrasiyab seem to have had appeal. It appears that the name Zahhak was popular in parts of eastern Iran in the early medieval period; the historian Gardizi's father was named Zahhak.[37] Fakhr al-Din Modabber Mobarakshah, historian and panegyirist for the Delhi sultans in the late twelfth and early thirteenth century, found a way to attach the dynasty to the Arabs by tracing their ancestry back to Zahhak.[38] Afrasiyab likewise seems to have had some stature among Iranians. We find the founding of the town of Fushanj near Herat attributed to his son.[39] It is more striking to find an Iranian dynasty adopting the name Al-e Afrasiyab; this was a Shi'i dynasty that held power on and off in parts of Mazandaran from the mid-fourteenth to the fifteenth century.[40] The use of the name was not just a peculiarity of the Caspian region, since we find the name Afrasiyab also in the ruling dynasty of Lor in Timur's time.[41]

Iranian history and legend worked for many people at many levels; what I want to examine next is its regional aspects. As I have shown, local Iranian rulers and elites were important actors in the political and the cultural sphere; they must therefore be counted among the users and creators of identity in Iran, and many acted within a confined geographical context.[42] Although the concepts of Iran and *Aniran* permeate the *Shahnama*, the geographical definition of Iran varies, and much of the text is concerned with heroes and rulers attached to smaller regions within or neighbouring Iran.[43] The legends of ancient Iran and the history of the Sasanians, who ruled regions through governors, were used by local rulers and nourished regional patriotism as well as imperial identity. Local histories chronicling regional dynasties often give genealogies of the rulers going back to the Sasanians and earlier legendary figures. A number of these have a distinctly local character, serving to give regions and their rulers a separate legitimation within the Iranian umbrella.

The province of Khorasan provides good material for analysing local legitimation. We have two works from the fifteenth century that give a description of Khorasan and the regions to the south, including local history and lore. The first of these is the so-called *Geography* of Hafez-e Abru (d. 833/1430) written at the court of Shahrokh.[44] Towards the end of the century, Mo'in al-Din Zamchi Esfezari (d. 915/1510), serving in the *divan* of Soltan-Hoseyn-e Bayqara, wrote a paean to Khorasan – the historical geography *Rowzat al-jannat fi owsaf madinat Harat*. For the region of Sistan specifically, we have a series of local histories covering a long historical period. From the fourteenth century on we depend on the *Ehya al-moluk* by Malek Shah Hoseyn b. Malek Gheyas al-Din Mohammad, who served under Shah 'Abbas.[45] In eastern Iran, not surprisingly, claims to historical roots often went back to the earlier and legendary sections of the *Shahnama*, particularly the cycle concerning the Kayanian line, which was based there. Hafez-e Abru writes that the Pishdadi Manuchehr erected a building in Balkh, but the city is connected primarily to the Kayanid Lohrasp, successor to Kay Khosrow, who built the city and made it his capital.[46] Lohrasp's successor Kay Goshtasp is credited with founding Herat, and the subsequent Kayanid kings Bahman and Darab with additional building.[47]

The region of Sistan, along with Kabul and other southeastern regions, was connected to the mythical lineage of the warrior Garshasp and his descendant Rostam, the subject of one of the most elaborate and popular cycles of the *Shahnama*, which chronicles the exploits of the lineage and its changeable interactions with the Kayanid kings. Garshasp was said to have founded Sistan and its major city Zarang. According to one myth, he was a descendant of Jamshid and the daughter of the king of Zabol.[48] Later, in granting Rostam freedom from servility to the monarch, the Kayanid monarch Kay Kavus is supposed to have awarded him Sistan and Zabolistan.[49] Still later, the Sasanian founder Ardashir Papagan (224–42) was said to have refounded the capital Zarang.[50]

According to Esfezari, the Mehrabanid maleks of Sistan, who ruled from 1236 to the mid-sixteenth century, traced their genealogy yet further back and connected themselves to the Kayanid lineage. He reproduces a genealogy attaching the Mehrabanids to the Saffarids, and going back through the Sasanian kings to Kay Lohrasp, then from Lohrasp's uncle Kay Khosrow to Adam via Gayumars. The kings of Farah, he wrote, were also a great ancient line, connected to that of the kings of Sistan.[51] Not surprisingly, local lore in Khorasan also enshrined the memory of Goshtasp, Rostam and Rostam's father Zal. According to Hafez-e Abru, Zar-e Morgh Mandish, one of the five great mountains of Ghur, was the location where the mythical bird Simorgh kept Zal. The dragon that Zal's father Sam had killed in the *Shahnama* was in the *boluk* (district) of Tabadkan, and the place was still marked by a red stain.[52]

In the more westerly regions of Iran, the Sasanian dynasty generally played a larger role in the regional lore. I will give a few examples here. In his *Geography*, Hafez-e Abru describes the five sections (*kurat*) of Fars, each named, he writes, after the king who developed it. These are Kurat-e Estakhr, Kurat-e Darabjerd, Kurat-e Ardashir Khurra, Kurat-e Shapur Khurra and Kurat-e Qobad (Kavad) Khurra (also called Kurat-e Arrajan). Estakhr was founded by Gayumars and built up by Jamshid, while Darabjerd was named after the great Dara b. Bahman b. Esfandiyar, a successor to Goshtasp. The founding or building of the other three *kurats* is ascribed to Sasanian kings: Ardashir I (224–39), his successor Shapur (240–72) and Kavad I (488–96 and 499–531). While all of these figures were kings over an empire (real or mythical), the districts named for them lie within the province of Fars.[53]

The city of Yazd, on the edge of Fars, produced two local histories in the fifteenth century, which were used and augmented in the seventeenth century by Mostowfi Bafqi in his *Jame'-e Mofidi*. These histories introduced a new founding legend centred on a newly positive view of Alexander, who was said to have founded Yazd and developed the city, originally as a camp for prisoners. The changing attitude towards Alexander has been connected to the rule of outside imperial powers – Mongols and Timurids – who coincided with a flourishing period for the city.[54] This founding myth also served to set Yazd apart historically, giving it a separate narrative. A different view of Alexander's activity, coming from an earlier period and focusing on his destructiveness, is found in the *Tarikh-e Qom*, written originally in Arabic, and preserved in a Persian translation from the early fifteenth century. In this story, Qom was destroyed almost totally by Alexander and restored by Kavad I, mentioned above.[55]

In the Caspian region, the founding legend of Ruyan, repeated by Mar'ashi from earlier histories, takes the story back to an early period starting with

Faridun, whose birthplace was identified as a village in Larijan. The founding of Ruyan was connected with the famous bowshot of Arash, which identified the Oxus as the boundary of Turan and Iran and gave Manuchehr control over the territory stretching to Marv. Having taken his revenge for the murder of Iraj, Manuchehr buried Tur and his brother Sam in Sari; Mar'ashi states that the dome over their grave was visible in his time.[56] Local histories also connect the region's history to the legendary king of Tabarestan, Gavbara, supposedly a great-grandson of the Sasanian king Jamasp (r. 496/7 to 498/9), who was a brother of Shah Kavad I. The founding of the town of Sari in Mazandaran was credited to Gavbara's grandson, who had moved from Gilan to Tabarestan. The Sasanian period was used further for the genealogies of local dynasties. The Baduspanid ostandars of Ruyan traced their genealogy back to Gavbara through his son Baduspan, and the Bavandid maleks of Mazandaran claimed kinship with the Sasanians through Bav, supposedly a great-grandson of Kavad I, who went to Tabarestan at the time of the Arab conquest and was elected ruler by its people.[57] The historian Mar'ashi, who belonged to the dynasty of sayyeds ruling Sari and Amol in the Timurid period, connected himself to this line through his Bavandid grandmother.[58]

Dick Davis has written, 'We quickly see that notions of an Iranian identity, as they are embodied in the *Shahnama*, are complicated, and often apparently self-contradictory, and that they strongly resist attempts to essentialize the concept'.[59] The ambiguity made the text useful for the population of medieval Iran. The *Shahnama* and other legendary accounts could be used and understood in quite different ways; they showed the glory and the universality of Iranian royal lines, but also the divisions within them. Regions could be connected to the history of the central monarchy but also given a separate place, sometimes antagonistic to the royal dynasty. Furthermore, while setting the Iranians in opposition to the Turks/Turanians, the *Shahnama* nonetheless gives almost equal prominence to the Turanians. The history it recounts is also a history of the Turks and Arabs; more than this, it connects them – especially the Turanians – not only to the central line but also to several of the most beloved and heroic figures of Iranian myth.

Conclusion

In this chapter I have tried to examine the concepts of Iran and Turan more as a complimentary pair than as an opposition of two unitary spheres. By the fifteenth century, Turks and/or Mongolians had been ruling much of Iran for almost 400 years, interacting with Iranian scholars, bureaucrats and soldiers. They continued to identify themselves with steppe traditions just as Iranians continued to emphasize their own heritage, and the texts that have come down to us preserve this difference by assigning a set of characteristics to each population, seen as appropriate to the position they held within state and society. We need to recognize that some of these differences are constructed ones, and that they are essentialized. Members of the Iranian landed elites were active, and trained, as soldiers and they could be an important factor in regional struggles. Local rule existed not only in the peripheral regions, such as the Caspian provinces and Sistan, but also at a somewhat lower level in many other parts of Iran, and in times of weak central rule, local rulers undoubtedly contributed to the friability of the state. Looking at the larger dynasties and their traditions, we see that the custom of shared rule and lateral succession usually attributed to the Turks was shared by Iranian dynasties as well.

While the accepted division was that between Iran and Turan, with a north/south boundary at the Oxus, the operative divisions were often east–west, for both Turko-Mongolian and Iranian populations. *Iran-zamin* was not an easy entity to keep together, or for that matter to define. As scholars have shown before, eastern and western Iran were more often separate than united, and numerous regions within both often sought and sometimes enjoyed various levels of independence and felt a strong local patriotism. The Mongol Empire was likewise no longer one entity. Rulers attempting to establish and legitimize their rule did not stick to one type of claim, but used what was available, identifying themselves with rulers both of the distant and of the recent past, with traditions both of the *Shahnama* and of the steppe, making claims to universal power, and to power over specific regions.

Notes:

1. Mo'in al-Din Zamchi Esfezāri, *Rowzāt al-jannāt fi owsāf madinat Harāt*, vol. II, pp. 13–14.
2. See particularly the works of Jürgen Paul, notably *Lokale und imperiale Herrschaft im Iran des 12. Jahrhunderts.*
3. For a discussion of these histories see Charles Melville, 'The Caspian provinces', pp. 45–91.
4. See C. Edmund Bosworth, 'Sistan and its local histories', pp. 31–43.
5. Mohammad b. 'Ali b. Mohammad Shabānkāra'i, *Majma' al-ansāb*, including the continuation by Faryumadi, pp. 342–43.
6. Beatrice Forbes Manz, *Power, Politics and Religion in Timurid Iran*, pp. 129–30.
7. Hāfez-e Abru, *Zobdat al-tavārikh*, pp. 347, 720.
8. See Martin B. Dickson, 'Sháh Tahmásp and the Úzbeks', p. 25.
9. See Joseph F. Fletcher, 'The Mongols'.
10. Vladimir Minorsky, 'The Aq-qoyunlu and land reforms', pp. 451–58; John E. Woods, *The Aqquyunlu*, pp. 143–45.
11. Maria Eva Subtelny, 'Centralizing reform and its opponents', pp. 123–51.
12. Tilman Nagel, 'Buyids'.
13. John Limbert, 'Inju dynasty'.
14. Peter Jackson, 'Muẓaffarids'.
15. Christine Noelle-Karimi, *The Pearl in its Midst*, pp. 6–8; Ehsan Yarshater, 'Iranian national history', p. 373.
16. See Jürgen Paul, 'Nachrichten arabischer Geographen aus Mittleasien', p. 181.
17. David Durand-Guédy, 'What does the History of Isfahan tell us about Iranian society during the Seljuq period?', pp. 62–70.
18. Woods, *The Aqqoyunlu*, pp. 7–9; Devin DeWeese, *Islamization and Native Religion in the Golden Horde*, pp. 85–86.
19. Charles Melville, 'Čobān'; Patrick Wing, *The Jalayirids*, p. 160.
20. Wing, *Jalayirids*, pp. 129–34; J.A. Boyle, 'Dynastic and political history of the Īl-Khāns', p. 416.
21. Jean Aubin, 'Le Quriltai de Sultân-Maydân', pp. 180–92.
22. Wing, *Jalayirids*, pp. 87–89; Jürgen Paul, 'Mongol aristocrats and Beyliks in Anatolia', p. 118.
23. Beatrice Forbes Manz, *The Rise and Rule of Tamerlane*, pp. 95–96.
24. Manz, *Power, Politics and Religion*, pp. 252–53.
25. Ibid., pp. 259–74.
26. 'Abd al-Hoseyn Navā'i, ed., *Asnād va makātebāt-e tārikhi-ye Irān*, p. 101.
27. Michele Bernardini, *Mémoire et propagande à l'époque timouride*, p. 151.
28. Beatrice Forbes Manz, 'The development and meaning of Čagatay identity', pp. 37–39; Maria Subtelny, 'Art and politics in early 16th century Central Asia', p. 133.
29. 'Ali Yazdi, *Zafarnāma*, vol. I, p. 445.
30. Beatrice Forbes Manz, 'Mongol history, rewritten and relived', pp. 143–46.
31. John E. Woods, 'Timur's genealogy', pp. 90–96; Manz, *Power, Politics and Religion*, pp. 41–42.
32. Anne Broadbridge, *Kingship and Ideology in the Islamic and Mongol Worlds*, p. 175.

33. See for example, Yazdi, *Zafarnāma*, vol. I, p. 401; Esfezāri, *Rowzāt al-jannāt*, vol. I, p. 364.
34. Bosworth, 'Sistan and its local histories', pp. 39, 41.
35. For the palace at Takht-e Soleyman, see Tomoko Masuya, 'Ilkhanid courtly life', pp. 98–99.
36. Dick Davis, 'Iran and *Aniran*', pp. 39–41.
37. C.E. Bosworth, 'Gardīzī', p. 314.
38. C.E. Bosworth, 'The heritage of rulership in early Islamic Iran', pp. 13–14.
39. Esfezāri, *Rowzāt al-jannāt*, vol. I, p. 54.
40. C.E. Bosworth, 'Āl-e Afrāsīāb (1)'.
41. Mo'in al-Din Natanzi, *Extraits du Muntakhab al-tavārīkh-i Mu'ini*, pp. 50–53.
42. For an earlier period see Sarah Bowen Savant, *The New Muslims of Post-Conquest Iran*, pp. 11–12.
43. Davis, 'Iran and *Aniran*', pp. 38–39.
44. For the sources and probable title of Hafez-e Abru's *Geography*, see Ono Hiroshi, 'Ḥāfiẓ-i Abrū's geographical work, the so-called *Jughrāfiyā*', pp. 53–68.
45. Bosworth, 'Sistan and its local histories', p. 39.
46. Hāfez-e Abru, ed. and trans. Dorothea Krawulsky, *Ḫorāsān zur Timuridenzeit nach dem Tārīḫ-e Ḥāfiẓ-e Abrū (verf. 817–823 h.)*, text, p. 65. For this myth see also Prods Oktor Skjærvø, 'Kayāniān viii. Kay Luhrāsp'.
47. Hāfez-e Abru, ed. Krawulsky, text, p. 14.
48. C.E. Bosworth, 'Tārik̲-e Sistān'; Yarshater, 'Iranian national history', pp. 429–33.
49. Bosworth, 'Sistan and its local histories', p. 32.
50. Ibid., p. 31.
51. Esfezāri, *Rowzāt al-jannāt*, vol. I, pp. 330–31, 336.
52. Hāfez-e Abru, ed. Krawulsky, text, pp. 33, 95.
53. Hāfez-e Abru, *Joghrāfiyā-ye Hāfez-e Abru*, vol. II, pp. 107–8, 116, 119, 129, 137; Christopher Brunner, 'Geographical and administrative divisions', pp. 750–52.
54. Derek J. Mancini-Lander, 'Memory on the Boundaries of Empire', pp. 161–234.
55. Hasan b. 'Ali b. Hasan b. 'Abd al-Malek Qomi, *Ketāb-e Tārikh-e Qom*, p. 24.
56. Melville, 'The Caspian provinces', pp. 70–72.
57. W. Madelung, 'Āl-e Bāvand', 'Baduspanids' and 'Dabuyids'.
58. Melville, 'The Caspian provinces', p. 53.
59. Davis, 'Iran and *Aniran*', p. 38.

Bibliography:

Aubin, Jean, 'Le Quriltai de Sultân-Maydân', *Journal Asiatique* 279 (1991), pp. 175–97.

Bernardini, Michele, *Mémoire et propagande à l'époque timouride. Studia Iranica*, cahier 37 (Paris: Association pour l'avancement des études iraniennes, 2008).

Bosworth, C. Edmund, 'The heritage of rulership in early Islamic Iran and the search for dynastic connections with the past', *Iranian Studies* 11, no. 4 (1978), pp. 7–34.

— 'Āl-e Afrāsīāb (1)', *Encyclopaedia Iranica*, vol. I (1985), pp. 742–43.

— 'Sistan and its local histories', *Iranian Studies* 33, no. 1–2 (2000), pp. 31–43.

— 'Gardīzī, Abū Saʿīd ʿAbd-al-Ḥayy', *Encyclopaedia Iranica*, vol. X (2001), pp. 314–15.

— 'Tārik̲-e Sistān', online at www.iranicaonline.org/articles/tarikh-e-sistan [accessed 15 March 2019].

Boyle, J.A., 'Dynastic and political history of the Īl-Khāns', in *The Cambridge History of Iran, vol. 5, The Saljuq and Mongol Periods*, ed. J. A. Boyle (Cambridge: Cambridge University Press, 1968), pp. 303–421.

Broadbridge, Anne, *Kingship and Ideology in the Islamic and Mongol Worlds* (Cambridge: Cambridge University Press, 2008).

Brunner, Christopher, 'Geographical and administrative divisions: Settlement and economy', in *Cambridge History of Iran, vol. 3(2), The Seleucid, Parthian and Sasanid Periods*, ed. Ehsan Yarshater (Cambridge: Cambridge University Press, 1983), pp. 747–77.

Davis, Dick. 'Iran and *Aniran*: The shaping of a legend', in *Iran Facing Others: Identity Boundaries in a Historical Perspective*, ed. Abbas Amanat and Farzin Vejdani (New York: Palgrave McMillan, 2012), pp. 37–48.

DeWeese, Devin, *Islamization and Native Religion in the Golden Horde: Baba Tükles and Conversion to Islam in Historical and Epic Tradition* (University Park, PA: Pennsylvania State University Press, 1994).

Dickson, Martin B., 'Sháh Tahmásp and the Úzbeks (The Duel for Khurásán with 'Ubayd Khán)', doctoral dissertation (Princeton University, 1958).

Durand-Guédy, David, 'What does the History of Isfahan tell us about Iranian society during the Seljuq period?', in *The Age of the Seljuqs: The Idea of Iran*, vol. 6, ed. Edmund Herzig and Sarah Stewart (London: I.B. Tauris, 2015), pp. 68–73.

Esfezāri, Mo'in al-Din Zamchi, *Rowzāt al-jannāt fi owsāf madinat Harāt*, ed. Sayyed Mohammad Kāzem Imām, 2 vols (Tehran: Dāneshgāh-e Tehrān, 1338/1959).

Fletcher, Joseph F. 'The Mongols: Ecological and social perspectives', in Joseph F. Fletcher, *Studies on Chinese and Islamic Inner Asia*, ed. Beatrice Forbes Manz (Aldershot: Variorum, Ashgate, 1995), Chap. IX.

Hāfez-e Abru, ed. and trans. Dorothea Krawulsky, *Ḫorāsān zur Timuridenzeit nach dem Tārīḫ-e Ḥāfiẓ-e Abrū (verf. 817–823 h.)*, vol. 1, edition and introduction, vol. 2, translation (*Beihefte zum tübinger Atlas des vorderen Orients*, Reihe B, Nr. 46) (Wiesbaden: Dr. Ludwig Reichert Verlag, 1982).

— *Zobdat al-tavārikh*, ed. Sayyed Kamāl Hājj Sayyed Javādi (Tehran: Sāzmān-e chāp va enteshārāt-e vezārat-e farhang-e ershād-e eslāmi, 1372/1993).

— *Joghrāfiyā-ye Hāfez-e Abru*, ed. Sādeq Sajjādi (Tehran: Bonyān, vol. 1, 1375/1997, vols 2 and 3, 1378/1999).

Hiroshi, Ono, 'Ḥāfiẓ-i Abrū's geographical work, the so-called *Jughrāfiyā*: Its significance and evaluation in relation to Rashīd al-Dīn's works', in *Chinese and Asian Geographical and Cartographical Views on Central Asia and its Adjacent Regions*, *Journal of Asian History* 9, no. 102 (2015), pp. 53–68.

Jackson, Peter, 'Muẓaffarids', *Encyclopedia of Islam*, 2nd edn, vol. VII (1993), pp. 820–22.

Limbert, John, 'Inju dynasty', *Encyclopaedia Iranica*, vol. XIII (2006), pp. 143–47.

Madelung, W. 'Āl-e Bāvand', *Encyclopaedia Iranica*, vol. I (1985), pp. 747–53.

— 'Baduspanids', *Encyclopaedia Iranica*, vol. II (1989), pp. 385–91.

— 'Dabuyids', *Encyclopaedia Iranica*, vol. VI (1993), pp. 541–44.

Mancini-Lander, Derek J., 'Memory on the Boundaries of Empire: Narrating Place in the Early Modern Local Historiography of Yazd', doctoral dissertation (University of Michigan, 2012).

Manz, Beatrice Forbes, *The Rise and Rule of Tamerlane* (Cambridge: Cambridge University Press, 1989).

— 'The development and meaning of Čagatay identity', in *Muslims in Central Asia: Expressions of Identity and Change*, ed. Jo-Ann Gross (Durham, NC: Duke University Press, 1992), pp. 27–45.

— 'Mongol history, rewritten and relived', in *Mythes historiques du monde musulman*, ed. Denise Aigle, *Revue du monde musulman et de la Méditerranée* 89–90 (2001), pp. 129–49.

— *Power, Politics and Religion in Timurid Iran* (Cambridge: Cambridge University Press, 2007).

Masuya, Tomoko, 'Ilkhanid courtly life', in *The Legacy of Genghis Khan: Courtly Art and Culture in Western Asia, 1256–1353*, ed. Linda Komaroff and Stefano Carboni (Metropolitan Museum of Art, New York: Yale University Press, 2002), pp. 74–103.

Melville, Charles, 'Čobān', *Encyclopaedia Iranica*, vol. V (1992), pp. 875–78.

— 'The Caspian provinces: A world apart. Three local histories of Mazandaran', *Iranian Studies* 33, no. 1–2 (2000), pp. 45–91.

Minorsky, Vladimir, 'The Aq-qoyunlu and land reforms', *Bulletin of the School of Oriental and African Studies* 27, no. 3 (1955), pp. 449–62.

Nagel, Tilman, 'Buyids', *Encyclopaedia Iranica*, vol. IV (1990), pp. 578–86.

Natanzi, Mo'in al-Din, *Extraits du Muntakhab al-tavārīkh-i Mu'ini (Anonym d'Iskandar)*, ed. Jean Aubin (Tehran: Khayyām, 1336/1957).

Navā'i, 'Abd al-Hoseyn, ed., *Asnād va makātebāt-e tārikhi-ye Irān* (Tehran: Bongāh-e tarjoma va nashr-e ketāb, 2536 shāhi/1977).

Noelle-Karimi, Christine, *The Pearl in its Midst: Herat and the Mapping of Khurasan (15th–18th Centuries)* (Vienna: Österreichische Akademie der Wissenschaften, philosophisch-historische Klasse Denkschriften 463, 2014).

Paul, Jürgen, 'Nachrichten arabischer Geographen aus Mittleasien', *Bamberger Mittelasienstudien: Konferenzakten Bamberg 15–16. Juni 1990* (Berlin: Schwarz, 1994), pp. 179–91.

— 'Mongol aristocrats and Beyliks in Anatolia. A study of Astarābādī's *Bazm wa Razm*', *Eurasian Studies* 9, no. 1–2 (2011), pp. 105–58.

— *Lokale und imperiale Herrschaft im Iran des 12. Jahrhunderts: Herrschaftspraxis und Konzepte* (Wiesbaden: Reichert, 2016).

Qomi, Hasan b. 'Ali b. Hasan b. 'Abd al-Malek, *Ketāb-e Tārikh-e Qom*, ed. Sayyed Jalāl al-Din Tehrāni (Tehran: Majles, 1313/1934).

Savant, Sarah Bowen, *The New Muslims of Post-Conquest Iran: Tradition, Memory, and Conversion* (Cambridge: Cambridge University Press, 2013).

Shabānkāra'i, Mohammad b. 'Ali b. Mohammad, *Majma' al-ansāb*, ed. M. H. Mohaddes, including continuation by Faryumadi (Tehran: Amir Kabir, 1363/1984).

Skjærvø, Prods Oktor, 'Kayāniān viii. Kay Luhrāsp, Kay Lohrāsb', *Encyclopaedia Iranica*, online at http://www.iranicaonline.org/articles/kayanian-viii [accessed 15 March 2019].

Subtelny, Maria, 'Art and politics in early 16th century Central Asia', *Central Asiatic Journal* 27, no. 1–2 (1983), pp. 121–48.

— 'Centralizing reform and its opponents in the late Timurid period', *Iranian Studies* 21, no. 1–2 (1988), pp. 123–51.

Wing, Patrick, *The Jalayirids: Dynastic State Formation in the Mongol Middle East* (Edinburgh: Edinburgh University Press, 2016).

Woods, John E., 'Timur's genealogy', in *Intellectual Studies on Islam, Essays Written in Honor of Martin B. Dickson*, ed. Michel M. Mazzaoui and Vera B. Moreen (Salt Lake City: University of Utah Press, 1990), pp. 85–126.

— *The Aqquyunlu: Clan, Confederation, Empire*, 2nd edn (Salt Lake City: University of Utah Press, 1999).

Yarshater, Ehsan, 'Iranian national history', in *The Cambridge History of Iran, vol. 3 (1), The Seleucid, Parthian and Sasanid Periods*, ed. Ehsan Yarshater (Cambridge: Cambridge University Press, 1983), pp. 359–477.
Yazdi, 'Ali, *Zafarnāma*, ed. Mohammad 'Abbāsi (Tehran: Amir Kabir, 1336 /1957).

3

An Idea of Iran on Mongol Foundations: Territory, Dynasties and Tabriz as Royal City (Seventh/Thirteenth to Ninth/Fifteenth Century)

Daniel Zakrzewski
(Marburg University)

The Mongol conquests in the seventh/thirteenth century had tremendous effects all over Eurasia. Hence it seems worthwhile to ask how the invasions of Chinggis Khan (d. 624/1227) and his descendants and subsequent Mongol rule in the Middle East affected the idea of Iran. Bert Fragner has raised this question most forcefully and attributed significant changes in the idea of Iran to the Mongol Ilkhanid dynasty.[1] Chinggis Khan's grandson Hülegü (d. 663/1265) founded this dynasty during his campaign to the Middle East, which entailed the extinction of the 'Abbasid caliphate of Baghdad in 656/1258.

According to Fragner, the Ilkhanid rulers revived the term 'Iran' as a territorial-political designation and adopted it as the official name of their realm at the turn of the eighth/fourteenth century. Fragner further argues that all political concepts of 'Iran' in later periods derived from this alleged Mongol notion and notes one particularly important aspect characterizing it, in addition to the territorial vision and the name. This additional core aspect is, in Fragner's words, 'the idea of Tabriz being the undisputed and so to say natural capital of Iran'.[2]

Tabriz is well known as the principal urban centre of the Mongols in Iran. The ruler most closely attached to the city was Hülegü's great-grandson Ghazan (d. 703/1304) who embraced Islam shortly before his accession to the throne in 694/1295, ultimately securing the conversion of the Ilkhanid dynasty.[3] Ghazan had a massive pious endowment (*vaqf*) complex erected just outside the walls of Tabriz, which included the mausoleum of the ruler, a congregational mosque and a number of other structures.

After the collapse of the house of Hülegü in the middle of the eighth/fourteenth century, several successor dynasties of the Ilkhans up to the early Safavids at the beginning of the tenth/sixteenth century likewise accorded Tabriz the distinction of being the principal urban centre. Fragner notes that in the ninth/fifteenth century, the leaders of the Turkmen Qara Qoyunlu and Aq Qoyunlu would proclaim themselves king (*kesra* or *padshah*) of Iran as soon as they captured Tabriz, like the Safavid Esma'il (d. 930/1524) when he took the city in 907/1501.[4]

This chapter attempts to refine Fragner's argument regarding the changes in the idea of Iran in the wake of the Mongol conquests and to develop it further. The ultimate objective is to trace the emergence and perpetuation of the idea of a territorially distinct Islamic kingdom named Iran for which Tabriz would stand as royal city, advancing a twofold thesis. First, the Ilkhan Ghazan epitomized this idea and his mosque-mausoleum *vaqf* complex at Tabriz became its foundational pillar signalling the special royal status of the city. Second, similar complexes or other royal monuments erected in and around Tabriz by major post-Ilkhanid rulers helped perpetuate the special status of the city through the eighth/fourteenth and ninth/fifteenth centuries. Such complexes and monuments continued to mark Tabriz as royal city and it was and is possible to view them as constantly renewed material manifestations of the idea that it stood for a territorially distinct Islamic kingdom named Iran.

Advancing this twofold thesis implies raising the question of whether the territorial vision of Iran and the application of the name to the realm of the Ilkhans does indeed represent a Mongol notion, as Fragner asserts. The same question arises with regard to the special status of Tabriz as royal city, especially as perpetuated in the eighth/fourteenth and ninth/fifteenth centuries.

In the Turko-Mongol nomadic tradition, it was not uncommon to associate notions of legitimacy and sovereignty with specific localities.[5] However, it seems unwise to assume that Ghazan and all other lords of Tabriz during the period under study shared the same notions of legitimacy and sovereignty. Moreover, one may doubt whether any of them considered Tabriz a royal city standing for the idea of a territorially distinct Islamic kingdom named Iran (hereafter referred to simply as Iran), or attached major importance to this idea.

The next section will continue with a brief review of Fragner's and other relevant research and further contextualize the thesis of this chapter, adding some remarks about concepts such as 'royal city' and 'capital'. It will also introduce the main sources for this study, which consist largely of Persian historiographical works written between the seventh/thirteenth and tenth/sixteenth centuries. Then, the analysis will proceed in two steps.

One section will examine the Mongol foundations or, in other words, the emergence of the idea that Tabriz stands for Iran as a specific Ilkhanid-Ghazanid legacy. A final section will trace the perpetuation of that idea under the successor dynasties of the house of Hülegü, especially the Turkmen Qara Qoyunlu and Aq Qoyunlu in the ninth/fifteenth century. In both sections, the focus will be on visions of Iran as a territorially distinct royal realm bearing this name and on the material and symbolic signs marking Tabriz as its royal city.

Scholarship, Sources and Concepts

Fragner situates the revival of the term 'Iran (or *Iran-zamin*)' as a territorial-political designation in the context of post-'Abbasid history and describes it as a deliberate policy pursued by the Mongols. He asserts that the Ilkhans reinvented that concept of the Sasanians, realizing that their dominions roughly corresponded to the realm of this pre-Islamic Persian dynasty. Still according to Fragner, the non-Muslim conquerors of the Iranian plateau eventually aimed at carving out a proper place for themselves in the political and cultural landscape of the Middle East against the background of disintegrative developments in the Mongol Empire at large. In Fragner's view, this process culminated in the adoption of the prestigious ancient name 'Iran' as the official designation of the Ilkhanid realm and in the conversion of Ghazan, who would 'proclaim himself "*pādishāh-i Īrān va Islām*"'.[6]

Specialists in ancient Iranian history disagree whether the territorial-political concept of Iran is, in fact, more ancient than the Sasanians, but apparently agree that the land bearing this name may originally have been located east of the Iranian plateau.[7] There also seems to have been some ambiguity regarding the exact territorial extension of Iran, both at the time of the Sasanians and under the Mongols. While the Oxus river was then widely accepted as Iran's eastern frontier, the Euphrates or even the Nile were regarded as its western boundary.[8] Be that as it may, the Ilkhanid realm was generally restricted to the lands between the Oxus and the Euphrates, despite occasional campaigns beyond these limits. In any case, it seems that the territorial vision of Iran was coupled with a historical vision insofar as the land had been ruled by successive royal dynasties since ancient times.

As Charles Melville has shown, such a territorial-historical vision that equated the realm of the Mongol Ilkhans with the kingdom of Iran and named it accordingly, clearly predated Ghazan.[9] This chapter will present additional evidence for the use of 'Iran' or 'Iran-zamin' as designations for the Ilkhanid dominions already in the middle decades of the seventh/thirteenth century. It will further argue that this rather reflects a vision adopted by the Persian elites and expressed mainly in works of history instead of a deliberate policy pursued by the Mongols. The term 'Iran' as a territorial designation formed part of the Persian historical tradition and geopolitical imagination and it seems more likely that the indigenous elites of the Iranian lands recognized the dominions of the Ilkhans as the realm of their own past kings.

In any case, Fragner's emphasis on the importance of Ghazan and his conversion is, of course, completely justified. Yet this chapter will not expand on the religious aspect of the idea of a territorially distinct Islamic kingdom which the Ilkhan epitomized. Suffice it to say that from Ghazan onwards, all rulers considered as kings of Iran professed Islam in one form or another and claimed legitimacy based on a combination of various religious and dynastic elements. The Mongols had brought with them the notion that the lineage of Chinggis Khan possessed a heavenly mandate to rule the world which other lineages could claim as the Chinggisids died out in the Iranian lands in the eighth/fourteenth and ninth/fifteenth centuries. Moreover, temporary non-Muslim rule and the effective extinction of the 'Abbasid caliphate contributed to the growth and spread of universalist models of sacral kingship which often drew on elements of Sufism and Shi'ism.[10]

Ghazan's importance for the purposes of this study does not so much derive from his conversion as such but from a related aspect which Fragner also stressed. The ruler represented the link between the territorial vision of Iran associated with the Ilkhanid dynasty and the special status of Tabriz as royal city. Fragner asserts that the city was granted the epithet *dar al-saltana*, the abode of sovereign rule, as its official designation in Ghazan's reign to indicate the special royal status of Tabriz. In Fragner's view it was in this way that the Mongol Ilkhans could be portrayed as legitimate successors to the 'Abbasids and Tabriz as successor to the former *dar al-khelafa*, Baghdad.[11]

Judith Pfeiffer recently edited a collective volume avowedly dealing with Tabriz between the seventh/thirteenth and ninth/fifteenth centuries but concentrating strongly on the period of the Ilkhans. In her introduction, Pfeiffer states that 'Mongol rule [...] paved the way for the establishment of the territorial regional empires of the Safavids, Ottomans and Mughals'.[12] But the volume does not explore the revival of the term 'Iran' as a territorial-political designation associated with the house of Hülegü. Hence, it also does not explore the idea that Tabriz itself came to stand for a kingdom bearing that name. The absence of this line of thought may be due to Pfeiffer's disagreement with Fragner on the question of whether the special status that Tabriz acquired under the Mongols was somehow unique, like the status of Baghdad had been under the 'Abbasids.[13]

Pfeiffer is certainly right to point out that even '[w]hen Tabriz was at the height of its cultural, political and economic importance, it never was the *only* city that mattered (original emphasis)'.[14] One might ask whether Baghdad was ever the only city that mattered when the 'Abbasid caliphate still existed there, but this question would have to be answered elsewhere. What is relevant here is that the epithet *dar al-saltana* was not used exclusively for Tabriz and that other epithets and expressions were used to signal the special status of the city as well. All in all, there was little consistency in the use of honorary epithets like *dar al-saltana* and as with 'Iran', Fragner insists perhaps a bit too much on the official character of such designations.

Nonetheless, the status of Tabriz as royal city indeed developed as something unique, especially after the collapse of the Ilkhanid dynasty. In order to trace the emergence and perpetuation of that status, the analysis will focus on honorary epithets applied to Tabriz, in particular when they are coupled with the term 'Iran' as a territorial-political designation. Most scholars tend to translate honorary epithets like *dar al-saltana* or *dar al-molk*, the abode of kingship, as 'capital', but David Durand-Guédy has argued convincingly that this kind of handy translation should perhaps be abandoned in contexts of Turko-Mongol nomadic domination.[15] Hence the terms 'principal city' or 'principal urban centre' will be employed here instead of 'capital', and the term 'royal city' when speaking about the significance of Tabriz for the idea of Iran.

The nomadism of the Mongols and other rulers of the Iranian lands between the seventh/thirteenth and the ninth/fifteenth centuries was a crucial practical precondition for the emergence and perpetuation of the idea that Tabriz itself stands for the kingdom named Iran. With its excellent pastures, the extended region of Azerbaijan and adjacent areas in southern Caucasia and eastern Anatolia attracted the Chinggisids as they attracted Turkic and Turko-Mongol nomadic rulers before and after them. This extended region had already gained in geopolitical centrality prior to the Mongol conquests, became increasingly integrated and central under the Ilkhans and maintained that level of integration and centrality during much of the post-Ilkhanid period.[16] Some preferred royal campsites were located in the environs of Tabriz and the city was a focal point of royal migration routes.[17] Thus nomadic political practice kept the courts of the Ilkhans and their successor dynasties physically close to Tabriz, enabling the building activities of Ghazan and other rulers in and around the city.

While this study understands honorary epithets like *dar al-saltana* or *dar al-molk* as symbolic signs of the emerging and perpetuating special royal status of Tabriz, the royal monuments are taken as its material signs, with Ghazan's mosque-mausoleum *vaqf* complex as its foundational pillar. Several scholars, including Charles Melville, Christoph Werner, Sandra Aube and Sussan Babaie, have analysed royal monuments of Tabriz from various angles, usually focusing on those built in the ninth/fifteenth century.[18] Almost all the relevant monuments are either poorly preserved or have, like Ghazan's complex, vanished completely. As material signs of the emerging and enduring idea that Tabriz stands for Iran, the royal monuments of the city will give support to the argument developed here rather than being the actual subjects of analysis.

The focus will be on the symbolic signs, honorary epithets applied to Tabriz mainly by Persian historians and, as noted above, especially when they are coupled with the term 'Iran' as a territorial-political designation. Works of Persian universal and dynastic history written between the middle of the seventh/thirteenth and the middle of the tenth/sixteenth century form the bulk of the sources. Those of the famous Ilkhanid court historians, such as Rashid al-Din (d. 718/1318) and Hamdollah Mostowfi (d. ca. 750/1349) will of course receive appropriate consideration.

Among the successors of the Mongols, the Timurids come to mind as great patrons of Persian historiography, and histories produced at Timurid courts will not be neglected. However, works emanating from the courts of their rivals will be examined in somewhat greater detail. Examples are the *Tavarikh-e Sheykh Oveys*, a universal history written for the Jalayerid Soltan Oveys (d. 776/1374) by Qotb al-Din Ahari, and the *Ketab-e Diyarbakriya*, which Abu Bakr Tehrani began on the orders of Jahanshah Qara Qoyunlu and completed after the latter's death in 872/1467 for his new patron Uzun Hasan Aq Qoyunlu (d. 882/1478).

Special attention will be paid to a recently discovered source from Tabriz, a versified universal history composed in the middle of the seventh/thirteenth century by the poet Zajjaji in emulation of the *Shahnama* and entitled *Homayun-nama*. Zajjaji's *Homayun-nama* was written a bit too early to be counted among the numerous Persian verse chronicles of the Mongol period, but it clearly foreshadows the increasing importance that the *Shahnama* would gain under the Ilkhans and subsequent rulers of the Iranian lands.[19] As a local source, the *Homayun-nama* also offers unique insights into visions of history cultivated among the notables of Tabriz while the first Ilkhanid rulers were consolidating their power in Iran.

The Persian histories of various kinds, some of which have been mentioned, will be supplemented by comparatively few sources of different sorts, including geographical works and travelogues written in the Iranian lands and beyond as well as documents, such as royal edicts and correspondence with foreign rulers. Another important local source is the Sufi pilgrimage guide to the cemeteries of Tabriz and surrounding villages written by Ebn-e Karbala'i (d. 997/1589), the *Rowzat al-jenan*. This work offers the most comprehensive information on the topography of Tabriz and a distinctly local perspective on the history of the Mongols in Iran and their successors.

The analysis, especially of the universal histories under consideration, will also examine how relevant authors arrange their narratives of individual dynasties and how they conceived the transfer of legitimacy from one dynasty to another. It is important to point out that the authors of these works had various options for envisioning the Mongol and post-Mongol periods which they lived through. The idea that Tabriz came to stand for a kingdom named Iran was associated with a specific Ilkhanid-Ghazanid legacy. The genesis of this legacy is the subject of the next section.

The Mongol Foundations: An Ilkhanid-Ghazanid Legacy

When Hülegü led his campaign to the Middle East in the 650s/1250s, founding the Ilkhanid dynasty, most of the Iranian lands had already been under Mongol rule for about 20 years. As will become evident below, the initial contact of Tabriz with the Mongols occurred during the first invasion in 617–18/1220–21. Since 628/1231, Azerbaijan and adjacent lands beyond the Iranian plateau had attracted the conquering armies and Tabriz gradually became the most important city in the Chinggisid far west during that period of pre-Ilkhanid Mongol rule, notably for financial administration.[20]

However, in spite of a considerable degree of continuity, Hülegü's arrival also brought significant changes. Not only did the 'Abbasid caliphate of Baghdad cease to exist in 656/1258, but a Chinggisid prince assumed direct control of the extended Iranian plateau area. But both Hülegü and his son and successor Abaqa (d. 680/1282) were challenged on different fronts, being surrounded by hostile powers. The Ilkhans fought several wars with the Mamluk sultans of Egypt to the west and with two rival Chinggisid dynasties to the east and north, the Chaghatayids in Transoxiana and the Jochids in the Qepchaq Steppe.[21]

Neither Hülegü nor Abaqa achieved lasting territorial gains but they were able to preserve their dominions between the Oxus and the Euphrates. These military developments were a necessary precondition for envisioning the Ilkhanid realm as a territorial-political entity named Iran. And some contemporary Persian authors did indeed envision the dominions of Hülegü and Abaqa in this way and named the realm accordingly.

The famous scholar Beyzavi, with his *Nezam al-tavarikh*, a short but very influential universal history written in 674/1275, is an excellent example. He states in the introduction that the subject of the work is 'the sequence of rulers and kings of Iran which extends from the Euphrates to the Oxus'.[22] Beyzavi closes his history with the Mongols, depicting the emerging house of Hülegü as the latest royal dynasty in this sequence: 'Among his [Chinggis Khan's] descendants who ruled in Iran and conquered the lands there was Hülegü Khan. [...] At present, his son Abaqa Khan is king of Iran and the land of Rum'.[23]

Melville, who thoroughly examined numerous manuscripts of Beyzavi's history in a series of articles, noted a degree of inconsistency as to how many and which dynasties are featured as predecessors of the Mongol Ilkhans.[24] Furthermore, Melville emphasized the innovative structure of Beyzavi's work with a fourfold division of history.[25] The first section is devoted to the prophets, the second to pre-Islamic kings of Iran, the third to the Umayyad and 'Abbasid caliphs and the fourth to the dynasties that ruled the Iranian lands in Islamic times down to the Mongols. At least two other contemporary Persian universal histories adopt this very structure. One is Juzjani's *Tabaqat-e Naseri*, completed in 658/1260, and the other is Zajjaji's *Homayun-nama*, composed in the same meter as the *Shahnama* between the 650s/1250s and 670s/1270s.[26] It seems that this fourfold division of history and its criteria were regarded as an adequate structural model by mid-seventh/thirteenth-century Persian authors.

While the similarity in structure indicates a common vision of history in general, there are also clear differences between the three works. The most obvious differences pertain to the portrayal of the Mongols and to the dynasties which Beyzavi, Juzjani and Zajjaji include in their histories as predecessors of the non-Muslim conquerors. Thus, Beyzavi includes the Salghorid Atabegs of his native region of Fars who persisted as vassals of the Mongols for some time and, as noted above, presents the Ilkhans as merely a new royal dynasty of Iran.

Juzjani, working in Delhi outside the Mongol dominions, focuses rather on dynasties of India and the eastern Iranian frontier lands and is openly hostile to the Mongols. Like Beyzavi, he puts the conquerors at the end of the fourth section but, unlike the *Nezam al-tavarikh*, the *Tabaqat-e Naseri* does not conclude with praise of Hülegü and Abaqa as kings of Iran. Instead Juzjani's history strikes a final optimistic note by narrating the conversion to Islam of the Jochid Berke Khan (d. 665/1267), an enemy of the Ilkhans.[27] Nonetheless, even Juzjani recognizes the territory conquered by Hülegü as the kingdom of Iran and names it accordingly (*mamlekat-e Iran va 'ajam*).[28]

Zajjaji likewise puts a strong local and regional flavour into his universal history, with special emphasis on Tabriz as royal city of Iran and on the Eldigüzid Atabegs of Azerbaijan. The *Homayun-nama* associates the special royal status of Tabriz with the Eldigüzid Atabeg Abu Bakr (d. 607/1210) who secured control of the city against two of his half-brothers in 589/1193 and continued to rule there after the end of the Seljuq dynasty in Iran in 590/1194. Zajjaji summarizes the result of Abu Bakr's fight against his half-brothers as follows, 'Finally, he was victorious against the bold ones, through manliness he gained kingship, the kingdom of Iran. In Tabriz Abu Bakr became shah, he established the royal court in that place.'[29]

In order to give even greater weight to his assertion that Abu Bakr instituted the status of Tabriz as royal city of Iran, Zajjaji changes the structure of the fourth section of the *Homayun-nama* for the time after the demise of the Seljuqs. Beginning with the reign of Abu Bakr, the author switches from narrating the history of dynasties to devoting individual chapters to the successive lords of Tabriz. It is only in this capacity that Zajjaji includes the Khvarazmshah Jalal al-Din (d. 628/1231), the heroic warrior against the Mongols. He states that Jalal al-Din's reign lasted seven years, meaning the period that he ruled Tabriz as successor of the Eldigüzids.[30] Unlike the works of Beyzavi and Juzjani, the *Homayun-nama* features no separate chapter on the Khvarazmshahs as a royal dynasty of Iran in its fourth section.

While Zajjaji makes it very clear that he regards the lords of Tabriz in the decades prior to the establishment of Mongol rule as kings of Iran, he does not explicitly indicate the territorial extension of the kingdom. However, the author was also not unaware of this. He blames Abu Bakr's half-brothers who went to the courts of the Sharvanshahs and the Georgian Bagratids to seek redress against the Eldigüzid ruler for leaving Iran (*z Iran beraftand*).[31] Zajjaji also makes special mention of Hülegü crossing the Oxus and calls the conqueror a 'glorious king (*shah-e sar-afraz*)'.[32] Yet he does not refer to the Ilkhanid dominions as Iran and, except for issues relating to his personal situation, reports no events after Hülegü's sack of Baghdad.

It is likely that Zajjaji was uncertain whether the Ilkhans would be able to maintain control of the extended Iranian plateau area against their Chaghatayid, and especially against their Jochid, enemies. Containing the Jochids was critical for the security of Azerbaijan, the Ilkhanid heartland with the principal city of Tabriz where the poet-historian lived. However, Zajjaji not only traces the status of Tabriz as royal city of Iran to the Eldigüzids as the last pre-Mongol regional Muslim dynasty; he also posits a special relation between Tabriz and Mongol rule, asserting that this relation was already forged at the time of Chinggis Khan himself.

It is important to bear in mind that Tabriz was one of the very few or perhaps even the only major city in Iran that had peaceful interactions with the Mongols from the outset, never offering resistance. Zajjaji reports the arrival of two generals of Chinggis Khan at the gates of Tabriz during the first invasion in 617–18/1220–21 and puts the following statement in their mouth, 'They said that this pleasant city has peacefully surrendered to us, supporting our army and cavalry; this golden city here forms private property of the khan, for no [city] is more amiable than it in the world'.[33]

The Mongols may indeed have seen Tabriz as a city with a particularly favourable disposition towards them when Hülegü came to Azerbaijan. In any case, one of the changes which his arrival entailed is that Tabriz became increasingly closely attached to an imperial court based in the region. Rashid al-Din reports in his account of the beginning of Abaqa's reign that the latter 'made the *dar al-molk* Tabriz the seat of the royal throne'.[34] He does not specify which throne here, and while Rashid al-Din designates Tabriz as *dar al-molk* or *dar al-saltana* many times in passages stretching from the time of the Eldigüzids to the reign of Ghazan, he never seems to couple these honorary epithets with the name 'Iran'.[35]

However, in general, references to Iran as a territorial-political entity abound in Rashid al-Din's history. Modern day scholars are rightfully fascinated by the global outlook of the work, containing not only the history of the Mongols but also of other peoples and nations such as the Turks, the Jews, the Christian Franks, Indians or Chinese. Some tend to overlook the fact that the structure of Rashid al-Din's work reflects a special focus on Iran.

Thus, in the history of the Mongols, each section on Chinggis Khan and his descendants down to Hülegü's campaign is followed by an account of the rulers of China, of the 'Abbasid caliphs as well as of the sultans, kings and atabegs of *Iran-zamin*, Syria, Egypt and other lands. The second volume of Rashid al-Din's massive work, which contains the histories of the other peoples and nations, also features a part on the Middle East. This part faithfully reproduces the structure adopted by Beyzavi, Juzjani and Zajjaji with its focus on the royal dynasties of Iran.[36]

The first volume containing the history of the Mongols leads, of course, up to Hülegü's takeover of the land and ultimately to Ghazan's reign as Muslim king of Iran. In his account of Hülegü's campaign, Rashid al-Din speaks several times of the dominions of Iran where the conqueror was heading and of the rulers of Iran who pledged allegiance to him. And he appears to be the earliest author to claim that Hülegü mounted a throne immediately after crossing the Oxus, meaning as soon as he set foot on the territory of Iran.[37] Then Rashid al-Din portrays Abaqa as 'dispensing justice and equity in the dominions of Iran'.[38] Finally, he quotes his patron, the convert Ilkhan Ghazan, as saying, 'I am not unaware of the fact that utmost gratitude to God is compulsory and necessary for out of favour and beneficence He has brought all creatures of Iran (*tamamat-e khalayeq-e Iran-zamin*) who are the deposits of the divine majesty under the yoke of obedience to me'.[39]

It is noteworthy that Rashid al-Din does not make Ghazan speak of being granted authority over all creatures of the world but only over those of Iran. He reports that Ghazan made this speech in summer 701/1302 at Ujan, the most valued royal campsite in the rural hinterland of Tabriz that had been used since pre-Mongol times. Rashid al-Din and many later authors would usually add the honorary epithet 'city of Islam (*shahr-e eslam*)' to the name of the site in remembrance of Ghazan's conversion and his construction activities there. Banakati (d. 730/1329–30), for instance, who became the principal court poet at the end of Ghazan's reign and then wrote an abridgment of Rashid al-Din's history, praised Ujan in verse highlighting a golden tent Ghazan had set up there while noting that the site was connected to Tabriz.[40]

According to Rashid al-Din, work on the golden tent had lasted three years so that Ghazan must have commissioned it just prior to his first Syria campaign in the winter of 699/1299–1300.[41] This campaign entailed a brief occupation of Damascus, where Ghazan reportedly asked the assembled notables who he was, with Rashid al-Din making them reply, 'You are shah Ghazan' and then enumerate all the Ilkhan's ancestors back to Chinggis Khan.[42] There is a strong element of anti-Mamluk propaganda in this passage and one may doubt whether the notables of Damascus did indeed address Ghazan as 'shah' and cite his Chinggisid lineage. In any case, stressing Ghazan's descent from Chinggis Khan certainly reflects the Ilkhan's own notion of legitimacy and sovereignty, whereas calling him 'shah' probably rather reflects Rashid al-Din's vision of the ruler as Muslim king of a territorially distinct kingdom named Iran.

Ghazan's conversion enabled Rashid al-Din and subsequent authors to envision the kingdom of Iran as fully Islamic. But the famous vizier and historian also did a lot to portray the house of Hülegü as a veritable dynasty. Rashid al-Din consistently tries to delegitimize Ilkhanid rulers who did not belong to the straight line of descent from Hülegü through Abaqa and Arghun (d. 690/1291) to Ghazan.[43] Arghun is the one who began construction works in the village of Sham to the west of Tabriz, where according to Rashid al-Din, he founded a city named Arghuniya. The historian writes, for instance, that Tabriz was like Egypt, with regard to population size, and that Arghuniya was like Cairo, the seat of the king (*padshah-neshin*).[44]

Ghazan expanded on the construction works of his father Arghun at Sham, building his mosque-mausoleum *vaqf* complex there so that the place became a thriving suburb of Tabriz. Being a Muslim, he was the first Mongol ruler whose place of burial was publicly known. Masashi Haneda has analysed Ghazan's complex in considerable detail, listing to the extent possible the religious and charitable institutions that accompanied the royal mausoleum. Haneda understands Ghazaniya as a separate city representing a new type of urbanism that suited the nomadic Mongols. He calls this type the 'pastoral and mausoleum city', discussing geographical, economic and political factors determining the choice of the location of Ghazaniya and ensuring its survival.[45] Haneda argues convincingly that the *vaqf* was of utmost importance for the continued existence of such places.

Other examples of pastoral and mausoleum cities which Haneda's study compares with Ghazaniya are Soltaniya and Nasriya. The first was likewise begun by Arghun and completed by Ghazan's brother and successor Öljeitü (d. 716/1316) in a major summer pasture area between Zanjan and Abhar and the second was an Aq Qoyunlu complex just north of Tabriz, which will be discussed below. Haneda stresses the similarities between all three, stating for instance that 'the sites of Sulṭāniyya and Shām were very similar in that they were nomad camps'.[46] But the two sites were also very different in that Sham was located in the immediate vicinity of Tabriz whereas Soltaniya was relatively remote from established cities.

Qashani, the chronicler of Öljeitü's reign, reports the beginning of this ruler's construction activities at Soltaniya in 705/1305–6, claiming that he built a city like the metropolis (*mahrusa*) Tabriz.[47] At that time and in subsequent decades, both places were designated as *dar al-molk* in official decrees issued either at Soltaniya or at Tabriz, but in some cases also named without any honorary epithet.[48] Yet it seems that Soltaniya could never become like Tabriz with its suburb of Sham, as Öljeitü did not leave a legacy matching that of Ghazan.

It is probably not only a local bias when Ebn-e Karbala'i, writing in the tenth/sixteenth century, praises Ghazan's good deeds, presenting his conversion to Islam as the most important one. He takes care to underline that none of Ghazan's forefathers was blessed with this fortunate turn, which is true for the ruler's line of ancestors but not for the whole Chinggisid lineage and not even for the house of Hülegü. It is probably also not just a local bias when Ebn-e Karbala'i states clearly that Ghazan's tomb was in Tabriz, in a complex called Shanb-e Ghazan, viewing the suburb of Sham as an integral part of the city.[49]

Construction works on Ghazan's mosque-mausoleum *vaqf* complex continued for several years after Öljeitü succeeded his brother in 703/1304.[50] Describing Öljeitü's enthronement at Ujan, which preceded the resumption of works at Soltaniya, Qashani could include a verse in his account that underlines the unique status of Tabriz as royal city unequivocally, 'As long as there is dynastic good fortune and kingship in Iran and Turan, Mohammed Öljeitü is khan in Turan and Iran. His army is in Iran and news of him in Constantinople, his seat is in Tabriz (*neshastash hast dar Tabriz*) and traces of him extend to Turkestan'.[51]

Although these verses depict Öljeitü as lord of Iran and Turan, the following account of the arrangement of government refers to the dominions of Iran exclusively and repeatedly.[52] And although Qashani notes in another passage that, 'the metropolis Tabriz is the fortunate place for the kings and khans of the house of Hülegü', the centre of power did indeed shift towards Soltaniya during the reigns of Öljeitü and his son and successor Abu Sa'id (d. 736/1335).[53] Nonetheless, prominent members of the courts of both Ilkhans, including Persian viziers as well as Mongol military aristocrats such as the Chupanids who will reappear shortly, built their primary residences and especially mosque-mausoleum *vaqf* complexes at Tabriz, which remained the principal urban centre of the realm.[54]

This final period of the Ilkhanid dynasty in the early eighth/fourteenth century also saw the eventual fully fledged integration of the Mongol conquerors and rulers into the history of Iran. The principal evidence for this integration and the principal tool to achieve it were illustrations in precious court-commissioned manuscripts, especially the 'Great Mongol *Shahnama*' but also in copies of Rashid al-Din's history.[55] One person who belonged most probably to the production team of the 'Great Mongol *Shahnama*' was the well-known author Hamdollah Mostowfi.[56] Given Mostowfi's enthusiasm for the *Shahnama*, it cannot be surprising that his works are replete with references to Iran as a territorial-political entity. They are also very clear in stating that the house of Hülegü had become the royal dynasty of this now Islamic kingdom.

Tensions between the Ilkhans and their Jochid and Chaghatayid rivals rose again after the end of Öljeitü's reign and Mostowfi declares that the rulers of these dynasties wrought destruction in Iran, almost annihilating the kingdom. The author goes so far as to call the Ilkhanid Mongol armies who fought the Chaghatayids and the Jochids 'the Iranians' even at the time of Hülegü.[57] Mostowfi is also the writer who expresses most clearly the unique status of Tabriz as royal city of Islamic Iran. Soltaniya may have been a *dar al-molk* and Öljeitü's mausoleum there a highly revered site, but Ghazan's mausoleum made Tabriz the 'dome of Islam of Iran (*qobbat al-Eslam-e Iran*)'.[58]

Ghazan had no offspring and, in consequence, the inheritance of the kingdom of Islamic Iran he epitomized could only be achieved through its royal city Tabriz. Such a vision must have gained additional appeal when Abu Sa'id died without a male heir in 736/1335 and the Ilkhanid dynasty effectively collapsed. Moreover, with Abu Sa'id's death, the realm of the house of Hülegü broke apart into several regional principalities, which probably lent further weight to the idea that Tabriz stood for the territory of the kingdom as a whole.

Built on Mongol Foundations: Post-Ilkhanid Dynasties and Royal Monuments of Tabriz

At the end of Ilkhanid rule, the idea that Tabriz was standing for a territorially distinct Islamic kingdom named Iran as epitomized by Ghazan appears to have been well established even outside the Iranian lands. Thus the Mamluk bureaucrat al-'Omari (d. 749/1349) states that the section on the Ilkhanid lands in his geography is about 'the kingdom of the Iranians (*mamlekat al-iraniyyin*)' which extends from the Oxus to the Euphrates and from Kerman to Rum.[59] Then al-'Omari notes that this kingdom fell to the house of Hülegü and goes on to explain that 'the seat of the king in it [this kingdom] is now Tabriz, then Soltaniya, and the house Hülegü sees kingship belonging to who sits on the throne at Ujan, in the environs of Tabriz'.[60] The author does not mention Ghazan's mausoleum, having apparently other reasons to state about Tabriz that 'it is nowadays the mother of the entire Iran'.[61]

Dynastic notions of legitimacy and sovereignty naturally remained highly influential after the death of Abu Sa'id. Various contenders for succession to the Ilkhans raised their claim in the name of actual or alleged descendants of Hülegü whom they had under tutelage. However, the vision in the account which the contemporary Persian historian Qotb al-Din Ahari gives of events is in conformity with al-'Omari's explanation of who could be considered a ruler. Ahari remarks, for instance, that one contender and his puppet sovereign 'came to Ujan and seized the kingdom' after a military victory in spring 736/1336.[62]

The next contender was the Jalayerid emir Sheykh-Hasan, known as Bozorg, who was then based in Anatolia and is portrayed in a very favourable light by the historian, being the father of Ahari's patron. Ahari notes that Sheykh-Hasan and his Chinggisid protégé set out to 'Iran and the foundation of the throne (*pa-ye takht*)' with their allies and that, after defeating an opposing army in Moharram 737/August 1336, they 'seized the kingdom', descending on Tabriz.[63] About a year later, an invasion attempt from Khorasan in the name of a rival Chinggisid claimant based there failed, which makes Ahari declare that Sheykh-Hasan gained 'complete kingship and command of Iran (*tamamat-e saltanat va emarat-e Iran-zamin*)'.[64]

Ahari must have been fully aware that complete kingship of Iran required at least some nominal suzerainty over all the former Ilkhanid territory, which neither Sheykh-Hasan nor any of his rivals achieved. Yet, bearing in mind the special status of Tabriz as royal city, Ahari is consistent in presenting only the puppet sovereigns based in Azerbaijan as successors to the Ilkhanid dynasty, whereas historians from eastern Iran also devote separate chapters to the Chinggisid claimant in Khorasan.[65] Ahari even retains this structuring pattern for the period after summer 738/1338, when the Jalayerid Sheykh-Hasan-e Bozorg was expelled from the Ilkhanid heartland by an opponent from the abovementioned Chupanid family who was likewise named Sheykh-Hasan and known as Kuchek.[66]

The Jalayerid had to be content with ruling Baghdad but continued trying to challenge his Chupanid rival. Relations between the two families were extremely complex and both also had matrimonial ties to the Ilkhanid dynasty.[67] With regard to the perpetuation of the special royal status of Tabriz, the Chupanid Sheykh-Hasan-e Kuchek may appear as the first veritable successor of Ghazan. He founded a congregational mosque in 742/1341–42 and it is possible that the complex also included a tomb for himself or for his puppet sovereign from the house of Hülegü; perhaps one for each. The mosque was known by the honorific titles of both but mainly as *ostad-shagerd* after the famous master calligrapher ʻAbdollah Seyrafi and his pupil Mohammad Bandgir, both of whom decorated it.[68]

Under Sheykh-Hasan-e Kuchek, the Chupanid realm extended southward to Fars and recurring invasion attempts from Khorasan remained unsuccessful. But there was also internal division and some of the ruler's relatives even allied with the Jalayerid Sheykh-Hasan-e Bozorg.[69] The complicated rivalry continued after Sheykh-Hasan-e Kuchek was murdered by his wife in 743 or 744/1343 and his brother Malek Ashraf assumed power. Persian historians unanimously describe Malek Ashraf's reign as tyrannical and none deplores the campaign of the Jochid Jani Beg Khan (d. 758/1357) to Tabriz, where he executed the Chupanid ruler in 758/1357, as an unjustified attack on Iran.[70]

The narrative conclusion of all accounts is the conquest of Tabriz by the Jalayerid Sheykh-Oveys, who succeeded his father Sheykh-Hasan-e Bozorg when the latter died in Baghdad in 757/1356.[71] Ahari is understandably the most outspoken, commenting that divine decree had destined 'this kingdom, throne and sovereignty (*in molk-o-mamlekat va in takht-o-saltanat*)' for his patron once Sheykh-Oveys secured control of the royal city in 760/1359.[72] In an earlier passage Ahari, whose history unfortunately breaks off immediately after the establishment of Sheykh-Oveys as lord of Tabriz, had already announced that 'the great sultan, the supreme king of kings (*soltan-e moʻazzam shahanshah-e aʻzam*)' would take over the Ilkhanid heartland.[73]

Sheykh-Oveys did indeed adopt the title *soltan* and is generally designated as such in the histories of the period. This title had been officially used by the Muslim Ilkhans, in particular from Ghazan onwards.[74] Sheykh-Oveys also did not install any puppet sovereigns from the house of Hülegü or recognize any Chinggisid overlord, which his father had already stopped doing at some point. Of all the regional rulers in the Iranian lands in the middle of the eighth/fourteenth century, Sheykh-Oveys had perhaps the strongest dynastic connection with the Ilkhans, his mother being a former wife of Abu Saʻid and his grandmother a full sister of Öljeitü.

But since Sheykh-Oveys lacked a patrilinear Chinggisid genealogy, Abolala Soudavar speaks of 'a semblance of legitimacy' which the Jalayerids inherited through their descent, but that 'to gain acceptance as successors to *il-khāns*, they had to act like *il-khāns* (original emphasis): following in the footsteps of

Abu Sa'id, they patronised the Il-Khānid library-atelier and the production of illustrated literary manuscripts, commissioning copies of the *Kalilé-o Demné* and the *Shahnamé*'.[75] The Jalayerids were indeed great patrons of literature and there is one particular work dedicated to Sheykh-Oveys suggesting that, with the conquest of Tabriz, he may rather have aspired to be a successor of Ghazan. This was a verse chronicle memorializing Ghazan in the style of the *Shahnama* which was evidently entitled *Ghazan-nama*.[76]

Another work dedicated to Sheykh-Oveys was Mohammed b. Hendushah Nakhjavani's *Dastur al-kateb fi ta'yin al-marateb*, a collection of sample chancellery writings. Among the honorifics which the author showers on the ruler is the Persian royal title *shahanshah*, which Ahari had likewise so proudly employed to designate Soltan Sheykh-Oveys. Nakhjavani combines *shahanshah* with *soltan-e eslam* but also uses the titles *bahador khan* for Oveys, utilizing the customary combination of Iranian, Islamic and Mongol elements to express notions of sovereignty and legitimacy.[77] He also makes numerous references to Iran as a territorial-political entity, relating it to several government offices and specifying in some instances that the land extended from the Oxus to Egypt.[78] Only in one sample document, a victory letter or *fathnama*, does Nakhjavani link the territorial-political concept of 'Iran' with the *dar al-molk* Tabriz, albeit indirectly.[79]

Erecting royal monuments in and around Tabriz was perhaps the best way to act like Ghazan and thereby to become his successor as king of 'Iran' even without coming close to controlling the entire former Ilkhanid realm. And the Jalayerid did erect royal monuments, leaving material traces in the urban and suburban fabric of Tabriz. He was credited with having built a palace known as *dowlatkhana*, which may have been an older structure enlarged by Sheykh-Oveys and which was probably located on the northern outskirts of the city.[80] And there must have been a mausoleum as the Jalayerid sultan was buried in a village called Shadabad, just south of Tabriz, where he appears to have been devoted to the local family of Sufi sheykhs. Ebn-e Karbala'i unfortunately does not describe the tomb but notes that, after succeeding his father, Sheykh-Oveys 'became the refuge of the sultans of Iran'.[81]

Sheykh-Oveys died in 776/1374 and under his son and successor Soltan Hoseyn, both internal conflicts and external pressure on the Jalayerid realm increased. In 778/1376, the Mozaffarids of Fars, who had already briefly occupied Tabriz before the conquest of Oveys, captured the city again. It seems that an eminent local leader had invited them to take over the 'great place of the throne (*takhtgah-e bozorg*)' but they were soon forced to retreat.[82] The same local leader, known as Khvaja Sheykh Kojoji, then procured the assassination of Soltan Hoseyn in 784/1382 and brought Hoseyn's brother Soltan Ahmad to the throne, but things would even get worse.[83]

In Zu'l-Qa'da 787/December 1385, the Jochid Toqtemish Khan (d. 809/1406) approached Tabriz and eventually sacked the city. Unlike Jani

Beg earlier, Toqtemish was not welcome at all. There is an anonymous local eyewitness account of the event that was written within a year of the attack, suggesting that the elites of Tabriz took great pride in its special status as royal city of Islamic Iran. The introduction deplores several times the catastrophe which befell the 'dome of Islam (*qobbat al-eslam*) Tabriz' and showers elaborate praise on a strongman emir of Soltan Ahmad named 'Adel Aqa who enjoyed much support in the city at the time. However, like the sultan, he was obviously absent and a regional ruler of Mazandaran who was in Tabriz, 'coveting the kingdom of Iran (*saltanat va mamlekat-e Iran-zamin-ra matmah-e nazar gardanida*)' could not help the city either. The dome of Islam of Iran, as Mostowfi had put it, fell prey to 'nearly 9000 infidel Turks'.[84]

This Jochid attack was part of the conflict between Toqtemish and the conqueror Timur, whose expansion had already thrown the Iranian lands into disarray.[85] Timur came to Tabriz in summer 788/1386, according to his chronicler Nezam al-Din Shami, who was a native of Sham-e Ghazan, to protect the *qobbat al-eslam*.[86] Soltan Ahmad retreated to Baghdad once more and Timur eventually had 'Adel Aqa executed after having made use of his services for some time.[87] Then he returned to his base in Transoxiana, having risen to power in the former Chaghatayid dominions. Timur still ruled in the name of a Chinggisid puppet sovereign and considered Chinggis Khan himself as his model rather than any other Mongol ruler.[88]

Persian historians working at Timurid courts, such as Sharaf al-Din 'Ali Yazdi or later Mirkhvand, were aware that the conqueror came from beyond the territory of Iran and had to take possession of the kingdom bearing this name by military means. They would usually note explicitly that Timur's western campaigns led him to Iran.[89] From the perspective of the Timurid court historians, the conqueror finally took over the royal realm of the Ilkhans from the Jalayerids during his second major western campaign, which began in 794/1392. In the following year, Timur expelled Soltan Ahmad from Baghdad, an achievement that marks the conclusion of the continuation of Rashid al-Din's history written by Hafez-e Abru.[90]

Prior to his escape from Baghdad, Soltan Ahmad had his erstwhile ally Khvaja Sheykh Kojoji executed there, probably because the latter's relatives in Tabriz had colluded with Timur's representatives.[91] After a few other battles and before returning to his principal city Samarqand, the conqueror installed his son Miranshah as governor of the Ilkhanid heartland of Azerbaijan and adjacent regions. Yazdi notes, quite in line with the broader Chinggisid legacy Timur tried to assume, that Miranshah was granted the 'throne of Hülegü'.[92]

Miranshah was based in Tabriz, where he soon attempted to assert his rule independently from Timur, as a decree issued in 798/1396 evinces.[93] He had certainly become dissatisfied with his position among the Timurid princes but local leaders of Tabriz such as the Kojoji family may also have resented the relegation of the royal city of Islamic Iran to secondary status and pushed

Miranshah to rebel against his father. In any case it is noteworthy that the rebellion of this prince in the city of Ghazan's mausoleum caused such obvious embarrassment to the Timurid court historians that they claimed Miranshah had gone mad.[94]

Be that as it may, Timur embarked on his third major western campaign in 802/1399, removed Miranshah from the governorship of Tabriz but left him in the area after the end of the campaign, assigning the realm of Hülegü and his throne in Tabriz to a son of Miranshah in 806/1404.[95] Soltan Ahmad Jalayer was still alive when Timur died the following year, shortly after his return to Samarqand. The Jalayerid managed to take Tabriz back briefly in 809/1406 but it was the Turkmen leader Qara Yusof Qara Qoyunlu who expelled the quarrelling Timurids from Azerbaijan a year later, taking possession of the city.[96]

Qara Yusof had fought Timur together with Soltan Ahmad but when the Jalayerid came to Tabriz again in 813/1411, he defeated him as well and eventually had him executed. Like most other Jalayerid rulers, Soltan Ahmad was buried in the Chupanid *Demashqiya* complex, which dated from the reign of Ilkhan Abu Sa'id.[97] Hafez-e Abru reports that, 'when Emir Qara Yusof had completely freed his mind from the preoccupation of dealing with Soltan Ahmad and taken independent control of the *takhtgah-e Tabriz,* he wanted the throne of sovereignty to remain among his descendants, manufacturing a golden throne'. Because of dynastic sensitivities, a son of Qara Yusof who had previously been adopted by Soltan Ahmad was supposed to occupy this golden throne as successor to the Jalayerids.[98]

These sensitivities are entirely absent from the work of the tenth/sixteenth-century historian Hasan Beg Rumlu. For him, the end of the Jalayerid dynasty and the succession of the Turkmen leader as lord of Tabriz were sufficient to open his report of the year 816/1413 with further exploits of '*padshah-e Iran, Qara Yusof Torkoman*'.[99] The Bavarian squire Johann Schiltberger, who was taken captive by the Ottomans at the battle of Nicopolis in 798/1396 and then by Timur at the battle of Ankara in 804/1402, seems to have grasped the reasoning behind the honour accorded to Qara Yusof by Rumlu. Schiltberger spent some time with Miranshah in Azerbaijan and gives a vivid, though of course often inaccurate account of the fights between the Timurids, Soltan Ahmad and Qara Yusof.[100] In spite of the inaccuracies, he learned that, 'the chief city of all the kingdoms of Persia is called Thaures'.[101]

Being the lord of Tabriz gave Qara Yusof a certain claim to the legacy of Ghazan as king of Islamic Iran. Tehrani calls the first Turkmen ruler of the royal city 'a great king (*padshahi-ye bozorgvar*)'.[102] The Timurid court historians were rather ambiguous about the significance of the Ilkhanid heartland which slipped back out of control so quickly. Shami, as a native, does speak about the 'sayyeds, grandees and notables of *Iran-zamin* and especially of the *qobbat al-eslam* Tabriz'.[103] Mirkhvand also acknowledges that

Azerbaijan was the '*takhtgah-e mamalek-e Iran*' but states at the same time that Timur's successor Shahrokh in Herat was sitting 'on the throne of the kingdom of Iran (*bar sarir-e mamlekat-e Iran*)'.[104]

The ambiguity resulted partly from the fact that the Timurid realm continued to extend beyond Iran under Shahrokh, while the dominions in Transoxiana remained central. Moreover, major historians working during Shahrokh's reign, such as Hafez-e Abru and Yazdi, strengthened the image of Timur as a dynastic founder in his own right as well as the link between the emerging Timurid dynasty and the Chaghatayids.[105] Timur's relation to Iran derived from his conquest of the former Ilkhanid realm and, as Shahrokh preserved much of this conquest, his territory still encompassed Iran and Turan.[106] Shahrokh may have tried to emulate Ghazan as an exemplary Muslim ruler but without control of Tabriz the foundation of the kingdom of Islamic Iran would be lacking.

Qara Yusof died in 823/1420 while Shahrokh was approaching Azerbaijan on the first of three campaigns against the Qara Qoyunlu and was succeeded by his son Eskandar after the return of the Timurid sultan to Herat. By the time of the second campaign, in 832/1429, the Qara Qoyunlu had erected buildings in Tabriz, which Shahrokh had one of his sons destroy.[107] After the third and final campaign in, 835–36/1432–33, Eskandar Qara Qoyunlu likewise first 'returned to the throne of Tabriz (*bar sarir-e Tabriz 'ayed gasht*)' according to Tehrani.[108] But then Eskandar was killed by one of his sons, having already lost out to his brother Jahanshah, who formally recognized Shahrokh as overlord at the time. By the time of Shahrokh's death in 850/1447, Jahanshah's rule in Azerbaijan had stabilized to such an extent that he expanded his dominions eastward at the expense of the Timurids and briefly occupied Herat in 863/1458.[109]

From his base in the Ilkhanid heartland, Jahanshah brought most of the former dominions of the house of Hülegü under his control. Hence nothing prevented Tehrani from presenting the ruler as the equal of the Timurids during the period following Shahrokh's death, recounting parts of the succession struggle under the title 'report of the Chaghatayid and Qara Qoyunlu sultans'.[110] The author declares that he was ordered to draft a *Tarikh-e soltani* while Jahanshah was occupying Herat and this draft must have developed into the *Ketab-e Diyarbakriya* over the years.[111] One reason why Jahanshah retreated from Herat was a rebellion of his son Hasan-'Ali, giving rise to the threat that 'the throne of Tabriz [might] be lost'.[112]

Jahanshah secured the throne and the Qara Qoyunlu further strengthened their connection to the royal city. In 870/1465, his wife set up a *vaqf* complex around the famous Blue Mosque in Tabriz, which included a mausoleum for the founder, her female descendants and the ruler, but which became known as the Mozaffariya after Jahanshah.[113] The mosque is located in the south-eastern part of Tabriz and especially famed for its mostly dark blue tile mosaic. It is possible that relevant artistic techniques had been transmitted locally at Tabriz since the time of the Ilkhans.[114] The Blue Mosque has an inscription above the main portal commemorating Abu'l-Mozaffar Jahanshah b. Yusof Shah Noyen Jahanshah, showing the ongoing blending of Mongol and Iranian concepts.[115]

While Jahanshah probably played a secondary role in the endowment and construction of the Mozaffariya complex, he left a royal monument of his own as well. According to Ebn-e Karbala'i, the Qara Qoyunlu ruler built a new *dowlatkhana* replacing the one attributed to the Jalayerid sultan Sheykh-Oveys. The *dowlatkhana-ye Jahanshahi*, as Tehrani calls it, was located in an area just north of Tabriz, known as Sahebabad, apparently not far from the older Jalayerid palace structure.[116] Most scholars stress that the Aq Qoyunlu rulers of Tabriz continued to develop the same area later and some note that the name Sahebabad derived from the Ilkhanid vizier Saheb-Divan Shams al-Din Joveyni (ex. 683/1284).[117] The latter had constructed a guest house there and the area which was known as the marketplace or *meydan* quarter under the Ilkhans also hosted religious buildings.[118]

It is uncertain what remained of these structures in the ninth/fifteenth century or what may have been added in the meantime. However, in view of the continuity that can be observed in other domains, the impression sometimes conveyed in scholarship that the Sahebabad area with its meydan was devoid of buildings before the Turkmen rulers erected their monuments is probably misleading. Jahanshah died on campaign against his enemy Uzun Hasan Aq Qoyunlu, in 872/1467. When the news spread, the Timurid sultan Abu Sa'id, a grandson of Miranshah, attempted to win the Ilkhanid heartland back for his dynasty but was defeated by Uzun Hasan in Rajab 873/January 1469 and executed a month later.[119]

According to Tehrani, who completed his history for Uzun Hasan, the defeat of Jahanshah marks a transfer of dynastic good fortune from the Qara Qoyunly to the Aq Qoyunlu that had been predicted in the Qur'an.[120] But the author also makes it clear that Uzun Hasan was not Jahanshah's successor as lord of the royal city. A succession struggle erupted in Tabriz among the Qara Qoyunlu, in which Jahanshah's son Hasan-'Ali gained the upper hand. Tehrani closes the chapter recounting these events by announcing that he will first go over to reporting the advance of the Timurid claimant Abu Sa'id and then 'return to the account of the affairs of Soltan Hasan-'Ali b. Jahanshah Mirza'.[121]

But Hasan-'Ali soon found himself in a desperate situation, committing suicide near Hamadan within just over a year of Jahanshah's death and Uzun Hasan brought the territory previously ruled by the Qara Qoyunlu under his control. Tehrani notes that Uzun Hasan entered the *dar al-saltana* Tabriz in Zu'l-Hejja 873/June 1469 from the side of the Mozaffariya complex. The author stresses that the new ruler promised to the people that he would respect the management of the complex and return for a visit of the king and princes (thus Jahanshah and his relatives were presumably buried there), before proceeding to the residence of Sahebabad which was 'a building of the deceased sovereign'.[122]

Having taken possession of Tabriz and the former Qara Qoyunlu dominions, Uzun Hasan attempted to extend his influence towards Khorasan by supporting a Timurid claimant and to check Ottoman expansion into Anatolia.[123] The Aq Qoyunlu ruler was in steady correspondence with the Ottoman sultan Mehmet II (d. 886/1481) and one of Uzun Hasan's letters is of particular interest for this study. This letter is a *fathnama* proclaiming an Aq Qoyunlu victory over the Georgians that seems to refer to Uzun Hasan's last campaign, after his defeat in battle against Mehmet II in 878/1473 and about a year before his death in 882/1478.

The letter appears as an attempt to present Uzun Hasan as a ruler on the same level as the Ottoman sultan, mainly by using royal titles which reflect their respective realms in historical depth. Thus it emphasizes the importance of continuing diplomatic relations between the Caesars or Emperors of Rum (*al-qayasera*) and the kings of Iran (*al-akasera*). One of the formulas used to politely address Mehmet II is *qeysar-makan*, the position of the Caesar, and one could speculate if this might also be a reference to Constantinople as the place where the Ottoman sultan was based since his conquest of the Byzantine capital in 857/1453.[124] In parallel, Uzun Hasan's chancellery officials who drafted the letter may have thought of Tabriz as *kesra-makan*, the place of the king of Iran.

In any case, the sequence of succession to Ghazan as the epitome of the idea of a territorially distinct kingdom named Iran, now extended to Uzun Hasan and the Aq Qoyunlu. Both the conqueror and his eventual successor Ya'qub acted like successors to Ghazan, leaving royal monuments in Tabriz and other members of the ruling family likewise constructed buildings there. The best known Aq Qoyunlu complexes are the Nasriya and the Hasht Behesht, both located in the Sahebabad area. The former was named after Uzun Hasan but, at least the greater part, was built during the reign of Ya'qub and it included their mausoleum as well as a congregational mosque and other religious structures. The latter was a palace which the Safavids continued to use as royal residence later.[125]

The historian Fazlollah Khonji-Esfahani who worked for Ya'qub left no doubt that, after Uzun Hasan, the throne of Iran (*takht-e Iran*) belonged to the member of the Aq Qoyunlu dynasty in possession of the royal city, so that in 883/1478 Ya'qub finally 'ascended the royal throne in the *dar al-saltana* Tabriz'.[126] And the Aq Qoyunlu ruler not only took on the Ghazanid legacy by erecting buildings in the immediate vicinity of the city but directed his attention to the major royal campsite of Ujan as well. Khonji relates that Ya'qub renovated a palace which Ghazan had built in Ujan and which had allegedly been falling into decay since the time of the Mongols.[127]

After Ya'qub's death in 896/1490, various Aq Qoyunlu factions kept fighting each other, installing successive rulers on the throne in Tabriz until Esma'il Safavi, a maternal grandson of Uzun Hasan, took over the city in 907/1501. This event is still viewed today as marking the transformation of the Safavid family into a royal dynasty of Iran. Like Uzun Hasan and Jahanshah before him, Esma'il was able to bring most of the former Ilkhanid realm under his control only after ascending the throne of Islamic Iran in the royal city Tabriz.

Hans Robert Roemer remarks with regard to the Turkmen predecessors of the Safavids that '[t]hough their rule extended deep into Persian territory, it represents from the point of view of the history of Persia merely peripheral formations beyond or on the frontiers of Iran'.[128] In fact, the opposite seems to be the case. Turkmen rule was highly influential in perpetuating the idea that Tabriz stands for a territorially distinct Islamic kingdom named Iran as it had emerged under the Mongols. As such, it strengthened the very foundation on which a central element of the Safavid claim to royal dignity rested.

Conclusion

This chapter has examined Tabriz as a royal city from the seventh/thirteenth to the ninth/fifteenth centuries and attempted to show that it came to stand for the idea of a territorially distinct Islamic kingdom named Iran. From the middle of the seventh/thirteenth century onwards, Persian historians tended to identify the dominions of the Mongol Ilkhanid dynasty with a territory they recognized as Iran and to name it accordingly. The conversion of the Ilkhan Ghazan at the turn of the eighth/fourteenth century allowed them to envision that territorial-political entity as a fully Islamic kingdom and his mosque-mausoleum complex at Tabriz allowed them to envision the city as its manifestation.

The analysis has revealed that only few authors explicitly combined the territorial-political concept of 'Iran' with honorary epithets applied to Tabriz to signal its special status as royal city. Yet, in many cases these epithets can still be related to this concept implicitly. In view of the variety of Islamic, Iranian and Turko-Mongol nomadic elements that made up contemporary notions of sovereignty and legitimacy, the idea that Tabriz stood for Iran may also not have appealed to everybody. Authors with a local background seem more inclined to conceive and express that idea.

After the collapse of the Ilkhanid dynasty in the middle of the eighth/fourteenth century, hardly any political entity was able to establish a realm centred on the Iranian plateau. This may explain why explicit definitions of the territory of Iran seem to decrease noticeably until the end of the ninth/fifteenth century compared with the time of the Ilkhans. Nonetheless, many Persian authors apparently also envisioned a world of political entities, both within and beyond Iran, that had as basic features a territory and a ruling dynasty. In most cases, notably that of Iran, the ruling dynasty was of course preceded and could be succeeded by others.

Tabriz was certainly very much a prize for the various nomadic formations that competed for succession to the Mongols and were generally portrayed as dynasties. However, only members of the Chupanid, the Jalayerid, the Qara Qoyunlu and the Aq Qoyunlu ruling families erected royal building complexes similar to that of Ghazan. Those rulers who did so could be considered as successors to Ghazan and kings of Islamic Iran, especially in the ninth/fifteenth century, when the Turkmen dynasties gradually managed to bring the territory previously ruled by the Mongol Ilkhans under their control. The royal monuments which Chupanid, Jalayerid, Qara Qoyunlu and Aq Qoyunlu rulers erected in and around Tabriz continuously marked the city as a royal site, which could be seen as standing for the idea of a territorially distinct kingdom named Iran. In doing so, these monuments also indicated a sequence of dynastic succession to that kingdom which was literally built on a Mongol foundation.

Notes:

1. Bert G. Fragner, 'Iran under Ilkhanid rule in a world history perspective', pp. 127–28; idem, 'The concept of regionalism in historical research on Central Asia and Iran', pp. 348–50; idem, 'Ilkhanid contributions to Iranian political culture', pp. 72–75.
2. Fragner, 'Iran under Ilkhanid rule', pp. 127–28.
3. Charles Melville, 'Padshāh-i Islām', pp. 159–77.
4. Fragner, 'Iran under Ilkhanid rule', p. 128.
5. Thomas T. Allsen, 'Spiritual geography and political legitimacy in the Eastern Steppe', pp. 116–35.
6. Fragner, 'Iran under Ilkhanid rule', p. 127; idem, 'The concept of regionalism', p. 348; idem, 'Ilkhanid contributions', pp. 72–73.
7. A. Shapur Shahbazi, 'The history of the Idea of Iran', pp. 102, 105.
8. Abolala Soudavar, 'Looking through *The Two Eyes of the Earth*', pp. 52–53; Charles Melville, 'From Adam to Abaqa', p. 76.
9. Melville, 'From Adam to Abaqa', pp. 81–84.
10. John E. Woods, *The Aqquyunlu*, pp. 4–10; Beatrice Forbes Manz, 'Mongol history rewritten and relived', pp. 129–49; Michal Biran, *Chinggis Khan*, pp. 81–84, 94–95; Anne F. Broadbridge, *Kingship and Ideology in the Islamic and Mongol Worlds*, pp. 6–11.
11. Fragner, 'Iran under Ilkhanid rule', p. 128.
12. Judith Pfeiffer, 'Introduction. From Baghdad to Marāgha, Tabriz and beyond', p. 3.
13. Ibid., p. 4.
14. Ibid., p. 5.
15. David Durand-Guédy, 'Introduction. Location of rule in a context of Turko-Mongol domination', p. 13. Also see Daniel Zakrzewski, 'Local elites and dynastic succession', pp. 355, 366–67, 387–88.
16. Andrew Peacock, 'Nomadic society and the Seljūq campaigns in Caucasia', pp. 205–30; David Durand-Guédy, '1147: The battle of Qara-Tegin', pp. 161–96; Sara Nur Yildiz, 'Post-Mongol pastoral polities in Eastern Anatolia', pp. 27–48.
17. While royal campsites in the immediate vicinity of Tabriz have not been analysed in detail, systematic studies exist on major grazing grounds in areas adjacent to Azerbaijan at the time of Hülegü's invasion and on migration routes in the reign of Ghazan's brother and successor Öljeitü. John Masson Smith Jr, 'Mongol nomadism and Middle Eastern geography', pp. 39–56. Charles Melville, 'The itineraries of Sultan Öljeitü, 1304–16', pp. 55–70. Migration and residence patterns shifted slightly away from Tabriz during Öljeitü's well-documented reign, but the city remained a central locality especially in the long run. A few important sites in the environs of Tabriz will be discussed but a detailed analysis of this matter through the entire period under study here is unfortunately beyond the scope of this chapter.
18. Charles Melville, 'Earthquakes and historical monuments in Tabriz', pp. 164–65, 170–71. Masashi Haneda, 'The pastoral and the mausoleum city', pp. 142–70; Christoph Werner, 'Ein Vaqf für meine Töchter. Ḥātūn Jān Bēgum und die Qarā Quyūnlū Stiftungen zur "Blauen Moschee" in Tabriz', pp. 94–109; Sussan Babaie,

Isfahan and its Palaces, pp. 30–45; Ertuğrul Ökten, 'Imperial Aqquyunlu construction of religious establishments', pp. 371–85; Sandra Aube, *La céramique dans l'architecture en Iran au xve siècle*, pp. 75–102.

19. For additional information on Zajjāji's *Homāyun-nāma* and a preliminary analysis of questions of content and patronage, see Daniel Zakrzewski, 'Malik Ṣadr al-Dīn Tabrīzī and the establishment of Mongol rule in Iran', pp. 1060–62, 1070–71. On the increasing importance of the *Shāhnāma* under the Mongols and their successors see, for instance, Eleanor Sims, 'The illustrated manuscripts of Firdausi's "Shāhnāma" commissioned by princes of the house of Timūr', pp. 43–68; Abolala Soudavar, 'The Saga of Abu-Sa'id Bahādor Khān', pp. 95–218; Charles Melville, 'Between Firdausī and Rashīd al-Dīn', pp. 45–65, and idem, 'The royal image in Mongol Iran', pp. 343–69.
20. Zakrzewski, 'Malik Ṣadr al-Dīn Tabrīzī', features a detailed analysis and additional references.
21. George Lane, *Early Mongol Rule in Thirteenth-Century Iran*, pp. 42–95; Michal Biran, 'The Battle of Herat', pp. 175–219. Biran is one of the few scholars who follow Fragner in regarding the delineation of Iran's boundaries as a legacy of the Mongols; also see Biran, *Chinggis Khan*, pp. 99–100.
22. Nāser al-Din Beyzāvi, *Nezām al-tavārikh*, ed. M.H. Mohaddes, p. 3, '*selsela-ye hokkām va moluk-e Irān-zamin keh tul-e ān az Forāt ast tā beh Jeyhun*'.
23. Beyzāvi, *Nezām al-tavārikh*, p. 132, '*va az owlād-e u keh dar Irān-zamin hokm kardand va mamālek gashudand Hulāku Khān bud. [...] in zamān pesar-e u Abāqā Khān pādshāh-e Irān va belād-e Rum*'.
24. Melville, 'From Adam to Abaqa (Part II)', pp. 8–9; idem, 'Qāḍī Bayḍāwī's *Niẓām al-tawārīkh* in the *Safīna-yi Tabrīz*, pp. 97–98.
25. Melville, 'From Adam to Abaqa (Part 1)', pp. 77–79.
26. Serāj al-Din Juzjāni, *Tabaqāt-e Nāseri*, ed. 'A. Habibi Qandahāri; Hakim Zajjāji, *Homāyun-nāma*, ed. 'A. Pir-neyā. This is the second part of the *Homāyun-nāma*, which comprises the universal history. The first part of the work, which is a biography of the Prophet Mohammed, was likewise edited by 'Ali Pir-neyā and published in 2011. For additional information see also the reference to my article given in note 19.
27. Juzjāni, *Tabaqāt-e Nāseri*, vol. II, pp. 212–22.
28. Ibid., pp. 188–89, also uses the phrase *belād-e Irān va 'ajam.*
29. Zajjāji, *Homāyun-nāma*, p. 1189, '*sar-anjām dast az delirān be-bord, be-mardi molk, molk-e Irān be-bord; beh Tabriz budi Abu Bakr Shāh, zadi andar ān bum-o-bar bargāh*'.
30. Ibid., p. 1227. It should in fact be six years as Jalāl al-Din conquered Tabriz in 622/1225.
31. Ibid., p. 1191.
32. Ibid., p. 1100.
33. Ibid., p. 1219, '*be-goftand ke-in shahr-e khush il-e mā-st, keh yāri-deh-e lashkar va kheyl-e mā-st; chenin shahr-e zarin bud khāss-e khān, keh khushtar nabāshad az in dar jahān*'.
34. Rashid al-Din Fazlollāh Hamadāni, *Jāme' al-tavārikh*, ed. M. Rowshan and M. Musavi, vol. II, p. 1061, '*dar al-molk Tabriz-rā maqarr-e sarir-e pādshāhi sākht*'.

35. Rashid al-Din, *Jāme' al-tavārikh*, vol. I, p. 553, vol. II, pp. 1102, 1110, 1113, 1259–60, 1293. There are at least two passages on Abaqa's reign where Bahman Karimi's edition of Rashid al-Din's history has the epithet *dār al-saltana* instead of *dār al-molk*, see Rashid al-Din, *Jāme' al-tavārikh*, ed. B. Karimi, vol. II, pp. 773, 775.
36. Charles Melville, 'Jāme' al-tawāriḵ', pp. 463–64.
37. Rashid al-Din, *Jāme' al-tavārikh* (Rowshan), vol. II, pp. 979–80.
38. Ibid., p. 1070, '*dar mamālek-e Irān beh nashr-e 'adl va ensāf mashghul bud*'.
39. Ibid., p. 1304, '*az ān ghāfel nistam keh shokrāna-ye ānkeh tamāmat-e khalāyeq-e Irān-zamin-rā keh vadāye'-e hazrat-e oluhiyat-and az rāh-e fazl va ehsān dar rabqa-ye tā'at-e man avarda beh sad hazār zabān vājeb va lāzem ast*'.
40. Dāvud b. Mohammad Banākati, *Rowzat owlā-l-albāb*, p. 466.
41. Rashid al-Din, *Jāme' al-tavārikh* (Rowshan), vol. II, p. 1303.
42. Ibid., pp. 1293–94.
43. Judith Pfeiffer, 'The canonization of cultural memory', p. 67.
44. Rashid al-Din, *Jāme' al-tavārikh*, ed. 'A.'A. 'Alizadeh, vol. III, p. 229.
45. Haneda, 'The pastoral and the mausoleum city', pp. 144–56.
46. Ibid., p. 161.
47. Abu'l-Qāsem Qāshāni, *Tārikh-e Uljāytu*, p. 45.
48. Gottfried Herrmann, *Persische Urkunden der Mongolenzeit*, pp. 84–87, 101–3, 115, 147–49, 151–53.
49. Ebn-e Karbalā'i, *Rowzāt al-jenān va jannāt al-janān*, vol. I, p. 528.
50. Qāshāni, *Tārikh-e Uljāytu*, p. 53.
51. Ibid., pp. 27–28.
52. Ibid., pp. 28–29.
53. Ibid., p. 31, '*mahrusa-ye Tabriz keh maghbut-e pādshāhān va khavāqin-e urugh-e Hulāku Khān-ast*'. Melville, 'The itineraries of Sultan Öljeitü', pp. 57, 64–66. Precise data is lacking for the reign of Abu Sa'id but it seems that the preference for Soltāniyeh initiated by Öljeitü continued.
54. Melville, 'Earthquakes and historical monuments', pp. 164, 170; Birgitt Hoffmann, 'In pursuit of *memoria* and salvation', pp. 171–85.
55. Melville, 'The royal image in Mongol Iran', pp. 347–56; Soudavar, 'The Saga of Abu-Sa'id', pp. 98–158.
56. Soudavar, 'The Saga of Abu-Sa'id', pp. 176–77.
57. Hamdollāh Mostowfi, *Tārikh-e gozida*, pp. 590, 609, 614, 616–17.
58. Hamdollāh Mostowfi, *Bakhsh-e nakhost az maqāla-ye sevvom-e Nozhat al-qolub*, p. 85.
59. Ebn Fadlollāh al-'Omari, *Masālek al-absār fi mamālek al-amsār*, p. 85.
60. Ibid., pp. 85–86.
61. Ibid., p. 88.
62. Qotb al-Din Ahari, *Tavārikh-e Sheykh-Oveys*, p. 220.
63. Ibid., pp. 221–222.
64. Ibid., pp. 221, 223.
65. Mohammad b. 'Ali Shabānkāra'i, *Majma' al-ansāb*, pp. 301–11; Shehāb al-Din Hāfez-e Abru, *Zeyl-e Jāme' al-tavārikh-e Rashidi*, pp. 193–201.
66. Ahari, *Tavārikh-e Sheykh-Oveys*, pp. 224–27.

67. Charles Melville and ʻAbbās Zaryāb, ʻChobanids', pp. 498–99; Peter Jackson, ʻJalayerids', pp. 416–18.
68. Ahari, *Tavārikh-e Sheykh-Oveys*, p. 228; Hāfez-e Abru, *Zeyl*, p. 213; Ebn-e Karbalā'i, *Rowzāt al-jenān*, vol. I, pp. 44–45, 369–70; Melville, ʻEarthquakes and historical monuments', pp. 165, 170.
69. Ahari, *Tavārikh-e Sheykh-Oveys*, pp. 227–31; Zeyn al-Din b. Hamdollāh Mostowfi, *Zeyl-e Tārikh-e gozida*, pp. 27–30; Hāfez-e Abru, *Zeyl*, pp. 204–18.
70. Ahari, *Tavārikh-e Sheykh-Oveys*, pp. 231–39; Zeyn al-Din, *Zeyl*, pp. 31–64; Hāfez-e Abru, *Zeyl*, pp. 219–36.
71. Ahari, *Tavārikh-e Sheykh-Oveys*, pp. 240–47; Zeyn al-Din, *Zeyl*, pp. 64–70; Hāfez-e Abru, *Zeyl*, pp. 236–39.
72. Ahari, *Tavārikh-e Sheykh-Oveys*, p. 246.
73. Ibid., p. 225.
74. Jackson, ʻJalayerids'; Thomas T. Allsen, *Culture and Conquest in Mongol Eurasia*, pp. 26–32.
75. Soudavar, ʻThe Saga of Abu-Saʻid', p. 169.
76. Charles Melville, ʻĠāzān-nāma', p. 383.
77. Mohammad b. Hendushāh Nakhjavāni, *Dastur al-kāteb fi taʻyin al-marāteb*, vol. I, pp. 13–21.
78. Nakhjavāni, *Dastur al-kāteb*, vol. I, pp. 127, 134, 270, 325, 352; vol. II, pp. 9–10, 40, 75, 88, 126, 316.
79. Nakhjavāni, *Dastur al-kāteb*, vol. II, pp. 255–58.
80. Rui Gonzales de Clavijo, *Embassy to Tamerlane*, p. 153; Ebn-e Karbalā'i, *Rowzāt al-jenān*, vol. I, p. 470; Zeyn al-Din, *Zeyl*, p. 64; Hāfez-e Abru, *Zeyl*, pp. 235–36.
81. Ebn-e Karbalā'i, *Rowzāt al-jenān*, vol. II, pp. 6–7, includes a photograph of the tombstone of Sheykh-Oveys in Shadabad. Meanwhile, the tombstone has been transferred to a museum in Tabriz (personal observation of the author, 2012).
82. Zeyn al-Din, *Zeyl*, pp. 95–96; Shabānkāra'i, *Majmaʻ al-ansāb*, p. 318.
83. Zakrzewski, ʻLocal elites', pp. 377–78.
84. Ebn-e Karbalā'i, *Rowzāt al-jenān*, vol. II, pp. 640–49; Zeyn al-Din, *Zeyl*, pp. 153–67.
85. Beatrice Forbes Manz, *The Rise and Rule of Tamerlane*, p. 71.
86. Nezām al-Din Shāmi, *Zafarnāma*, pp. 97–98.
87. Zeyn al-Din, *Zeyl*, pp. 113–22; Hāfez-e Abru, *Zeyl*, pp. 266–88; Sharaf al-Din ʻAli Yazdi, *Zafarnāma*, vol. I, pp. 555–62.
88. Manz, *The Rise and Rule of Tamerlane*, pp. 12–15.
89. Yazdi, *Zafarnāma*, vol. I, pp. 559–60, 681–83; Mohammad Mirkhvānd, *Tārikh-e Rowzat al-safā'*, vol. VI, pp. 144, 203–4.
90. Hāfez-e Abru, *Zeyl*, pp. 301–2.
91. Zakrzewski, ʻLocal elites', p. 379.
92. Yazdi, *Zafarnāma*, vol. I, p. 724.
93. John E. Woods, ʻTurco-Iranica II', pp. 333–34.
94. Manz, *The Rise and Rule of Tamerlane*, pp. 72–73.
95. Yazdi, *Zafarnāma*, vol. II, pp. 1188, 1227.
96. Hāfez-e Abru, *Zobdat al-tavārikh*, vol. III, pp. 168, 222–29.
97. Ibid., pp. 399–403.
98. Ibid., p. 446.

99. Hasan Beg Rumlu, *Ahsan al-tavārikh*, vol. I, p. 202.
100. Johann Schiltberger, *The Bondage and Travels of Johann Schiltberger*, pp. 29–33.
101. Schiltberger, *The Bondage and Travels*, p. 44.
102. Abu Bakr Tehrāni, *Ketāb-e Diyārbakriya*, p. 74. For a study of Tehrani's history, see Daniel Zakrzewski, 'Terms of politics and pastoral nomadism in two works', pp. 159–85.
103. Shāmi, *Zafarnāma*, p. 242.
104. Mirkhvānd, *Tārikh-e Rowzat al-safā'*, vol. VI, pp. 500, 509.
105. Beatrice Forbes Manz, 'Family and ruler in Timurid historiography', pp. 58–65.
106. Yazdi, *Zafarnāma*, vol. I, p. 849; Hāfez-e Abru, *Zobdat al-tavārikh*, vol. III, pp. 565, 579–81; 'Abd al-Razzāq Samarqandi, *Majma'-e bahreyn*, vol. III, pp. 129–30, 391.
107. Samarqandi, *Majma'-e bahreyn*, vol. III, p. 409.
108. Tehrāni, *Ketāb-e Diyārbakriya*, p. 139.
109. Samarqandi, *Majma'-e bahreyn*, vol. IV, pp. 828–47.
110. Tehrāni, *Ketāb-e Diyārbakriya*, p. 285.
111. Ibid., p. 353.
112. Ibid., p. 359.
113. Werner, 'Ein Vaqf für meine Töchter', pp. 101–3.
114. Sheila S. Blair, 'Tabriz: International entrepôt under the Mongols', pp. 346–48; Aube, *La céramique*, pp. 77–92.
115. Aube, *La céramique*, p. 82.
116. Ebn-e Karbalā'i, *Rowzāt al-jenān*, vol. I, p. 470; Tehrāni, *Ketāb-e Diyārbakriya*, p. 437.
117. Aube, *La céramique*, pp. 76–78; Sussan Babaie, *Isfahan and its Palaces*, pp. 19–21, 31–43; Haneda, 'The pastoral and the mausoleum city', pp. 163–67; Melville, 'Earthquakes and historical monuments', p. 170.
118. Ebn al-Fowati, *Majma' al-ādāb fi mo'jam al-alqāb*, vol. III, p. 175.
119. Woods, *The Aqquyunlu*, pp. 96–99.
120. Tehrāni, *Ketāb-e Diyārbakriya*, p. 406.
121. Ibid., pp. 434–42.
122. Ibid., pp. 522–23.
123. Woods, *The Aqquyunlu*, pp. 112–22.
124. Mehmet Şefik Keçik, *Briefe und Urkunden aus der Kanzlei Uzun Ḥasans*, pp. 216–21 (document no. 15).
125. Aube, *La céramique*, pp. 77–79; Babaie, *Isfahan and its Palaces*, pp. 30–31; Haneda, 'The pastoral and the mausoleum city', pp. 164–65; Melville, 'Earthquakes and historical monuments', pp. 170–71; Ökten, 'Imperial Aqquyunlu construction of religious establishments'.
126. Fazlollāh b. Ruzbehān Khonji-Esfahāni, *Tārikh-e 'ālam-ārā-ye Amini*, pp. 93–96, 158.
127. Ibid., pp. 364–65.
128. H.R. Roemer, 'The Safavid period', p. 189.

Bibliography:

Primary Sources

Ahari, Qotb al-Din, *Tavārikh-e Sheykh-Oveys*, ed. Iraj Afshār (Tabriz: Sotuda, 2010).

Banākati, Dāvud b. Mohammad, *Rowzat owlā-l-albāb fi ma'refat al-tavārikh wa'l-ansāb*, ed. Ja'far She'ār (Tehran: Anjoman-e āsār-e melli, 1969).

Beyzāvi, Nāser al-Din, *Nezām al-tavārikh*, ed. M.H. Mohaddes (Tehran: Bonyād-e mowqufāt-e Doktor Mahmud Afshār, 2003).

Clavijo, Rui Gonzales de, *Embassy to Tamerlane*, trans. G. Le Strange (London: Routledge & Sons, 1928).

Ebn al-Fowati, Kamāl al-Din 'Abd al-Razzāq al-Baghdādi, *Majma' al-ādāb fi mo'jam al-alqāb*, ed. M. al-Kāzem (Tehran: Sāzmān-e chāp va enteshārāt-e vezārat-e farhang va ershād-e eslāmi, 1995).

Ebn-e Karbalā'i, Hāfez Hoseyn-e Karbalā'i Tabrizi, *Rowzāt al-jenān va jannāt al-janān*, ed. Ja'far Soltān al-Qorrā'i (Tehran: Bongāh-e tarjoma va nashr-e ketāb, 1965–70).

Hāfez-e Abru, Shehāb al-Din 'Abdollāh Khvāfi, *Zeyl-e Jāme' al-tavārikh-e Rashidi*, ed. K. Bayāni (Tehran: Enteshārāt-e Dāneshgāh-e Tehrān, 1971).

— *Zobdat al-tavārikh*, ed. K.H.S. Javādi (Tehran: Sāzmān-e chāp va enteshārāt-e vezārat-e farhang va ershād-e eslāmi, 2001).

Juzjāni, Serāj al-Din, *Tabaqāt-e Nāseri*, ed. 'A. Habibi Qandahāri (Kabul, 1964–65).

Khonji-Esfahāni, Fazlollāh b. Ruzbehān, *Tārikh-e 'ālam-ārā-ye Amini*, ed. M.A.'Āsheq (Tehran: Mirās-e Maktub, 2003).

Mirkhvānd, Mohammad b. Sayyed Borhān al-Din Khvāndshāh, *Tārikh-e Rowzat al-safā'*, ed. N.A. Sabuhi (Tehran: Enteshārāt-e markazi Khayyām-Piruz, 1959).

Mostowfi, Hamdollāh, *Bakhsh-e nakhost az maqāla-ye sevvom-e Nozhat al-qolub*, ed. Mohammad Dabir Seyāqi (Tehran: Tahuri, 1958).

— *Tārikh-e gozida*, ed. 'Abd al-Hoseyn Navā'i (Tehran: Amir Kabir, 1960).

Nakhjavāni, Mohammad b. Hendushāh, *Dastur al-kāteb fi ta'yin al-marāteb*, ed. 'A.'A. 'Alizadeh (Moscow: Nauka, 1964–71).

al-'Omari, Ebn Fadlollāh, *Masālek al-absār fi mamālek al-amsār*, partial ed. and trans. K. Lech, *Das mongolische Weltreich* (Wiesbaden: Harrassowitz, 1968).

Qāshāni, Abu'l-Qāsem, *Tārikh-e Öljeitü*, ed. Mahin Hambly (Tehran: Bongāh-e tarjoma va nashr-e ketāb, 1970).

Rashid al-Din Fazlollāh Hamadāni, *Jāme' al-tavārikh*, ed. 'A.'A. 'Alizadeh (Baku: Academy of Science of the Socialist Soviet Republic of Azerbaijan, 1957).

— *Jāme' al-tavārikh*, ed. B. Karimi, 2 vols (Tehran: Enteshārāt-e Eqbāl, 1988).

— *Jāme' al-tavārikh*, ed. M. Rowshan and M. Musavi, 4 vols (Tehran: Alborz, 1994).
Rumlu, Hasan Beg, *Ahsan al-tavārikh*, ed. 'Abd al-Hoseyn Navā'i, 3 vols (Tehran: Enteshārāt-e asātir, 2005).
Samarqandi, 'Abd al-Razzāq, *Majma'-e bahreyn va matla'-e sa'deyn*, ed. 'Abd al-Hoseyn Navā'i (Tehran: Pazhuheshgāh-e 'olum-e ensāni va motāle'āt-e farhangi, 2004).
Schiltberger, Johann, *The Bondage and Travels of Johann Schiltberger, a Native of Bavaria, in Europe, Asia and Africa, 1396–1427*, trans. J.B. Telfer (London: The Hakluyt Society, 1897).
Shabānkāra'i, Mohammad b. 'Ali, *Majma' al-ansāb*, ed. M.H. Mohaddes (Tehran: Amir Kabir, 1984).
Shāmi, Nezām al-Din, *Zafarnāma. Fotuhāt-e Amir Timur Gurgāni*, ed. M.A. Panāhi Semnāni (Tehran: Bāmdād, 1984).
Tehrāni, Abu Bakr, *Ketāb-e Diyārbakriya*, ed. Faruk Sümer (Ankara: Türk Tarih Kurumu Basımevi, 1964).
Yazdi, Sharaf al-Din 'Ali, *Zafarnāma*, ed. S.S.M.M. Sādeq and 'Abd al-Hoseyn Navā'i (Tehran: Ketābkhāna-ye muza va markaz-e asnād-e majles-e shurā-ye eslāmi, 2008).
Zajjāji, Hakim, *Homāyun-nāma*, ed. 'A. Pir-neyā (Tehran: Mirās-e Maktub, 2004).
Zeyn al-Din b. Hamdollāh Mostowfi, *Zeyl-e Tārikh-e gozida*, ed. Iraj Afshār (Tehran: Majmu'a-ye enteshārāt-e adabi va tārikhi-ye mowqufāt-e Doktor Mahmud Afshār Yazdi, 1993).

Secondary Sources

Allsen, Thomas T., 'Spiritual geography and political legitimacy in the Eastern Steppe', in *Ideology and the Formation of Early States*, ed. H.J.M. Claessen and J.G. Oosten (Leiden: Brill, 1996), pp. 116–35.
— *Culture and Conquest in Mongol Eurasia* (Cambridge: Cambridge University Press, 2001).
Aube, Sandra, *La céramique dans l'architecture en Iran au xve siècle. Les arts qarâ quyûnlû et âq quyûnlû* (Paris: Presses de l'université Paris-Sorbonne, 2017).
Babaie, Sussan, *Isfahan and its Palaces: Statecraft, Shi'ism and the Architecture of Conviviality in Early Modern Iran* (Edinburgh: Edinburgh University Press, 2008).
Biran, Michal, 'The Battle of Herat', in *Warfare in Inner Asian History (500–1800)*, ed. N. Di Cosmo (Leiden: Brill, 2002), pp. 175–219.
— *Chinggis Khan* (Oxford: Oneworld, 2007).
Blair, Sheila S., 'Tabriz: International entrepôt under the Mongols', in *Politics, Patronage and the Transmission of Knowledge in 13th–15th Century Tabriz*, ed. J. Pfeiffer (Leiden: Brill, 2014), pp. 321–56.

Broadbridge, Anne F., *Kingship and Ideology in the Islamic and Mongol Worlds* (Cambridge: Cambridge University Press, 2008).

Durand-Guédy, David, 'Introduction. Location of rule in a context of Turko-Mongol domination', in *Turko-Mongol Rulers, Cities and City Life*, ed. D. Durand-Guédy (Leiden: Brill, 2013), pp. 1–20.

— '1147: The Battle of Qara-Tegin and the rise of Azerbayjan', *Der Islam* 92, no. 1 (2015), pp. 161–96.

Fragner, Bert G., 'Iran under Ilkhanid rule in a world history perspective', in *L'Iran face à la domination mongole*, ed. D. Aigle (Tehran: Institut Français de Recherche en Iran, 1997), pp. 121–31.

— 'The concept of regionalism in historical research on Central Asia and Iran (A macro-historical interpretation)', in *Studies on Central Asian History in Honor of Yuri Bregel*, ed. D. DeWeese (Bloomington: Indiana University Research Institute for Inner Asian Studies, 2001), pp. 341–54.

— 'Ilkhanid contributions to Iranian political culture', in *Beyond the Legacy of Genghis Khan*, ed. L. Komaroff (Leiden: Brill, 2006), pp. 68–80.

Haneda, Masashi, 'The pastoral and the mausoleum city: Nomadic rule and city construction in the Eastern Islamic World', in *Islamic Urbanism in Human History: Political Power and Social Networks*, ed. T. Sato (London: Kegan Paul International, 1997), pp. 142–70.

Herrmann, Gottfried, *Persische Urkunden der Mongolenzeit: Text- und Bildteil* (Wiesbaden: Harrassowitz, 2004).

Hoffmann, Birgitt, 'In pursuit of *memoria* and salvation: Rashīd al-Dīn and his Rab'-i Rashīdī', in *Politics, Patronage and the Transmission of Knowledge in 13th–15th Century Tabriz*, ed. J. Pfeiffer (Leiden: Brill, 2014), pp. 171–85.

Jackson, Peter, 'Jalayerids', *Encyclopaedia Iranica*, vol. XIV (2008), pp. 415–19.

Keçik, Mehmet Şefik, *Briefe und Urkunden aus der Kanzlei Uzun Ḥasans. Ein Beitrag zur Geschichte Ost-Anatoliens im 15. Jahrhundert* (Freiburg: Klaus Schwarz Verlag, 1976).

Lane, George, *Early Mongol Rule in Thirteenth-Century Iran: A Persian Renaissance* (London: Routledge Curzon, 2003).

Manz, Beatrice Forbes, *The Rise and Rule of Tamerlane* (Cambridge: Cambridge University Press, 1989).

— 'Mongol history rewritten and relived', ed. Denise Aigle, *Revue des mondes musulmans et de la Méditerranée* 89/90 (2000) pp. 129–49.

— 'Family and ruler in Timurid historiography', in *Studies on Central Asian History in Honor of Yuri Bregel*, ed. D. DeWeese (Bloomington: Indiana University Research Institute for Inner Asian Studies, 2001), pp. 57–78.

Masson Smith Jr, John, 'Mongol nomadism and Middle Eastern geography: Qīshlāqs and Tümens', in *The Mongol Empire and Its Legacy*, ed. R. Amitai-Preiss and D.O. Morgan (Leiden: Brill, 1999), pp. 39–56.

Melville, Charles, 'Earthquakes and historical monuments in Tabriz', *Iran* 19 (1981), pp. 159–77.
— 'Padshāh-i Islam: The conversion of Sultan Maḥmūd Ghāzān Khān', in *Persian and Islamic Studies in Honour of P.W. Avery* (Pembroke Papers 1), ed. C. Melville (Cambridge: Centre for Middle Eastern Studies, 1990), pp. 159–77.
— 'The itineraries of Sultan Öljeitü, 1304–16', *Iran* 28 (1990), pp. 55–70.
— 'Ḡāzān-nāma', *Encyclopaedia Iranica*, vol. X (2000), p. 383.
— 'From Adam to Abaqa: Qāḍī Baiḍāwī's rearrangment of history', *Studia Iranica* 30 (2001), pp. 67–86.
— 'Between Firdausī and Rashīd al-Dīn: Persian verse chronicles of the Mongol period', *Studia Islamica* 104/105 (2007), pp. 45–65.
— 'From Adam to Abaqa: Qāḍī Bayḍāwī's rearrangement of history (Part II)', *Studia Iranica* 36 (2007), pp. 7–64.
— 'Qāḍī Bayḍāwī's *Niẓām al-tawārīkh* in the *Safīna-yi Tabrīz*: an early witness to the text', in *The Treasury of Tabriz: The Great Il-Khanid Compendium*, ed. A.A. Seyed-Gohrab and S. McGlinn (Amsterdam: Rozenberg Publishers; West Lafayette: Purdue University Press, 2007), pp. 91–102.
— 'Jāme' al-tawārik̲', *Encyclopaedia Iranica*, vol. XIV (2008), pp. 462–68.
— 'The royal image in Mongol Iran', in *Every Inch A King: Comparative Studies on Kings and Kingship in the Ancient and Medieval Worlds*, ed. L. Mitchell and C. Melville (Leiden: Brill, 2013), pp. 343–69.
Melville, Charles and 'Abbās Zaryāb, 'Chobanids', *Encyclopaedia Iranica*, vol. V (1991), pp. 496–502.
Ökten, Ertuğrul, 'Imperial Aqquyunlu construction of religious establishments in the late fifteenth century Tabriz', in *Politics, Patronage and the Transmission of Knowledge in 13th–15th Century Tabriz*, ed. J. Pfeiffer (Leiden: Brill, 2014), pp. 371–85.
Peacock, Andrew, 'Nomadic society and the Seljūq campaigns in Caucasia', *Iran and the Caucasus* 9, no. 2 (2005), pp. 205–30.
Pfeiffer, Judith, 'The canonization of cultural memory: Ghāzān Khan, Rashīd al-Dīn and the construction of the Mongol past', in *Rashīd al-Dīn: Agent and Mediator of Cultural Exchanges in Ilkhanid Iran*, ed. A. Akasoy et al. (London: The Warburg Institute, Turin: Nino Aragno Editore, 2013), pp. 57–70.
— 'Introduction. From Baghdad to Marāgha, Tabriz and beyond: Tabriz and the multi-cephalous cultural, religious, and intellectual landscape of the 13th to 15th century Nile-to-Oxus region', in *Politics, Patronage and the Transmission of Knowledge in 13th–15th Century Tabriz*, ed. J. Pfeiffer (Leiden: Brill, 2014), pp. 1–11.
Roemer, H.R., 'The Safavid period,' in *The Cambridge History of Iran, vol. 6, The Timurid and Safavid Periods*, ed. P. Jackson (Cambridge University Press, Cambridge, 1986), pp. 189–347.

Shahbazi, A. Shapur, 'The history of the Idea of Iran', in *The Idea of Iran, vol. 1, Birth of the Persian Empire*, ed. V. Sarkosh Curtis and S. Stewart (London: I.B. Tauris, 2005), pp. 100–111.

Sims, Eleanor, 'The illustrated manuscripts of Firdausi's "Shāhnāma" commissioned by princes of the house of Timūr', *Ars Orientalia* 22 (1992), pp. 43–68.

Soudavar, Abolala, 'The Saga of Abu-Sa'id Bahādor Khān. The Abu-Sa'idnāmé', in *The Court of the Il-Khans, 1290–1340*, ed. T. Fitzherbert and J. Raby (Oxford: Oxford Studies in Islamic Art, 1996), pp. 95–218.

— 'Looking through *The Two Eyes of the Earth*: A Reassessment of Sassanian rock reliefs', *Iranian Studies* 45, no. 1 (2012), pp. 29–58.

Werner, Christoph, 'Ein Vaqf für meine Töchter. Ḥātūn Jān Bēgum und die Qarā Quyūnlū Stiftungen zur "Blauen Moschee" in Tabriz', *Der Islam* 80 (2003), pp. 94–109.

Woods, John E., 'Turco-Iranica II: Notes on a Timurid decree of 1396/798', *Journal of Near Eastern Studies* 43, no. 4 (1984), pp. 331–37.

— *The Aqquyunlu. Clan, Confederation, Empire. Revised and extended edition* (Salt Lake City: The University of Utah Press, 1999).

Yildiz, Sara Nur, 'Post-Mongol pastoral polities in Eastern Anatolia during the late Middle Ages', in *At the Crossroads of Empires: 14th – 15th Century Eastern Anatolia*, ed. D. Beyazit (Paris: Institut Français d'Études Anatoliennes, 2012), pp. 27–48.

Zakrzewski, Daniel, 'Terms of politics and pastoral nomadism in two works of fifteenth-century Persian historical writing', *Eurasian Studies* 9, no. 12 (2001), pp. 159–85.

— 'Malik Ṣadr al-Dīn Tabrīzī and the establishment of Mongol rule in Iran', *Asiatische Studien/Études Asiatiques* 71, no. 4 (2017), pp. 1059–73.

— 'Local elites and dynastic succession: Tabriz prior to, under and following Mongol rule (Sixth/Twelfth to Ninth/Fifteenth Centuries)', *Eurasian Studies* 16 (2018) pp. 352–94.

4

Two Later Ninth/Fifteenth-Century Iranian Travellers

John E. Woods
(University of Chicago)

Ninth/fifteenth-century Iran-zamin produced a wealth of literature on cosmography and travel in the form of treatises in Persian and accounts of ambassadors, merchants and pilgrims, both foreign and domestic. In the first connection, the most important geographical work of this period is the unfinished and untitled historical geography of the Timurid courtier and chronicler Hafez-e Abru. Commissioned by Shahrokh in 817/1414, Hafez-e Abru was charged with translating Arabic works on routes and regions into Persian, supplementing his translation with data from other sources, including his own personal observations as he travelled

> west and north to the lands of Transoxiana, Turkestan, the Qepchaq Steppe, Khorasan, the two 'Eraqs, Fars, Azerbaijan, Arran, Mughan, Gorjestan, Greater and Lesser Armenia, the breadth of Anatolia and Syria, the banks of the Euphrates, Takrit, Mosul, Diyar Bakr, Gorjestan, the shores of the Caspian, Darband, Sharvan, Gilan, Rostamdar, Amol, Sari, and Jorjan; south and east to Zabol, Kabol, Send, Hend, Moltan, Uch, Delhi, and to the banks of the Ganges....[1]

References in his other historical writings attest to the fact that, beginning with the Three-Years' Expedition – *Yuresh-e seh sala*, 788–90/1386–88 – when he joined Timur, Hafez-e Abru participated in all the conqueror's major campaigns. Later, in the service of Timur's son Shahrokh, he took part in the first two of the three Azerbaijan expeditions of that ruler in 823–24/1420–21 and in 832–33/1429–30.

In the course of the ninth/fifteenth century, the political and military exploits of Timur and Uzun Hasan attracted the attention of observers in both West Europe and East Asia as well as in other parts of the Islamic world. The travel accounts of foreign diplomats such as the Spanish envoy Ruy Gonzalez de Clavijo,[2] the Venetian businessman Giosafat Barbaro,[3] the Mamluk military judge Ebn Aja,[4] the Ming ambassador Fu An[5] and many others furnish ample testimony to this fact. There also exist two very well-known Persian travel accounts from the first half of this century. Both reflect encounters of Iran-zamin with other civilizations. The earlier of the two is Gheyas al-Din Naqqash's account of the Timurid embassy to the Yongle Emperor of Ming China from its departure in 822/1419 until its return in 824/1422. Hafez-e Abru subsequently inserted Gheyas al-Din's report of this embassy in his annalistic narrative *Zobdat al-tavarikh*, dedicated to Shahrokh's son Baysunghor, on whose orders Gheyas al-Din had been sent to China along with a number of other Timurid envoys.[6] The second is the account of the mission of 'Abd al-Razzaq Samarqandi, who was sent by Shahrokh to the Vijayanagara Empire in 845/1442, returning to Herat in late 848/1444. Samarqandi's personal observations on his travels form an integral part of his Timurid annals *Matla'-e sa'deyn va majma'-e bahreyn*.[7] Finally, the lengthy cosmographic epilogues appended to the universal chronicles of Mirkhvand and his grandson Khvandmir at the end of the ninth/fifteenth and the beginning of the tenth/sixteenth century should also be mentioned.[8]

This chapter will focus on the works of two Iranian travellers from the second half of the ninth/fifteenth century: Sayyed Mir 'Ali Tusi, 'Ma'ali' and Amir Sayyed Kamal al-Din Hoseyn Abivardi, 'Feyzi'. Near contemporaries, both individuals were natives of Timurid Khorasan, both were descendants of the Prophet, both travelled to the west to perform the pilgrimage to the Holy Cities (Figure 1), and both utilized the *masnavi* poetic form in their works in contrast to the prose narrative accounts of the travel literature previously mentioned. One of the major differences between them, however, is that Abivardi was much more closely associated with aristocratic circles than Tusi and this fact is clearly reflected throughout their writings.

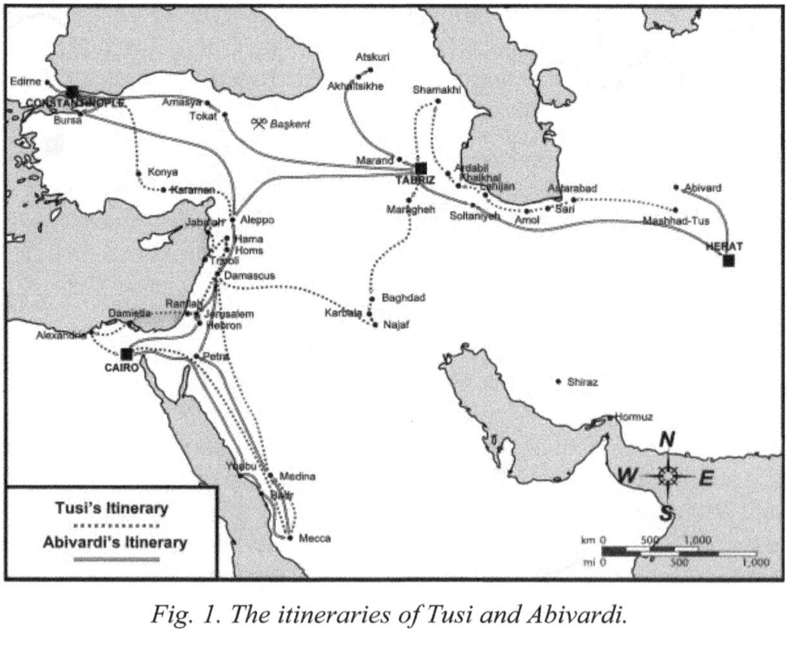

Fig. 1. The itineraries of Tusi and Abivardi.

These travelogues appear to exist only in unique manuscript copies and therefore probably did not circulate widely. Similarly, although made known to the scholarly community decades ago, neither seems to have had an appreciable effect on modern studies of the period since. Finally, if the travel accounts of Gheyas al-Din Naqqash and Samarqandi serve to define Iran-zamin in the earlier ninth/fifteenth century vis-à-vis the Chinese and Indian 'other', the works of Tusi and Abivardi situate the region firmly within the context of the history and civilization of the Islamic metropoles of Western Asia in the second half of the ninth/fifteenth century. I will first consider the life, work and travels of Tusi before turning to a discussion of Abivardi and his writings.

Sayyed Mir 'Ali Tusi, 'Ma'ali'

Tusi – known by his *makhlas* or pen name Ma'ali – and his work entitled *Khondkarnama* were first introduced in 1949 in an article published in Turkish by the German scholar Robert Anhegger.[9] While conducting research in Istanbul during the previous year, he had come across manuscript No. 1417 in the Topkapi Saray Hazine Library identified in the library catalogue as an anonymous Ottoman history. An inscription added above the *shamsa* on the top of folio 2r in fact states that the work is 'a history of the Ottoman House—a versified history in Persian of Soltan Mohammad Khan, the son of Morad Khan and others'. The *shamsa* on folio 1v is the ex-libris of Fateh Soltan Mehmet (r. 848–50/1444–46, 855–86/1451–81) and in the facing *shamsa* on folio 2r the title of the work, *Khondkarnama*, the dedication to Fateh Soltan Mehmet and the date early Zu'l-Hejja 878 (late April 1474) are written, but the name of the author is not recorded (see Plate I).

The manuscript, possibly a holograph, has never been published. It consists of 183 gold-ruled folios of 15 clear *nasta'liq* lines per folio, totalling more than 2,700 verses, for the most part in *masnavi* form. The headings – of which there are 133 – are written in gold ink, some on a cobalt blue background. In the first sections of the manuscript, the words *shahinshah*, Mohammad, *amir*, *shah*, *soltan*, *khonkar* and *khan* are also written in gold, especially when referring to the dedicatee. There is no formal colophon, but the date 877 AH appears in the last verse on the final folio (see Plate II).

The text of the *Khondkarnama* can be divided into five somewhat disconnected sections: fols. 2v–8r, exordium and praise of Fateh Soltan Mehmet; 8r–70v, Ottoman history I; 70v–137v, Iranian history; 137v–168r, Travels; and 168r–183v, Ottoman history II. Robert Anhegger was particularly interested in sections two and five and therefore much of his analysis concentrates on them. In the first section on Ottoman history, after glorifying Fateh Soltan Mehmet's conquests and campaigns in Serbia, Morea, Bosnia, Albania, Wallachia, Sinop, Trabzon and Mytilene, Tusi turns to a lengthy and detailed account of the Ottoman conflict with Uzun Hasan that began with the Aq Qoyunlu destruction of Tokat in 877/1472 and culminated in Fateh

Mehmet's resounding victory over the Turkmen invaders at the Battle of Başkent the following year – Tusi's is the only contemporary Persian account of this decisive event. There are important references to the Ottoman use of artillery, caissons and laagers (wagons) in the description of this campaign. The section concludes with a flashback to the victory of Fateh Soltan Mehmet's father Murad II over the Hungarians in the Second Battle of Kossova in 852/1448.

The second Ottoman section deals with the author's arrival in Konya – which at that time was under the control of Ebrahim Beg Qaramani (d. 869/1464) – and his sojourn in Laranda. It is not exactly clear when or how he entered Ottoman service, but after his account of Karaman, he returns to a continuation of the description of the aftermath of the Ottoman victory at Başkent dealt with in the first section on Ottoman history. He then writes of the exploits and death of Fateh Soltan Mehmet's son Prince Mostafa in 879/1474 and the execution of Mahmud Paşa Angelović later that same year, at which point he begins to give prominence to Fateh Soltan Mehmet's eldest son and eventual successor Prince Bâyezid. This section and the work close with the author's supplication to the sultan, reminding him that he had been in his service for 21 years, implying that he must have come to Anatolia in approximately 857/1453.

Section three on Iranian history begins with an account *in media res* of the career of Timur Khan (also called Beg) and his conflict with the Mozaffarid Shah-Mansur in 795/1393. After a description of the conquest of Damascus in 803/1401, Timur's conflict with Bâyezid I is mentioned, omitting any reference to the Ottoman defeat at the Battle of Ankara in 805/1402. A report of Timur's invasion of India in 801/1398 is anachronistically inserted just before his projected eastern campaign in 807/1405. The long reign of Shahrokh and the other successors of Timur are similarly condensed, although some space is devoted to the rebellion of Shahrokh's grandson Soltan-Mohammad, implicating the sovereign's wife Gowhar-Shad in the prince's fall from favour – to the best of my knowledge, Ahmed Zeki Velidi Togan is the only scholar to have made use of this part of Tusi's work.[10] After touching briefly on the rivalry between the Timurids and the Qara Qoyunlu and Aq Qoyunlu Turkmens, Tusi ends this historical section with Uzun Hasan's defeat of the Timurid Soltan-Abu Sa'id in 873/1469. His focus then shifts to the rise of the Mosha'sha' and the complex relationship between this messianic movement and the rulers of Hormuz and Lahsa, and the activities of the renegade Qara Qoyunlu prince Alvand, material that remains as yet largely unexploited.

Section four on the author's travels is also the only source of information on his life. Although he introduces his pen name Ma'ali early in the manuscript on folio 5v in the last line of a *qasida* in praise of the Ottoman sultan and repeats it numerous times throughout the poem,[11] he does not give us his full name – Sayyed Mir 'Ali – until folio 138r. Here we learn that he was originally from

Mashhad and was the third son of Mozaffar Tusi, whose death had evidently left him in very difficult circumstances. He had two older brothers, Sayyed Ahmed and Amir Mahmud, from whom he seems to have been estranged at the time of his father's death. After announcing to his betrothed his intention to travel, he bid her a bitter farewell and departed Mashhad for Astarabad to seek support for his journey from one of his brothers who lived there with his two sons Mozaffar Mortaza and 'Ali Miri. Although he was welcomed by his family members, they were unable or unwilling to provide him with assistance and he was forced to continue his travels with great hardship, of which he complains throughout this section, a situation that may only have been finally alleviated by Fateh Soltan Mehmed's munificence.

Leaving Astarabad, Tusi progressed westward along the southern Caspian coast through Sari, Amol and Lahejan; based on the regnal dates of the rulers of those locales mentioned by Tusi in his text, Anhegger calculates that he must have begun his travels between 851/1448 and 856/1452.[12] From Gilan, he entered the region of Azerbaijan, eventually reaching the town of Ardabil via Khalkhal, where he was received by Sheykh Ja'far, who had been installed as master of the Safavid religious order in place of his nephew Juneyd by the Turkmen ruler Jahanshah Qara Qoyunlu. Sheykh Ja'far welcomed him, appointed him a guide, and presented him with a horse and saddle to facilitate his onward journey. At this point, he diverted his route northward to Shamakhi – seat of the government of the Sharvanshah – before travelling south to the city of Tabriz. At the time of Tusi's visit, Tabriz was under the control of Jahanshah and the traveller commented on some of the political issues of the day. He also marvelled at the magnificence of the dome of the mausoleum of the Chinggisid Mahmud Ghazan Khan in the suburb of Shanb-e Ghazan where his quarters were located. Reaching Maragha in great distress, he obtained some relief from one of the local inhabitants before leaving Azerbaijan on his way to Baghdad.

After a dangerous passage through Kurdistan, Tusi arrived at Baghdad, where he made a visitation to the sanctuaries of the Imami Shi'ite Musa al-Kazem,[13] his companion Buhlul and the gnostics Juneyd, Shebli, Ma'ruf al-Karkhi, Ebrahim ebn Adham and Mansur al-Hallaj,[14] and he invoked their spirits to guide him on his pilgrimage. At the shrines of Hoseyn at Karbala[15] and 'Ali at Najaf,[16] Tusi passionately declared his reverence for the 'Alids and claims to have circumambulated the tomb of 'Ali – *Amir al-mo'menin, Shah-e velayat* – for three days and nights in midwinter. Joining a caravan of some 400 camels led by a young Kurd, whom he described as a devotee of the Prophet and his family, he crossed the Syrian Desert and reached Damascus. Travelling south from Damascus, he visited the tombs of the Patriarchs in Hebron[17] before proceeding to Jerusalem. There he worshipped at the Dome of the Rock (the Rock of God, *sakhra-ye Allah*, curiously misspelled with a *sin* instead of a *sad*) and then travelled to the Mediterranean coast via Ramla in the company of a

Circassian officer. He boarded a ship bound for Egypt and disembarked at the port of Damietta.

Noting the well-stocked markets of Damietta and the lushness of its hinterland, planted with bananas and sugar cane, Tusi also visited the hospices and shrines of several holy men in Lower Egypt, including the tomb of the 'Alid sheykh Ebrahim al-Dasuqi. After spending a brief time in the company of a certain Sheykh 'Abd al-Razzaq in Alexandria, he set out for Cairo, travelling along the banks of the Nile. Overwhelmed by the tumult and the crowds in the city, he was relieved to meet a person from his hometown Mashhad, who escorted him to see the tomb of Imam Shafe'i. At this point, Tusi inserts a short panegyric of the Mamluk sultan al-Malek al-Zaher Jaqmaq – 'King of Egypt and the Holy Sanctuary, succor of sayyeds, the pride of heaven and earth; no other ruler is so revered' in conjunction with a discussion of the Nilometer ([*al*]-*meqyas*), which he mistakenly calls *omm al-qeyas*. The reference to Jaqmaq as the ruler of Egypt and Syria at the time of Tusi's pilgrimage indicates that his journey to the Hejaz must have taken place before Zu'l-Hejja 856/December 1452, as Jaqmaq had abdicated in favour of his son 'Osman on 21 Moharram 857/1 February 1453 and died 11 days later.

Under the leadership of the *amir al-hajj*, the pilgrimage caravan left Cairo and proceeded overland to Mecca. Depicting the major rituals of the Hajj sequentially in considerable detail, Tusi then described his departure from Mecca for Medina. There, in addition to the tomb of the Prophet, Tusi visited the graves of the Prophet's daughter Fatema and his grandson Hasan before leaving Arabia for the return journey to Syria.

The final part of Tusi's travelogue becomes more compressed at this point: the account of his journey from Mashhad to Medina occupies 21 folios while his itinerary from Medina to Ottoman territory fills only six – Homs, Hama, Tripoli, Jabla and Aleppo. In Jabla, he visited the tomb of Ebrahim ebn Adham, which he also claims to have seen in Baghdad.[18] From Aleppo, he travelled north to Anatolia, first stopping at Karamanid Laranda (Karaman) and Konya before finally entering the service of Fateh Soltan Mehmet. Nothing else is known of Tusi and it may be presumed that he died in Ottoman territory, never returning to his homeland.

Amir Sayyed Kamal al-Din Hoseyn Abivardi, 'Feyzi'

Although listed and described in Tornberg's catalogue of the Arabic, Persian and Turkish manuscripts in the Uppsala University library in the middle of the nineteenth century,[19] the works of Sayyed Kamal al-Din Hoseyn Abivardi only became better known nearly a hundred years later when they were published in 1968 by Iraj Afshar, who had come across them during a visit to Sweden.[20] In recent years, Ali Muhaddis has again catalogued the Uppsala Persian manuscripts – including the compilation (*majmu'a*) of Abivardi's writings.[21] It is made up of 122 folios and includes two separate works, *Chartakht* (pp. 9–

84/1v–60r)[22] and *Anis al-'asheqin* (pp. 85–160/65r–122r). After the end of *Chartakht*, five blank folios (60v–64v) have been inserted before the beginning of *Anis al-'asheqin*. It is written in what is described by Muhaddis as 'fine Nastaliq', 13 lines per folio, with red headings. *Chartakht* is composed in *masnavi* form and consists of over 1,400 verses divided into 44 sections. Mixing poetry and prose, *Anis al-'asheqin* was written in imitation of Sa'di's *Golestan*, according to the author. On page 8/folio 1v his name appears: *jenab-e seyadat-ma'ab, sa'adat-ektesab, manzur-e anzar al-salatin, jame'-e al-fazayel va al-kamalat, hajj al-Harameyn, al-ghazi fi sabil Allah* Mir Sayyed Hoseyn Abivardi; the name of the copyist: Pir Ahmad;[23] and the date of the copying of *Chartakht*: Rabi' I, 898/December 1492. *Anis al-'asheqin* was completed by the same copyist about six months later in Ramazan 898/June–July 1493 (p. 160/122r). This folio also contains a record of the various owners of the manuscript and in some cases the dates on which they acquired it. The final entry in this series is Adolph Frederik Sturtzenbecker (d. 1784), chaplain of the Swedish legation in Constantinople, who bought the manuscript in 1783 (see Plate III). It subsequently entered the Uppsala Library as a part of the Sturtzenbeckeriana collection and is so indicated by the siglum *St.* in Tornberg's catalogue.

Unlike Tusi, a great deal is known about the life of Abivardi before and after his travels, thanks to information found in the writings of Khvandamir and others.[24] Moving from Abivard to Herat to continue his education, he became a member of the entourage of the Miranshahid prince Mohammad-Soltan, known as Kichik Mirza (d. 889/1484), who had arrived in Khorasan after the execution of his kinsman Soltan-Abu Sa'id in Azerbaijan in 873/1469.[25] After an incident of *lèse-majesté* involving his uncle the king Soltan-Hoseyn-e Bayqara (r. 873–911/1469–1506), this prince fell from favour and was arrested, later resolving to leave Khorasan for the Hejaz, probably in the year 888/1483.[26] Although Abivardi had planned to accompany his patron on the pilgrimage, he was unable to do so at this time and his Hajj seems to have been postponed until the following year.[27] Abivardi was also son-in-law of the powerful bureaucrat Khvaja Majd al-Din Mohammad Khvafi (d. 899/1494),[28] who had served in the administrations of both Kichik Mirza and Soltan-Hoseyn-e Bayqara.[29]

Following his period of travels extending from 889/1484 to some time before 892/1486, Abivardi returned to Herat, where he entered the service of Mir 'Ali-Shir Nava'i (d. 906/1501), who sent him as an envoy to the court of Soltan Ya'qub Aq Qoyunlu in 894/1489.[30] Khvandamir relates the following anecdote about this embassy.

> During the time that he was attendant upon Amir 'Ali-Shir, he was nominated for a mission to Soltan Ya'qub Mirza. It was decided that he would take the complete works of Mowlana 'Abd al-Rahman Jami along with other precious books from the royal library as presents to

> Qazi 'Isa and His Majesty. When the librarian Mowlana 'Abd al-Karim was delivering those books to His Excellency the Sayyed, he made a mistake and instead gave him a copy of [Ebn 'Arabi's] *Fotuhat-e Makki*[*ya*] that resembled Jami's complete works in size and appearance. Amir Hoseyn did not notice this and placed the volume along with the other gifts and presents. When he came before Soltan Ya'qub Mirza to present these gifts, the king, graciously remarked "I hope you did not find your long journey fatiguing." Amir Hoseyn replied, "I had a travelling companion that kept me from feeling weary." Soltan Ya'qub asked him what he meant by these words and the Sayyed answered, "I was in the company of Mowlana Jami's collected works that the Royal Intimate [Mir 'Ali-Shir] had sent for the Qazi, and whenever I grew tired, I would read a little of that extraordinary book." The king said, "Bring me the book so that I may see it" and Amir Hoseyn had the volume brought into the assembly. When they opened it, they discovered that it was the *Fotuhat-e Makki*[*ya*], not the collected works of Mowlana Jami. As a result, the Sayyed was disgraced and humiliated and therefore never again found favour with Amir 'Ali-Shir.[31]

Despite this embarrassment, Abivardi continued to serve the Timurid family and was employed by Soltan-Hoseyn's eldest son Badi' al-Zaman until his retirement in 910/1504-5, when he returned to his hometown. After the Ozbek conquest of Khorasan and the fall of the Timurids, Mohammad Shibani Khan sent him as ambassador to the court of the Safavid ruler Shah Esma'il in 914/1508–9. He died in Abivard in 920/1514.[32]

Abivardi, using the pen name Feyzi, evidently wrote both *Chartakht* and *Anis al-'asheqin* after returning to Herat from his travels; as stated previously, both were copied by Pir Ahmad in 898/1492–93, during the author's lifetime. In the current state of our knowledge, the Uppsala manuscript appears to be unique and, with the exception of Khvandamir's passing reference to a single anecdote from *Anis al-'asheqin*,[33] other writers do not seem to have been familiar with either work.

He claims to have been inspired to write *Chartakht* while he was in Mecca: a voice from the unseen world told him (p. 10/2v):

> There are but four thrones in all the climes of earth;
> Each occupied by a Solomon of the age.
> There are no other thrones like these;
> No other magnificence like theirs.
> You know all their secrets,
> Reveal to all their hallmarks.
> When you finally complete this work,
> Call it *Chartakht* [Four Thrones], *wa'l-salam*.

The first 'throne' is Constantinople or *mamalek-e Rum*, seat of the Ottomans (pp. 11–25/3r–14v); the second, Cairo or *mamalek-e 'Arab*, seat of the Mamluks (pp. 26–42/14v–28r); the third, Tabriz or *mamalek-e Azerbaijan*, seat of the Aq Qoyunlu (pp. 43–59/28r–41r), and the fourth, Herat or *mamalek-e Khorasan*, seat of the Timurids (pp. 60–83/41r–59r). Each of the four sections has certain features in common: an outline of the itinerary, praise of the ruler and other elite personages, descriptions of landmarks and, in some instances, accounts of events.

Although not explicit in his text, Abivardi began his journey in Herat whence he travelled to Tabriz. There he met the Ottoman general Ahmed Paşa – who is probably to be identified with Hersekzade Ahmed Paşa (d. 923/1517) – in the service of the Ottoman sultans Bayezid II and Selim I. This individual was returning from a mission to India (Hindustan) via Hormuz and Shiraz to Constantinople – an otherwise undocumented episode in his life – when he encountered Abivardi in Tabriz. He invited the author to accompany him and the two travelled via Tokat and Amasya to the Ottoman capital Constantinople. Abivardi first praises the sultan Bayezid II (r. 886–918/1481–1512), *padshah-e Eslam, qeysar-e saheb-qeran*, emphasizing the strength and vastness of his military power. Artillery and handguns (*tup o tofang*) are mentioned twice in this connection as are the Janissaries, referred to as *gholaman* and *ichughlanan*. After eulogizing his travelling companion Ahmed Paşa, he turns to a panegyric of Bayezid's eldest son Soltan Ahmed Çelebi (d. 919/1513), before describing sites in *takht-e Estanbol keh mashhur'ast beh Qostantiniya*, such as the great mosque of Aya Sofya and *shahr-e Farang* (Galata) – this is the longest single section in *Chartakht*. He also apparently made a side trip to the other Ottoman capital city of Edirne. Returning to Constantinople, he mentions an exchange of embassies with the Hungarians and that he himself delivered a letter from the Aq Qoyunlu ruler Ya'qub.

Setting out from Constantinople in late 889/1484, Abivardi travelled to Bursa, eventually entering Mamluk Syria. On his arrival in Jerusalem, he describes both the Dome of the Rock and the Aqsa Mosque. Like Tusi, he also visited the Tomb of the Patriarchs in Hebron before continuing by caravan to Egypt. Again like Tusi, in Cairo he met a fellow townsman, Mowlana Hafez 'Obeyd Abivardi, who presented him to the Mamluk sultan al-Malek al-Ashraf Qayetbay (r. 872–901/1468–96). After a brief passage in praise of the Mamluk ruler, *soltan-e Harameyn*, he includes a much longer eulogy of the Aq Qoyunlu prince Mirza Hoseyn (d. 897/1492), the son of Ughurlu Mohammad, who had taken refuge with Qayetbay seven years earlier after the rebellion and death of his father.[34] Among the sights of Cairo, he mentions 'the three domes built by Ahriman' (*seh gonbad bana-ye Ahriman*), by which he must mean the Pyramids of Giza; it is difficult to say whether he intended thereby to designate them as the work of the Zoroastrian evil spirit or whether he possibly misheard the Arabic words (al-)*haram*, (*al-*) *haraman*, or (*al-*)*ahram*, much as Tusi may have incorrectly heard *al-meqyas*.[35] He then follows a description of the Nile with a long account of the Nilometer and how it functions.

The Egyptian pilgrim caravan departed Cairo and travelled by way of Berka (al-Hajj), Buweyb in the Sinai, Yanbo‘, Badr and Honeyn to Mecca. In comparison with Tusi, Abivardi's account of the pilgrimage rituals in both Mecca and Medina is quite sketchy, after which he describes his joining the Syrian caravan for the return journey. This stage of his travels that took him northward from Medina through Petra (*shahr-e Saleh*) to Damascus seems to have been much more difficult than what he had experienced previously.

Before beginning his account of the Third Throne, Aq Qoyunlu Tabriz, Abivardi inserts an elegy on the death of his patron Mohammad-Soltan, Kichik Mirza, the news of whose death in Khorasan after his return from the Hajj must have reached him about this time.[36] Personages honoured in this section include Soltan Ya‘qub (r. 883–96/1478–90), his brother Mirza Yusof, the sultan's powerful magistrate and preceptor Qazi ‘Isa Savaji and the bureaucrat Najm al-Din Mas‘ud. The Hasht Behesht palace and its gardens is the only landmark in Tabriz mentioned in this section – the fact that Abivardi visited it in early 890/1485 supports the earlier date 888/1483–84 for its laying out and completion, found in two tenth/sixteenth-century sources,[37] over the later date 891/1486, recorded in Khonji-Esfahani's contemporary report.[38] The major political event in which Abivardi took part at this time was Soltan Ya‘qub's invasion of Georgia in Ramazan-Shavval 890/September–October 1485, in return for participating in which he received the title of *al-ghazi fi sabil Allah* found on page 8/folio 1r of the manuscript. His account of this campaign is particularly important for its use of terminology (*tup*, *dig*, *ra‘d*) referring to the use of gunpowder weaponry in the siege activities of the Turkmens against their Georgian adversaries.[39] Back in Tabriz, Abivardi was entreated by his friend the poet and gnostic ‘Abd al-Rahman Jami to end his travels and return to Herat.

Abivardi devotes the final part of *Chartakht* to Herat, the centre of *mamalek-e Khorasan*, one of the two surviving Timurid rump kingdoms in Khorasan and Transoxiana. He includes praise of the king Soltan-Hoseyn; his sons, the princes Badi‘ al-Zaman (d. 921/1515), Mozaffar-Hoseyn (d. 913/1508) and Abu Torab (d. before 915/1509–10); the statesman and litterateur ‘Ali-Shir Nava'i; and, finally, his father-in-law Majd al-Din Mohammad Khvafi. There are also brief descriptions of two well-known gardens in Herat, the Bagh-e Zaghan and the Bagh-e Jahan-ara. It is not known how much time he spent at the Timurid court before he was again sent to Tabriz as envoy to Soltan Ya‘qub – possibly the notorious 894/1489 debacle referred to in Khvandamir's anecdote quoted above. The manuscript of *Chartakht* abruptly comes to an end at this point; at the bottom of folio 60r there is a note, presumably by the copyist Pir Ahmad, acknowledging the unfinished state of the work at the time of its copying in Rabi‘ I, 898/December 1492,[40] and allotting the five blank folios, 60v–64v, for its completion (see Plate III).

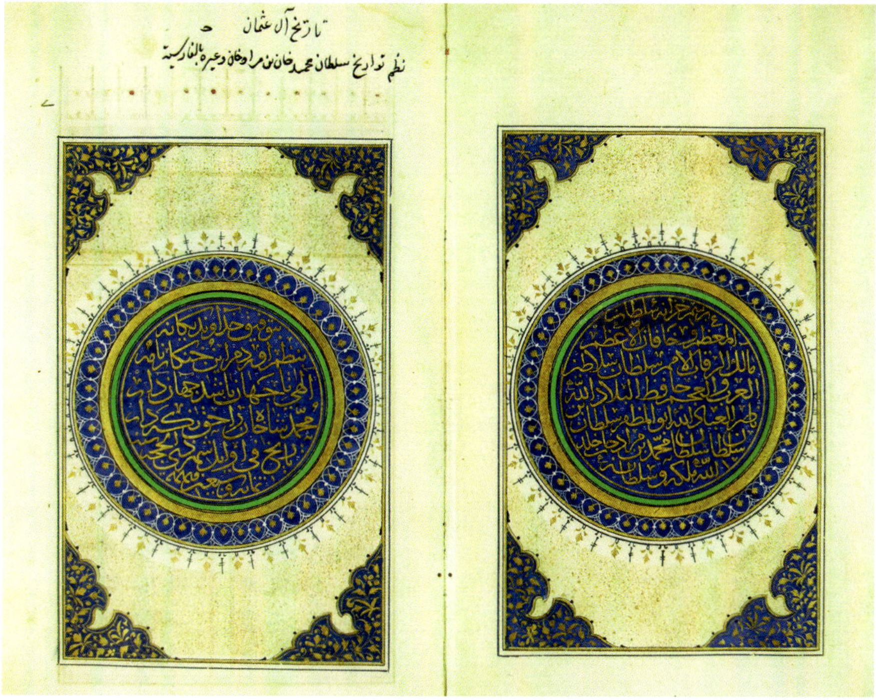

Plate I - Tusi, 'Ma'ali', *Khondkarnama*, folios 1v and 2r. Courtesy of Topkapi Saray Library, Istanbul, Turkey.

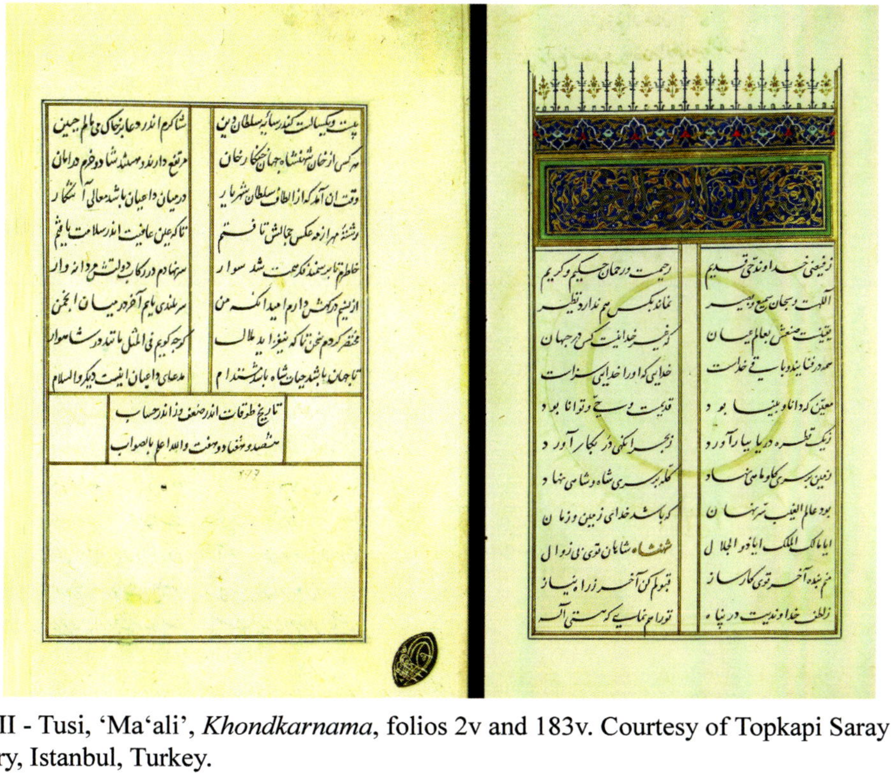

Plate II - Tusi, 'Ma'ali', *Khondkarnama*, folios 2v and 183v. Courtesy of Topkapi Saray Library, Istanbul, Turkey.

Plate III - Abivardi, ‘Feyzi’, Chartakht and Anis al-‘asheqin, *Majmu‘a*, folios 1r and 60r. Courtesy of Uppsala University Library, Uppsala, Sweden.

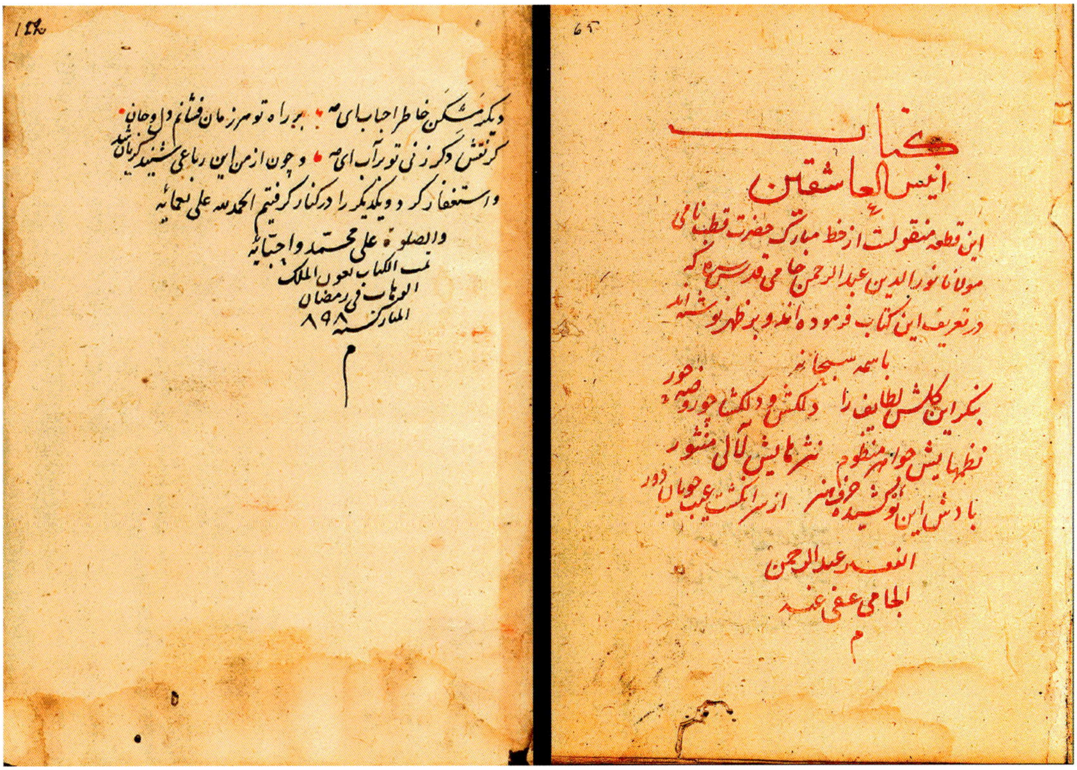

Plate IV - Abivardi, 'Feyzi', Chartakht and Anis al-'asheqin, *Majmu'a*, folios 65r and 122r.
Courtesy of Uppsala University Library, Uppsala, Sweden.

Plate V - Homay's dream: He sees Homayun in a garden at night. Paris, Musée des arts decoratifs 3727, on long-term loan to the Musée du Louvre since 2006.

The second work contained in the Uppsala *majmu'a* is Abivardi's *Anis al-'asheqin*. On the 'title page', page 85/folio 65, are three verses ascribed to Jami extolling its value (see Plate IV), possibly in response to the negative judgement of Abivardi given in Nava'i's *Majales al-nafayes*:

> In accordance with [the statement of Imam Shafe'i] "Leave your homeland in quest of the sublime ..." [Abivardi] travelled to 'Eraq, Fars, and Anatolia where he met with the scholarly and saintly of those lands and learned from all of them. Nevertheless, he could not escape the slanders of the envious who claimed that he was insane, based on a single verse that he had written, insisting that its meter was incorrect and that it was meaningless.[41]

In any event, Jami's death in Moharram 898/November 1492, therefore, gives us a certain terminus ad quem for the composition of *Anis al-'asheqin*. Later in the work, a reference to the 'thrones' of Cairo, Constantinople, Tabriz and Herat also suggest that it was written after *Chartakht*.[42]

As mentioned previously, Abivardi claims to have modeled *Anis al-'asheqin* on the *Golestan* and therefore, unlike *Chartakht*, it is composed in prose interspersed with verse. Dedicated to the Timurid ruler Soltan-Hoseyn, it is divided into three sections: an introduction (pp. 86–89/65v–68r), a long allegory (pp. 89–108/68r–83r), and a group of 19 stories (*hekayat*, pp. 108–160/83r–122r). In the introductory section, Abivardi states his reasons for writing the work:

> Long tempered in the crucible of the effort of travel, I – Hoseyn Abivardi – drove the stallion of exertion in every direction. At times, I sat with enthroned potentates or handsome princes; other times, I accompanied respected generals and conversed with high-ranking lords. In every land, I was stricken with the pain of intimacy and wounded by the sting of conceit. When I returned to Herat, I realised that nothing remained of the attractions and affections of my youth but a handful of stories in my memory. I decided to set down those stories of loves and lovers in writing and call them *Anis al-'asheqin* (*The Intimate of Lovers*) so that it might be a companion to the forlorn and an intimate to the vain beloved ....

This brief prologue is followed by an extended allegory on the struggle of reason and passion. The following passage is characteristic of this section:

> God founded two cities in the microcosm of man's body: one is called Head – of which Reason is the ruler – and the other is called Heart, which is also subject to Reason, who has deputized Patience to govern Heart and see to its welfare. Reason enlists an informer named Insight; Patience also has an informer called Vision. In Heart, there lives a madman called Passion and a youth named Beauty – they are both

> completely intertwined. Passion is always tumultuous and therefore Heart is invariably tense. Reason orders Patience to put Passion in chains and confine it to the prison of Separation. Because of this disunion, Beauty is forced to leave Heart and travel the path of Parting … When Patience learns of the departure of Beauty from Heart, it closes the gates of the city and strengthens its fortifications so that Beauty cannot return and the upheaval would be quelled. One day, Vision – the informer of Patience – gazes out and sees the approach of a rider mounted on the steed of Coquetry coming from the city of Sincerity on the highroad of Fidelity. The horseman secretly rides around Heart, hoping to gain some news of Love. Recognizing him immediately, Vision informs the people of Heart and a great disturbance breaks out. When Passion learns of the faithfulness of Beauty, he subdues Patience, bursts the chains of Reason, and mounts the ramparts of Heart. When Beauty sees Passion, he lays siege to Heart. Passion breaches the walls of Heart, chases Patience away, and goes out to welcome Beauty. In sum, Passion conquers Heart and makes it the capital of Beauty … By chance, Insight, the spy of Reason, learns of these events and rushes to Head with the news. Reason then makes ready for battle with Passion (pp. 89–91/68r–69v).

Finally, Abivardi combines the sense of the novelty and arduousness of travel with the nostalgia for lost relationships in 19 vignettes of his personal adventures, encounters and involvements during his journeys, related in the form of first-person narratives. Both the longest and probably the most interesting and significant part of *Anis al-'asheqin*, these anecdotes complement the matter-of-fact tone of *Chartakht* with an infusion of humor and humanity. Though Abidvardi invokes the *Golestan*, this part of *Anis al-'asheqin* is perhaps more reminiscent in substance – if not in form – of the *Maqamat* of Badi' al-Zaman and Hariri.

Of the 19 stories, four have no specific geographical locale; the remaining 15 are set in the following cities in alphabetical order: Aleppo, Ankara, Ba'lbak, Cairo (two stories), Constantinople (two stories), Damascus, Edirne, Galata, Hama, Jerusalem, Sivas, Soltaniya and Tabriz. The arrangement of the anecdotes does not follow Abivardi's itinerary in *Chartakht*, nor are they grouped in any discernible thematic order, although almost all follow a similar storyline. The scene is usually clearly and concretely established: 'In the mosque of 'Amr ebn al-'As in Old Cairo, on Friday, the last day of Ramazan' (Story 17); 'One day, I was sitting in the Haram-e Qods in front of the Aqsa Mosque' (Story 4); 'Once I was sitting in front of a church in Galata' (Story 7); 'Passing through a neighbourhood in Constantinople' (Story 11); 'I was sitting on the banks of the Orontes River near the Mohammadiya water wheel' (Story 15). He is able to make his way in all these regions and situations by virtue of his knowledge of Persian, Arabic and Turkish.[43] In each setting, Abivardi usually fixates upon a handsome youth and many of the ensuing narratives chronicle his infatuation, disappointment or reconciliation with the object of his ardour. Story 1, the longest in the collection, furnishes a typical example of this scenario: one moonlit night in the Beyn al-Qasreyn district of Cairo, he sets his sights upon an apparently highborn youth and begins to follow him. The youth suddenly stops, turns on Abivardi, and addresses him:

> "Young man, you seem to be Iranian (*'ajam*)." I said, "Yes." He said, "I too am of Iranian origin (*dar asl 'ajam-am*), but I grew up in Egypt [the Aq Qoyunlu prince Mirza Hoseyn?]. What is your name?" I said, "So and so." He said, "What talents do you have?" I said, "I have no talents." He said, "Can you read and write?" I said, "Yes." He said, "Do you know poetry and enigmas?" I said, "Yes, to the extent of my understanding." He said, "What talents could be greater than these?" He then said, "Where are you staying?" I said, "With such and such Iranian, who is a courtier of the sultan" [Mowlana Hafez 'Obeyd?]. He said, "That Iranian is my courtier." I was so amazed and taken aback that I couldn't even speak. When he left, I was chagrined and cursed myself for not asking his name ...

After many vicissitudes, the two are eventually united.

In many of the stories set in Islamic contexts, Abivardi is referred to or refers to himself or other Iranians as *'ajam*.[44] This term does not merely indicate ethno-linguistic identity, but has other connotations for Abivardi's interlocutors in some of the stories. In Story 2,[45] for example, the author becomes the broker of a relationship between a good-looking Arab youth Soheyl and the daughter of the governor of Ba'lbak. Having already recognized Abivardi as Iranian, Soheyl tells him, 'Easterners are powerful sorcerers and I am sure you know that art very well'.[46] Whereupon Abivardi – no sorcerer – acts on Soheyl's stereotype and concocts as spell, but his hoax ultimately fails, and he is forced to leave for Damascus. There, in Story 3,[47] he decides to present himself as an alchemist based on a remark by the person of his desires to a second Iranian man: 'You Iranians are experts in alchemy. Let me know if an Iranian skilled in this art shows up.'[48] When this ploy also founders, the targeted individual reacts in anger, 'Iranians are all faithless liars!'[49] Finally, in Story 9, when Abivardi sends an unenthusiastic young pigeon flyer in Edirne a lovesick Persian verse attached to one of his birds, the youth – who obviously cannot read the poem – responds in exasperation, 'You have dealt me an Iranian insult!'[50] Abivardi then curses himself and the youth and gets out of town.

Religious issues also appear in the stories. Abivardi's descent from the family of the Prophet is mentioned in Stories 6 and 15.[51] In a learning circle in the Omayyad Mosque in Damascus in Story 3, he is decried as a Shi'ite heretic (*rafezi*) when he corrects the teacher's allegedly prejudicial reading of a passage about ‘Ali and Mo‘awiya in the text under consideration. In Stories 6 and 11,[52] both set in Constantinople, he engages in dialogues with Christians and Jews in an effort to turn them to Islam, debating the roles of Mohammad, Jesus and Moses in Islam with a young worshipper and discussing the relative merits of the Torah and the Qur’an with a rabbi. In Story 7,[53] he is the only Muslim attending the ceremony for a bridegroom in a church (*deyr*) in Galata (*yaki az shahrha-ye Farang*). In these non-Islamic contexts, therefore, it is his religion that forms the basis of his identity, not his geographical or ethnic provenance. The consumption of alcohol in Story 16,[54] or the question of homoeroticism that permeates the entire work, however, are never specifically addressed. Abivardi’s failed encounter with a youth in Sivas (-e Rum) in Story 18 is perhaps enlightening in the latter connection:[55]

> When [the youth] realized how dejected I was, he came toward me out of sympathy and declared, “Give me such-and-such an amount of money.” I replied, “I am a poor man and have no money.” He indignantly retorted, “How can a person with no money have anything to do with love?” On hearing this, I lost my composure and responded, “Young man, money has nothing to do with love! That which demands payment is entirely something else!” When I had finished, he cursed me; I responded in kind, turned my back on his crassness, and left that city in anger.[56]

Conclusion

It is certainly no longer necessary to remind historians of the importance of the consideration of literary works in their efforts to grasp those intangible aspects of the study of the past not reflected in conventional narrative sources.[57] The travelogues of Tusi and Abivardi present a series of unique and vivid impressions of social, political, economic and cultural life in Iran-zamin and Western Asia in the final decades of the Later Middle Period just prior to the momentous changes that ushered in the Early Modern Age: the Ozbek conquest of Timurid lands in Central Asia, 1500–1507; the foundation of the Safavid Empire and the advent of political Shi‘ism, 1501; the Ottoman conquest of the Mamluks of Syria and Egypt and transformation from a *ghazi* state into an Islamic empire, 1516–17; and the revival of a Timurid dynastic project in India, 1526.

Notes:

1. Hāfez-e Abru, *Joghrāfiyā-ye Hāfez-e Abru*, vol. I, pp. 49–50.
2. Ruy Gonzalez de Clavijo, *Embajada a Tamorlán*, ed. F. López Estrada.
3. Giosafat Barbaro, 'Viaggio di Iosafa Barbaro alla Tana e nella Persia', vol. III, pp. 481–576.
4. Mohammad ebn Mahmud ebn Ajā, *Tā'rikh al-amir Yashbak al-Zāheri.*
5. See, e.g., Felicia J. Hecker, 'A fifteenth-century Chinese diplomat in Herat', pp. 85–98.
6. Gheyās al-Din Naqqāsh's account was first translated into English by K.M. Maitra and reprinted with a new introduction by L. Carrington Goodrich. There is a new English translation by Wheeler Thackston, 'Ghiyathuddin Naqqash's report on a Timurid mission to China', pp. 279–98, and 'Ghiyathuddin Naqqash, Report to Mirza Baysunghur on the Timurid legation to the Ming Court at Peking', pp. 53–67.
7. First published by M. Quatremère, *Notice de l'ouvrage persan qui a pour titre: Matla-assaadeïn ou-madjma-albahreïn*, subsequently translated into English by Richard Henry Major and published in his *India in the Fifteenth Century*, pp. 3–49. The text of Samarqandi's *Matla'-e sa'deyn* was partially edited by Mohammad Shafi' (Lahore, 1941–49) and has been published in its entirety in Iran by 'Abd al-Hoseyn Navā'i (Tehran, 1993, 2004). Wheeler Thackston has also published a new English translation of Samarqandi's travelogue as 'Kamaluddin Abdul-Razzaq Samarqandi's Mission to Calicut and Vijayanagar', pp. 299–321, and 'Kamaluddin Abdul-Razzaq Samarqandi, Mission to Calicut and Vijayanagar', pp. 68–87.
8. Mohammad Mirkhvānd, *Rowzat al-safā'*, vol. XI, pp. 6087–323; Gheyās al-Din Khvāndamir, *Habib al-seyar*, vol. IV, pp. 619–701.
9. Robert Anhegger, 'Fatih devrinde yazılmış Farsça manzum bir eser', pp. 145–66.
10. Ahmed Zeki Velidi Togan, 'Büyük Türk hükümdarı Şahruh', pp. 520–38.
11. For example, in addition to f. 5v, see e.g., ff. 42v, 45v, 56r, 62v, 66r, 70v, 125r, 138r, 168r and 182v.
12. Anhegger, 'Fatih devrinde yazılmış Farsça manzum bir eser', p. 148.
13. See 'Ali ebn Abi Bakr al-Harawi, *Kitab al-isharat ila ma'refat al-ziyarat*, pp. 186, 187.
14. Ibid., pp. 192–93, 196–97.
15. Ibid., pp. 198–99.
16. Ibid., pp. 198–99, 200–203.
17. Ibid., pp. 78–81.
18. Ibid., pp. 44–45.
19. C.J. Tornberg, *Codices arabici, persici et turcici bibliothecæ Regiæ Universitatis Upsaliensis*, No. 177 = *St.* 168, pp. 109–10.
20. Iraj Afshār, 'Do āsār az Hoseyn-e Abivardi', pp. 5–160.
21. Ali Muhaddis, *Catalogue of the Persian Manuscripts in Uppsala University Library*, pp. 146–47; *A Concise Catalogue of the Persian Manuscripts in Uppsala University Library*, pp. 11, 42. The manuscript listed as No. 177 and *St.* 168 by Tornberg is listed as 167.1–2 by Muhaddis.
22. Since, in the Iranian edition, the manuscript is incorrectly foliated, both page and folio numbers will be cited in this chapter, e.g., p. 55/37v.

23. Afshar's assertion that the manuscript is a holograph (introduction, p. 7) is revised by Muhaddis, *Catalogue of the Persian Manuscripts*, pp. 146–47.
24. On Abivard in modern Turkmenistan, see V. Minorsky, 'Abīward' and C.E. Bosworth, 'Abīvard'. In *Chartakht*, only his pen name Feyzi appears (pp. 55/37v, 57/39v, 73/51r, 75/53r, 81/58r), whereas in *Anis al-'āsheqin*, he does not use Feyzi and refers to himself as Hoseyn Abivardi, Mir Hoseyn Bāvardi or Hoseyn (pp. 87/66r, 111/85r, 151/115v).
25. Khvāndamir, *Habib al-seyar*, vol. IV, pp. 138, 350. According to Khvāndamir, p. 174, Kichik Mirzā studied with Mowlānā Kamāl al-Din *Sheykh Hoseyn, who may be identical to Abivardi.
26. Khvāndamir, *Habib al-seyar*, vol. IV, pp. 174–75.
27. A chronogram in *Chartakht*, p. 22/12r, suggests that Abivardi began his travels in 889/1484, the year of Kichik Mirza's death.
28. *Chartakht*, p. 83/59v.
29. Khvāndamir, *Habib al-seyar*, vol. IV, pp. 160, 167–68, 180–82, 187–89, 195–98; Gheyās al-Din Khvāndamir, *Dastur al-vozarā'*, pp. 400–18; Zahir al-Din Mohammad Bābor, *Bābur-nāma (Vaqāyi')*, ff. 176v–177r.
30. On the possible date of this embassy, see Fazlollāh Khonji-Esfahāni, *Tārikh-i 'ālam-ārā-yi Amini*, text, p. 375; trans., p. 83.
31. Khvāndamir, *Habib al-seyar*, IV, pp. 350–51.
32. Ibid., pp. 351, 504.
33. Ibid., pp. 699–700; Abivardi, *Anis al-'āsheqin*, Story 7, pp. 155–56/118v–119r: the street entertainer and the talking crow in Old Cairo.
34. On this prince in Mamluk lands, see Henriette Devonshire, 'Al-Qowl al-mostazraf fi safar mawlana al-malek al-Ashraf', pp. 15–16; Shams al-Din Mohammad al-Sakhāwi, *al-Zow' al-lāme' le ahl al-qarn al-tāse'*, No. 592, vol. III, pp. 156–57; and Mohammad Ebn Eyās, *Ketāb badā'e' al-zohur fi waqā'e' al-dohur*, part 3, pp. 139, 286.
35. See Alexander Fodor, 'The origins of the Arabic legends of the Pyramids', pp. 335–63 and Martyn Smith, 'Pyramids in the medieval Islamic landscape', pp. 1–14.
36. Khvāndamir, *Habib al-seyar*, vol. IV, p. 176.
37. Qāzi Ahmad Ghaffāri Qazvini, p. 254; Sharaf Khān Bidlisi, *Shèref-nāmeh*, vol. II, p. 126.
38. Khonji-Esfahāni, *Tārikh-i 'ālam-ārā-yi Amīnī*, text, p. 226; trans., p. 46 and n. 2.
39. Ibid., text, pp. 218–25; trans., pp. 43–45 and Annexes, pp. 99–100, 103–4; see also John E. Woods, 'Turco-Iranica I: An Ottoman intelligence report', pp. 1–9.
40. Pir Ahmad's note is not reproduced in Afshar's edition but is included by Muhaddis, *Catalogue of the Persian Manuscripts*, p. 145.
41. 'Ali-Shir Navā'i, *Majāles al-nafāyes*, No. 269, p. 273. The Persian translator Hakim Shāh Mohammad Qazvini suggests a correction to the offending verse and suggests, 'However, it is probable that he wrote it thus, the meter of which is correct and it has meaning. The fact that he had no poetic aptitude is not a sign of his insanity – many learned and saintly people cannot write poetry.'
42. *Anis al-'āsheqin*, p. 138/105v.
43. Abivardi has the Hebrew and 'Frangi' spoken in the anecdotes set in Constantinople translated into Turkish. See Jonathan Hys, *Trading Tongues, Merchants, Multilingualism, and Medieval Literature*, on multilingual merchants in Europe.

44. *Anis al-'āsheqin*, pp. 109/83v, 110/84v, 115/88r, 117/89v, 118/90v, 120/91v–92r, 121/92v–93r, 124/94v–95r, 125/96r, 126/96v, 127/97r, 129/98v, 134/102v, 135/103v, 137/105r, 151/115r, 152/116r, 155/118v, 156/119r.
45. *Anis al-'āsheqin*, pp. 115–19/87v–91r.
46. Ibid., p. 116/88v: *mashreqiyān sāherān-e 'azim'and va marā e'teqād be to ānast keh to in fann-rā nik midāni.*
47. Ibid., pp. 119–23/91r–94r.
48. Ibid., p. 121/92v: *'ajamān shomā kimiyā nik dānand, agar 'ajami keh in fann dānad peydā shavad, marā khabar kon.*
49. Ibid., p.122/93v: *'ajamān hama dorugh guy va bivafā'and.*
50. Ibid., p. 137/105r: *marā tashni'-e 'ajami kardi.*
51. Ibid., pp. 130–32/99v–101r; 150–53/114v–116v.
52. Ibid., pp. 130–32/99v–101r; 142–43/108v–109v.
53. Ibid., pp. 132–33/101r–v.
54. Ibid., pp. 153–55/116v–118r.
55. Ibid., pp.156–58/119r–120v.
56. See Khaled El-Rouayheb, *Before Homosexuality in the Arab-Islamic World*, especially chapter two.
57. See, for example, Charles Melville, 'Between Firdausī and Rashīd al-Dīn, pp. 45–65 and his comments in *Persian Historiography*.

Bibliography:

Afshār, Iraj, 'Do āsār az Hoseyn-e Abivardi', *Farhang*-e *Irān-Zamin* 15 (1347/1968), pp. 5–160.

Anhegger, Robert, 'Fatih devrinde yazılmış Farsça manzum bir eser, Mu'âli'nin Hünkârnamesi', *Tarih Dergisi* 1 (1949), pp. 145–66.

Bābor, Zahir al-Din Mohammad, *Bābur-nāma (Vaqāyi')*, 2nd edn, Eiji Mano (Kyoto: Syokado, 2006).

Barbaro, Giosafat, 'Viaggio di Iosafa Barbaro alla Tana e nella Persia', in Giovanni Battista Ramusio, *Navigazioni e Viaggi*, ed. Marica Milanese, 6 vols (Turin: Einaudi, 1978–88), vol. III (1980), pp. 481–576.

Bidlisi, Sharaf Khān, *Shèref-nāmeh, ou, Histoire des Kourdes, par Shèref, Prince de Bidlis*, ed. V. Véliaminof-Zernof, 2 vols (St Petersburg: Académie Impériale des Sciences, 1860–62).

Bosworth, C.E., 'Abīvard', *Encyclopaedia Iranica*, vol. I, fasc. 2 (1982), pp. 218–19.

Clavijo, Ruy Gonzalez de, *Embajada a Tamorlán*, ed. F. López Estrada (Madrid: Consejo superior de investigaciones científicas, Instituto Nicolás Antonio, 1943).

Devonshire, Henriette, 'Al-Qowl al-mostazraf fi safar mawlana al-malek al-Ashraf, Relation d'un voyage du sultan Qâitbây en Palestine et en Syrie', *Bulletin de l'Institut Français d'Archéologie Orientale* 20 (1920), pp. 1–43.

Ebn Ajā, Mohammad ebn Mahmud, *Tā'rikh al-amir Yashbak al-Zāheri* ([Cairo]: Dār al-Fekr al-'Arabi, [1974]).

Ebn Eyās, Mohammad, *Ketāb badā'e' al-zohur fi waqā'e' al-dohur/Die Chronik des Ibn Ijas*, 2nd edn, Mohammad Mostafa (Wiesbaden: Steiner, 1963).

El-Rouayheb, Khaled, *Before Homosexuality in the Arab-Islamic World, 1500–1800* (Chicago: University of Chicago Press, 2005).

Fodor, Alexander, 'The origins of the Arabic legends of the Pyramids', *Acta Orientalia Academiae Scientiarum Hungaricae* 23, no. 3 (1970), pp. 335–63.

Ghaffāri Qazvini, Qāzi Ahmad, *Nosakh-e Jahān-ārā*, ed. Hasan Narāqi (Tehran: Hāfez, 1342/1964).

Hāfez-e Abru, *Joghrāfiyā-ye Hāfez-e Abru*, ed. Sādeq Sajjādi, 3 vols (Tehran: Mirās-e Maktub, 1375–78/1996–69).

al-Harawi, 'Ali ebn Abi Bakr, *Kitab al-isharat ila ma'rifat al-ziyarat, A Lonely Wayfarer's Guide to Pilgrimage*, ed. and trans. Josef W. Meri (Princeton: Darwin Press, 2004).

Hecker, Felicia J., 'A fifteenth-century Chinese diplomat in Herat', *Journal of the Royal Asiatic Society* 3rd Series, 3, no. 1 (1993), pp. 85–98).

Hys, Jonathan, *Trading Tongues, Merchants, Multilingualism, and Medieval Literature* (Columbus: Ohio State University Press), 2013.

Khonji-Esfahāni, Fazlollāh/Faḍlullāh b. Rūzbihān Khunjī-Iṣfahānī, *Tārīkh-i 'ālam-ārā-yi Amīnī. Persian Text Edited by John E. Woods with the Abridged English Translation by Vladimir Minorsky, Revised and Augmented by John E. Woods* (London: Royal Asiatic Society, 1992).

Khvāndamir, Gheyās al-Din, *Dastur al-vozarā'*, ed. Sa'id Nafisi (Tehran: Eqbāl, 1317/1938).

— *Habib al-seyar fi tā'rikh afrād-e bashar*, ed. Jalāl Homā'i and Mohammad Dabir-Seyāqi, 4 vols (Tehran: Khayyām, 1333/1954).

Melville, Charles, 'Between Firdausī and Rashīd al-Dīn: Persian verse chronicles of the Mongol period', *Studia Islamica* 104/105 (2007), pp. 45–65.

— ed., *Persian Historiography. A History of Persian Literature*, volume X (London: I.B. Tauris, 2012).

Minorsky, V., 'Abīward', in *Encyclopaedia of Islam*, 2nd edn., vol. 1 (1960), pp. 99–100.

Mirkhvānd, Mohammad, *Rowzat al-safā' fi sirat al-anbiyā' wa'l-moluk wa'l-kholafā'*, ed. Jamshid Kiyānfar, 11 vols (Tehran: Enteshārāt-e asātir, 1380/2001).

Muhaddis, Ali, *Catalogue of the Persian Manuscripts in Uppsala University Library/Fehrest-e ketābhā-ye khatti-ye fārsi dar ketābkhāna-hā-ye dāneshgāh-e Uppsala (Acta Bibliothecae R. Universitatis Upsaliensis)*, vol. 45 (Uppsala: Uppsala Universitet, 2012).

— *A Concise Catalogue of the Persian Manuscripts in Uppsala University Library, English Edition* (*Acta Bibliothecae R. Universitatis Upsaliensis*) vol. 47 (Uppsala: Uppsala Universitet, 2013).

Naqqāsh, Gheyās al-Din, trans. K.M. Maitra, *A Persian Embassy to China, being an Extract from Zubdatu't Tawarikh of Hafiz Abru* (Lahore in 1934), repr. with a new introduction by L. Carrington Goodrich (New York: Paragon Books, 1970).

— trans. Wheeler M. Thackston, 'Ghiyathuddin Naqqash's report on a Timurid mission to China', in *A Century of Princes, Sources on Timurid History and Art*, pp. 279–98 (Cambridge, MA: The Aga Khan Program for Islamic Architecture, 1989).

— trans. Wheeler M. Thackston, 'Ghiyathuddin Naqqash, Report to Mirza Baysunghur on the Timurid legation to the Ming Court at Peking', in *Album Prefaces and Other Documents on the History of Calligraphers and Painters, Studies and Sources in Islamic Art and Architecture*. Supplements to *Muqarnas*, vol. 10 (Leiden: Brill, 2001), pp. 53–67.

Navā'i, 'Ali-Shir, *Majāles al-nafāyes* [Two Persian Translations], ed. 'Ali Asghar Hekmat (Tehran: Bānk-e Melli-ye Irān, 1323/1944).

al-Sakhāwi, Shams al-Din Mohammad, *al-Zow' al-lāme' le ahl al-qarn al-tāse'* (Cairo: Maktabat al-Qodsi, 1934–36).

Samarqandi, 'Abd al-Razzāq, ed. M. Quatremère, *Notice de l'ouvrage persan qui a pour titre: Matla-assaadeïn ou-madjma-albahreïn, et qui contient l'histoire des deux sultans Schahrokh et Abou-Saïd* (*Notices et extraits des manuscrits de la Bibliothèque du roi et autres bibliothèques*, vol. 14) (Paris: Imprimerie royale, 1843).

— ed. Richard Henry Major, *India in the Fifteenth Century: Being a Collection of Narratives of Voyages to India, in the Century Preceeding the Portuguese Discovery of the Cape of Good Hope* (London: Printed for the Hakluyt Society, 1857), pp. 3–49.

— *Matla'-e sa'deyn va majma'-e bahreyn*, ed. Mohammad Shafi', 2 vols (Lahore: Chāpkhāna-ye Gilāni, 1941–49).

— trans. Wheeler M. Thackston, 'Kamaluddin Abdul-Razzaq Samarqandi's Mission to Calicut and Vijayanagar', in *A Century of Princes, Sources on Timurid History and Art* (Cambridge, MA: The Aga Khan Program for Islamic Architecture, 1989), pp. 299–321.

— trans. Wheeler M. Thackston, 'Kamaluddin Abdul-Razzaq Samarqandi, Mission to Calicut and Vijayanagar', in *Album Prefaces and Other Documents on the History of Calligraphers and Painters, Studies and Sources in Islamic Art and Architecture*. Supplements to *Muqarnas*, vol. 10 (Leiden: Brill, 2001), pp. 68–87.

— ed. 'Abd al-Hoseyn Navā'i, vol. I, pt. 1 (Tehran: Mo'assesah-ye motāle'āt va tahqiqāt-e farhangi, 1372/1993), vol. I, pt. 2 and vol. II, pts 1–2 (Tehran: Pazuheshgāh-e 'olum-e ensāni va motāle'āt-e farhangi, 1383/2004).

Smith, Martyn, 'Pyramids in the medieval Islamic landscape: Perceptions and narratives', *Journal of the American Research Center in Egypt* 43 (2007), pp. 1–14.

Togan, Ahmed Zeki Velidi, 'Büyük Türk hükümdarı Şahruh', *İstanbul Üniversitesi Edebiyat Fakültesi, Turk Dili ve Edebiyat Dergisi* 3 (1949), pp. 520–38.

Tornberg, C.J., *Codices arabici, persici et turcici bibliothecæ Regiæ Universitatis Upsaliensis* ([Upsala]: Impensis Reg. universitatis upsaliensis, 1849).

Woods, John E., 'Turco-Iranica I: An Ottoman intelligence report on late fifteenth/ninth century Iranian foreign relations', *Journal of Near Eastern Studies* 38, no. 1 (1979), pp. 1–9.

5

Imitational Poetry as Pious Hermeneutics? Jami and Nava'i/Fani's Rewritings of Hafez's Opening Ghazal

Marc Toutant
(CNRS Paris)

He was the unique of the age (*nadera-ye zaman*) and a prodigy of the world (*o'juba-ye jahan*). These are the first words with which Dowlatshah Samarqandi begins the notice he devotes to Hafez in his *Tazkerat al-sho'ara'* in 1486. Then he adds: 'His excellence (*fazilat*) and his perfection (*kamal*) are endless and the art of poetry is unworthy of his rank. He is incomparable in the science of Qur'an and he is illustrious in the sciences of the exoteric (*zaher*) and the esoteric (*baten*).'[1]

Although Hafez died in 1389, his poetry was widely celebrated one century later, as shown by Dowlatshah's eulogy. Reflective of the poet's importance in later Timurid culture were the many sumptuous court objects, such as the several types of drinking vessels that were inscribed with his verses.[2] In the final years of the dynasty, one of Soltan-Hoseyn's sons, Faridun Hoseyn Mirza, even commissioned a 'revised edition' of his *Divan*.[3] Undoubtedly, Hafez's verses contributed to shaping the poetry of this era. In a period that has been described as the pinnacle of imitational poetry,[4] Hafez's ghazals were among the most imitated. Specifically, his poetry influenced two of the major poets of the Timurid Empire: Nur al-Din 'Abd al-Rahman Jami (1414–1492) and Mir 'Ali-Shir Nava'i (1441–1501). Famous for his achievements in Central Asian Turkish poetry, Nava'i also versified in Persian under the pen name Fani. In one of his last works, Nava'i wrote that he composed his Persian *Divan* in imitation of the great poet of Shiraz.[5]

Hafez's influence on these two poets has been the subject of several studies. In his book about Jami's lyrical output, A'lakhan Afsahzad devoted a short section to this issue of imitation.[6] After examining how Jami talked about his famous predecessor, the Tajik scholar discussed Jami's rewritings of a few *beyt*s in order to illustrate how he approached this type of exercise. Paul Losensky also analysed the way Jami responded to the great poets of the past, including Hafez. He observed that Jami's rewritings, especially compared with the imitations composed by others, were representative of the Timurid efforts towards codification and systematization of the Persian literary tradition.[7] As for Nava'i, Tajik and Uzbek scholars have published short articles in which they generally compared several parent ghazals of Hafez with later rewritings by the Timurid poet.[8] However, these articles rarely go beyond the specific analysis of the examined ghazals, except their argument that Nava'i did not restrict himself to writing a pale copy of the model but rather that he produced something fundamentally original and new. Riccardo Zipoli has studied two 'replies' (*javab*) of Nava'i which were composed in response to Hafez and Jami respectively, and this work stands out for its precision.[9] One of Zipoli's conclusions is that the connections between the poems of Nava'i and Jami are much more direct than those between Nava'i and Hafez's ghazals, indicating that Nava'i was careful not to use the same approach when he responded to either poet.[10] Finally, Benedek Péri recently published a study on Nava'i's imitation of Hafez's first ghazal. One of Péri's most important findings is that Nava'i's rewriting is part of a paraphrase network of poems that were linked 'not only to the base poem but through an intricate network of intertextual allusions to each other as well'.[11]

Several of these aforementioned investigations have opened new avenues for research and remain critical to our understanding of the intellectual life in this period. However, since they focused on poetical aspects and mostly approached these rewritings as practices of literary emulation, none of these studies have taken into consideration the importance of the religious dimension.[12] But did Jami and Nava'i regard their imitations of Hafez's poetry as mere poetic exercises? Were they only driven by a literary impetus when they emulated their model? Did their religious concerns play no role in this process? These are by no means meaningless questions, especially when one considers the two poets' roles and commitments to the Naqshbandiya Sufi order. Jami was the most prominent Naqshbandi-Sufi thinker in Herat in the late Timurid empire. His poetry bears the trace of this mystical commitment and was itself a vehicle for spreading his mystical thoughts. Similarly, Nava'i, who was initiated into the order by Jami and who remained extremely close to his spiritual master throughout his life, also used his poetry in order to spread Sufi conceptions. Recently, Chad Lingwood has shown that Jami's rewriting of Salaman and Absal's story could be read as a Naqshbandi Mirror for Princes for Ya'qub Beg, the Aq Qoyunlu ruler, to whom the book was dedicated.[13] Likewise, I have advocated that the *Khamsa* that Nava'i composed in imitation of Nezami's 'Pentalogy' (or 'Quintet') could also be seen as a Naqshbandi Mirror for Princes for Soltan-Hoseyn, to whom this work was dedicated.[14] These two examples are related to the *masnavi* genre, which given its narrative form seems particularly suited to delivering homiletic messages. However, we know that Sufi poets also borrowed from the secular tradition of the ghazal, which originally belonged to Persian court literature, in order to convey their mystical ideas.[15]

Superseding those approaches that consider the writing of *naziras* (poetic emulation) more as an exhibition of artistic mastery, I will therefore examine the extent to which religious concerns influenced Jami and Nava'i in their crafting of imitational verses. This will be achieved first by a quick survey of the texts in which Jami and Nava'i talked about Hafez and his poetry as a whole. I will then focus on their rewritings of the first ghazal of Hafez's *Divan*. The choice of this ghazal as a case study is not solely on account of the fact that both Jami and Nava'i rewrote it. The sheer number of rewritings of this opening ghazal, from the early fifteenth to the early sixteenth century, by numerous poets suggests that Hafez imitation was a phenomenon that extended beyond the exclusive connoisseurs of Hafez.

Hafez's Ghazals: An Unparalleled Poetry for Sufis

Our knowledge about how Timurid literati in Soltan-Hoseyn's court considered Hafez, especially as compared with other important poets, has benefited from their impulse to codify and chronicle the Persian poetic tradition. In 1486, Dowlatshah Samarqandi dedicated his *Tazkerat al-sho'ara'* to Nava'i. A year later, Jami composed the *Baharestan* for his son, in the seventh chapter of which he includes a *tazkera* of Persian poets which begins with Rudaki. Besides these examples, in 1490, Nava'i began to work on the *Majales al-nafayes*, the first *tazkera* that dealt almost exclusively with contemporary poets who composed both in Persian and Central Asian Turkish (hereafter referred to simply as Turkish), while a few years later, he translated into Turkish and expanded Jami's *Nafahat al-ons*, a compendium of Sufi biographies, as *Nasa'em al-mahabba men shama'em al-fotowwa*.

Dowlatshah's statement about Hafez's poetry (see *supra*) is representative of the privileged status given to the poet in all these biographical compendiums. In the mini-*tazkera* offered by Jami in the *Baharestan*, his notice begins with these words:

Hāfez Shirāzi – rahmat-allāh ta'ālā – aksar-e ash'ār-e vey latif va matbu' ast va ba'zi qarib beh sarhadd-e e'jāz[16]	Hafez Shirazi – upon whom be the mercy of God – most of his poems are pleasant and laudable and some of them are almost border upon the miracle (*e'jaz*)

Jami significantly uses the term *e'jaz* to characterize Hafez's poetry. As already observed by previous scholars, this word serves as a hyperbolic compliment, for it was traditionally employed in reference to the miraculous nature of the Qur'an, which made it impossible to imitate.[17] Stating that Hafez's poetry was inimitable amounted to awarding it the highest marks, especially during a period when many poets tried to prove their virtuosity by rewriting pieces that were considered *momtan' al-javab* ('impossible to imitate').[18]

In his *tazkera* entitled *Majales al-nafayes* (1490–91), Nava'i also pays tribute to Hafez's poetry. Actually, Nava'i did not provide a notice to the Persian poet since his *tazkera* did not include entries about people who were already dead during his lifetime. However, Nava'i makes several references to Hafez while highlighting the merits of other poets. In the few lines that he allots to each notice, he consistently mentions how such-and-such a poet imitated Hafez's verses; most of the time, he quotes the verses that were composed in response to Hafez, and sometimes these verses are the only ones he quotes. This is the case with a man named *Mo'ayyad-e Divana*:

Khāja Mo'ayyad-e Dīwāna	Khvaja Mo'ayyad-e Divana
Hazrat sheykh ewlādïdïndur. Özi āshufta-dimāgh kishi erdi ammā nazmï rawān o salīs wāqi' bolur erdi. Anga saltanat da'wāsi bar erdi. Hamol ish üstigä anï zā'i' qïldïlar. Bu matla' khāja Hāfiz jawābïda anïng dur kim:	He is a descendant of the venerated sheykh [Abu Sa'id Abu'l-Kheyr]. He was a disturbed person, but his poetry was fluid and easy. He had claim to power. Because of that they eliminated him. This *matla'* in response of Khvaja Hafez is his own:
Cheshm dārim az ān sham'-e sa'ādat partow Keh jahān-rā bedehad rowshani az sar-e now	*We hope for a ray from that lamp of felicity* *That gives light to the world again*
Gūyā anï talaf qïlghanda söngäkin tapmadïlar ki bir yerdä qoyghaylar[19]	It seems that when they killed him they could not find his bones to bury him.

Hafez's poetry is so important for Nava'i that an accomplished imitation by a poet can be highlighted as one of the most significant events in the latter's life.

In one of his last works, *Mohakamat al-loghateyn*, Nava'i claims that 'of the *Divans* [of Persian poetry] to be read there were few that [he] did not study'.[20] He further adds that three of them particularly impressed him: the *Divan* of Amir Khosrow Dehlavi, whose poetry was especially appreciated during the Timurid era; the *Divan* of his spiritual master Jami and the *Divan* of Hafez, whom he describes as 'the general and commander of the lovers of truth, [who] produced works with originalities and profundities that were adorned by the breath of the Holy Spirit of God'.[21] The celebration of Hafez's poetry actually permeates Nava'i's works. In *Mahbub al-qolub* (ca. 1500), Hafez is referred as *ma'ani adasïgha lafez*, that is 'the one who produces the expression of the [invisible] meaning'.[22] And in the preface to his Turkish *Divan*, he reiterates his admiration for 'the confidant of the keepers of the mysteries of love and passion'.[23] It is as if the figure of Hafez outshines all other great

Persian poets, such as Sa'di Shirazi or Rumi, with the two notable exceptions being Amir Khosrow and Jami.

In other works, Jami and Nava'i acknowledge the importance of Hafez on the basis of the mystical significance of his poetry. In his compendium of biographies of Sufis, *Nafahat al-ons* (ca. 1475), Jami portrays Hafez as follows:

Vey lesān al-gheyb va tarjomān al-asrār ast. Basā asrār-e gheybiya va ma'āni-ye haqiqiya keh dar kesvat-e surat va lebās-e majāz bāz namuda ast. Har chand ma'lum nist keh vey dast-e erādat-e piri gerefta va dar tasavvof beh yeki az in tā'efa nesbat dorost karda, ammā sokhanān-e vey chonān bar mashrab-e in tā'efa vāqe' shoda ast keh hich kas-rā ān ettefāq nayoftāda. Yeki az 'azizān-e selsela-ye khājagān qaddasa allāh ta'ālā asrārahom farmuda ast keh: hich divān beh az divān-e Hāfez nist agar mard sufi bāshad[24]

He is the tongue of the invisible and the translator of secrets. He has shown many secrets of the unknown and meanings of the reality with the help of metaphors and allegories. Although it is not clear whether he ever stretched out the hand of discipleship to an elder and affiliated with a Sufi brotherhood, his words correspond to those of the Sufis to the degree that no other poet's work does. One of the dear ones of the Khvajagan, may God sanctify their secrets, has said that: no *Divan* is better than the *Divan* of Hafez, if the man is a Sufi.

Jami was not sure if Hafez had studied with a Sufi, but he agreed that his *Divan* was one of the best works that a Sufi could read. In his translation-adaptation of this work (*Nasa'em al-mahabba men shama'em al-fotowwa*, ca. 1495–96), Nava'i, after repeating the words of Jami, quotes Qasem al-Anvar (d. 1433), who went as far as labelling the *Divan* of Hafez 'The Persian Qur'an':

Khājalar qaddasa allāhu ta'ālā asrārahom silsilasidin 'azīzi debdur ki: 'hīch dīwān Hāfiz dīwānïdïn yakhshïraq emäs agar kishi sūfī bolsa.' Bu faqīrgha andaq ma'lūm bolubtur wa mashhūr mundaqdur ki hazrat Mīr Qāsim qaddasa allāhu sirrahu alarnïng dīwānï 'Qur'ān-i fārsī' der ermishlär.[25]

A Khvaja, may his secrets be sanctified, who is a dear one of the chain said: 'No *Divan* is better than Hafez's *Divan* if the man is a Sufi.' It became so certain to your servant and so famous that his excellence Mir Qasem, may his secrets be blessed, called his *Divan* the Persian Qur'an.

While Jami and Nava'i were unsure whether Hafez had been initiated formally into a mystical order, they nonetheless agreed that his poetry was full of mystical significance. The question thus arises as to what extent this mystical dimension was reflected in their own rewritings of Hafez.

Rewriting Hafez's First Ghazal: A Matter of Consistency

Imitation is the sincerest form of flattery, they say.[26] This may explain why Jami wrote so many of his poems in imitation of Hafez's ghazals despite explicitly acknowledging their 'inimitability' (see *supra*). Within only the first one hundred or so poems of his *Divan* (those rhyming in the letter *alef*), there are some ten imitations of Hafez, seven of these replying to just the first poem of his *Divan*.[27] As far as Nava'i is concerned, the mid sixteenth-century historian Mirza Heydar Dughlat tellingly frames Nava'i's Persian poetry as 'reply to the divan of Khwaja Hafiz of Shiraz'.[28] In the *Mohakamat al-loghateyn*, Nava'i himself states that he wrote his Persian collection of lyrical poetry in the style of Hafez.[29] Of the 485 ghazals in the Divan of Fani,[30] compiled at the end of the 1490s, there are no less than 227 ghazals emulating Hafez, a little less than half of the Persian ghazals of Nava'i. Furthermore, the structure of his *Divan* itself reveals Nava'i's desire to have his collection of Persian poems understood with reference to the great Shirazi poet. While Nava'i begins his *Divan* with two devotional ghazals – the first one being devoted to God (*hamd*) and the second one to his Prophet (*na't*) – it is significant that the third is a rewriting of the poem that introduces Hafez's *Divan* itself.[31] The imitation of Hafez's first ghazal thus opens Fani's *Divan*, if we set aside the religious prolegomena that Nava'i regarded as a requirement for any collection of ghazals, according to the preface he composed for his Turkish *Divan*.[32]

Hafez's opening ghazal is a programmatic poem. The poet himself may have placed it or instructed that it be placed at the beginning of his *Divan*.[33] Its importance was well understood for the poem became the starting point of a series of imitations in the early fifteenth century. Before Jami and Nava'i, poets such as Katebi Torshizi (d. 1434–36), Fattahi Nishapuri (d. 1448) and Amir Shahi Sabzavari (d. 1453) all composed responses to it. When they rewrote it, our two Timurid poets thus consciously immersed themselves in a real imitation network.[34] But before we discuss the way they approached this type of exercise, here is the text and a translation of Hafez's first ghazal:

1	*A-lā yā ayyohā as-sāqī ader ka'san wa-nāwelhā*	O cupbearer proffer the cup and pass it around
	Keh 'eshq āsān namud avval vali oftād moshkel-hā	For love at first appeared easy, but difficulties have occurred
2	*Beh bu-ye nāfa'i k-ākher sabā z-ān torra bo-gshāyad*	In the hope of [smelling] the perfume of the musk-pod that in the end the breeze looses from that forelock
	Z-e tāb-e ja'd-e moshkinash cheh khun oftād dar del-hā	From the shining twist of his black curl, what blood befell the hearts

3	*Beh mey sajjāda rangin kon gar-at pir-e moghān guyad*	Colour the prayer-mat with wine, if the Magian elder bids you to
	Keh sālek bi-khabar nabvad z-e rāh-o rasm-e manzel-hā	For the traveller is not ignorant of the way and customs of the stages
4	*Ma-rā dar manzel-e janān cheh amn-e 'eysh chun har dam*	In the stage of the beloved what security of enjoyment have I
	Jaras faryād mi-dārad keh bar bandid mahmel-hā	When at every moment the bell gives voice saying: 'Bind on the camel-litters'?
5	*Shab-e tārik-o bim-e mowj-o gerdābi chonin hā'el*	The dark night, the fear of the wave, and the whirlpool so dreadful
	Kojā dānand hāl-e mā sabokbārān-e sāhel-hā	How do they know of our state, the light-burdened ones of the shore?
6	*Hama kār-am z-e khod-kāmi beh badnāmi keshid ākher*	All my work, because of my own fancy, has led at last to bad repute
	Nehān key mānad ān rāzi k-az u sāzand mahfel-hā	How can that secret remain concealed about which they make gatherings?
7	*Hozuri gar hami khāhi az-u ghā'eb ma-show Hāfez*	If you desire presence, Hafez, do not hide from him
	Matā mā talqa man tahwā da' ed-dunyā wa-ahmelhā[35]	When you have found the one you desire, abandon the world and ignore it

The structure of the ghazal may disconcert the modern reader who is looking for a clear progression of narrative. Even in the fourteenth century, Hafez's poems were being criticized for their 'incoherence', to use Meisami's words.[36] Hafez's patron Shah-e Shoja' himself is reported to have critiqued the poet for his poems' incongruity, saying:

> The beyts ... in your ghazals ... do not happen to be of one kind, instead in each ghazal there are three or four beyts about wine and two or three beyts about Sufism and one or two beyts about the characteristics of the beloved. The changeableness of each ghazal is contrary to the way of the eloquent.[37]

Whether apocryphal or not, this statement is consistent with those of many critics, including modern scholars, who speak of 'lines deprived of a true and proper "dramatic" succession of events and united more by a common inspiration than by precise and direct links of a semantic kind'.[38] As stated by de Bruijn, 'several studies have focused on the question of whether or not it is possible to find the rules of composition leading unity to the seemingly random sequence of images and lyrical motives in a typical Ḥāfiẓean poem'.[39] Admittedly, a first reading of this ghazal might give the impression of a paratactic juxtaposition of different ideas and a series of vaguely related couplets. This feeling of disunity is probably due to the absence of 'transitional devices,' as Michael Hillman suggested.[40] What word or image links the first couplet to the second one? And what about the third and the fourth one?

Nonetheless, this kind of issue did not prevent Jami from composing no fewer than seven imitations of this poem. Interestingly, he was careful to introduce the kind of transitional devices that were lacking in his model. By way of example, here is a translation of one of Jami's rewritings:

1	*Nasīm es-subhi zor menni robā Najdin wa qabbelhā*	Ah, morning breeze, visit the hills of Najd and kiss them
	Keh bu-ye dust mi-āyad az ān farsuda manzel-hā	For the perfume of the Friend comes from those decayed stages
2	*Chu gardad showq-e vasl afzun cheh jā-ye ta'n agar Majnun*	When longing for union grows why blame Majnun if
	Beh bu-ye howdaj-e Leyli fotad donbāl-e mahmel-hā	He follows camel-litters because of the perfume of Leyli's litter
3	*Del-e man por z-e mehr-e yār va u fāregh nabud-ast ān*	My heart is filled with love for the Friend and He is not unaware of it
	Keh mi-guyand rāhi hast del-hā-rā su-ye del-hā	For they say 'Hearts have a path to hearts'
4	*Rasid inak z-e rah Salmā-va man az za'f-e tan z-in sān*	Here is Salma who has arrived from the road yet I am like this because of the weakness of my body
	Fakhoz yā sāhi ruhi tohfatan menni wa aqbelhā	So, my Friend, take my spirit as a gift from me and accept it
5	*Ma-riz ey abr-e dida āb-e hasrat bar sar-e rāhesh*	O cloud-like eye, do not shed regret's rain on her path
	Keh dur owlā som-e asbesh z-e āsib-e chonin gel-hā	Best that her horse's hoof be far from the calamity of such mires
6	*Ma-rā az hejr-e u dar del gereh mi-bud sad moshkel*	In my heart a hundred difficulties were knotted by separation from that One
	Chu didam shekl-e u fi'l-hāl hall shod jomla-ye moshkel-hā	When I saw that One's form all difficulties were solved instantly
7	*Z-e jur-e dur-e gham-farjām Jāmi qossa-hā dārad*	Jami suffers sorrows from the harshness of this painful cycle
	Wa-lāken khowf emlāl en-nadāmā lam yotawwelhā[41]	But fearing the annoyance of penitents he did not prolong them

The first and the second beyts are linked by the idea of 'the perfume of the Friend'. In beyt 3, 'love for the Friend' (*mehr-e yar*) continues to dwell on the theme of the longing for the beloved, while the word 'path' in the second hemistich connects this couplet with beyts 4 and 5. The last phrase of this hemistich, 'the calamity of such mires,' sets up the last linking device, which is provided by a series of terms referring to pain and suffering. In this way, Jami creates a narrative whose progression is simpler to grasp than that of his model. At the outset, the poem depicts a lover, who (like Majnun) is longing for union with Leyli, the archetype of all beloveds. Suddenly the beloved appears in the form of Salma, another archetype of the beloved in Arabic poetry. However, the lover is already too weak because of his tormented condition. Nonetheless, the coming of the beloved allows for an immediate resolution of all difficulties. The moral could be summed up like this: although the condition of the lover is a difficult one, he has no reason to complain about it, for sorrow and pain are inseparable from love, and thus should be accepted with joy and gratefulness.

As already noted by Afsahzad, there are fewer themes in Jami's rewritings. He makes no mention of wine, nor does he evoke the debauchee's (*rend*) way of life. In his imitation, he only focuses on the painful condition of the lover. While Hafez's ghazal is polythematic, Jami's rewriting is firmly monothematic. His imitation, therefore, lacks those layers of meaning that make Hafez's ghazal so much more complex and open to various kinds of interpretations. However what Jami's verses lose in complexity, they gain in clarity.[42]

In Nava'i's rewriting, we also find these logical links that connect one verse to the next:

1	*Romuz ol-'eshq kānat moshkelan be'l-kā'si hallelhā*	The enigmas of love were difficult. Solve them by way of a cup
	Keh ān yāqut-e mahlul-at namāyad hall-e moshkel-hā	For that dissolved ruby of yours shows the solution of difficulties.
2	*Su-ye deyr-e moghān beh-khrām tā bini du sad mahfel*	March to the convent of the magi to see two hundred gatherings
	Sar-ā-sar z-āftāb-e mey foruzān sham'-e mahfel-hā	All the candles of the gatherings are brightened by the sun of the wine.
3	*Del-o mey har du rowshan shod nemi-dānam keh tāb-e mey*	Heart and wine, both shone brightly and I do not know whether the heat of the wine
	Zad ātesh-hā beh del yā tāb-e mey shod z-ātesh-e del-hā	Lit the fire of the heart or the fire of the heart heated up the wine.
4	*Beh maqsad garcheh rah dur ast agar ātesh resad az 'eshq*	Even if it is a long way until we reach our goal, if the fire comes from love
	Chu barq-āsā tavān kardan beh gāmi qat'-e manzel-hā	We can traverse all the stages with one step like a lightning

5	*Man-o bi-hāseli k-az 'elm-o zohd-am āncheh hāsel shod*	The fruitless harvest I gained from science and asceticism
	Yek-ā-yek dar serr-e ma'shuq-o mey shod jomla hāsel-hā	became entirely fruitful through the secrets of wine and the beloved
6	*Bovad chun abr seyr-e nāqa-ye Leyli keh dar vādi*	The coming of Leyli's she-camel is like a cloud, for in the valley [there is]
	Feghān az chāk-e del Majnun keshad ni zang-e mahmel-hā	[the sound] of Majnun's lamentation because of his broken heart, not [that of] the bell of the camel litters
7	*Chu dar dasht-e fanā manzel koni yek ruz ey Fāni*	If you stop even just one day in the desert of annihilation, o Fani
	Z-e man ān jānfezā atlāl-rā f-asjad wa qabbel-hā[43]	Prostrate before those soul-enlightening ruins and kiss them for me

The poet links the first three beyts by focusing on wine (*mey*). The logical link between the third and the fourth couplet is provided by the word *atesh* ('fire'). Beyts four and five are linked by terms denoting a result, an output, such as *maqsad* ('goal', 'destination') or *hasel* ('harvest'). The link connecting the fifth to the sixth couplet is the beloved, here embodied by the archetypal figure of Leyli. Finally, the closing couplet is linked to the previous one by the phrase *dasht-e fana* ('desert of annihilation'), which is the mystical metaphor of the valley, in which Majnun is waiting for Leyli.

As with Jami's poem, this succession of couplets provides the reader with a clear order of narrative: after stating that wine helps solve the difficulties of love, the poet invites his reader to 'march to the convent', so that his heart will be lit by the heat of the wine. Thanks to the fire produced by this heart, he will be able to traverse all stages with only one step. The poet is all the more confident in his assertions since his own experience (see the personal pronoun *man* as an emphatic 'I' in beyt 5) proved that nothing was more important in this journey than wine and the love for his beloved. Afflicted by the pain of love, just as Majnun longed for his Leyli, the lover can expect to reach his ultimate goal – the proximity of God through the annihilation (*fana*) of himself. Like Jami, Nava'i's imitation follows a simplified pattern, and does not take up 'the polythematic structure' of its model.

Actually, Nava'i seems to have been particularly attached to this poetic consistency. In the preface he wrote for his Turkish *Divan*, which appears to be a kind of *Ars Poetica*, the Timurid poet criticizes those who are not coherent in the writing of their ghazals:

Yana bukim, sā'ir dawāwīnda rasmī ghazal uslūbïdïnkim, shā'i' durur, tajāwuz qïlïb, makhsūs naw'larda söz 'arūsïnïng jilwasïgha namāyish wa jamālïgha ārāyish bermäydürürlär. Wa agar ahyānan matla'ī makhsūs naw'da wāqi' bolsa, hamol matla' uslūbï bilä itmām-i khil'atin wa anjām-i kiswatin kiydürmäydürürlär, balki tuganghuncha agar bir beyt mazmūni wisāl bahārida gul-ārāylïq qïlsa, yana biri firāq khazānida khār-namāylïq qïlïbdurur. Bu surat daghï munāsabatdin yïraq wa mulāyamatdin qïraq köründi. Ol jihatdin sa'y qïldïmkim, har mazmūnda matla'i wāqi' bolsa, andaq bolghaykim, maqta'ghacha surat heysīyatidin muwāfiq wa ma'nī jānibidin mutābiq tüshkäy[44]

Moreover, in other *Divan*s they blatantly transgress the conventional arrangement, and in specific genres they do not show the splendour[45] of the bride of speech and they do not provide ornament to her beauty. And if sometimes an opening verse is [written] in a specific genre, they do not finish dressing her in her garments in accordance with the arrangement of this opening verse. All too often, if the content of a couplet grows roses during the springtime of union, the next couplet brings out thorns during the autumn of separation. Such form appears to be far from consistent and showing no delicacy. For this reason, I have endeavoured that whatever the content of an opening verse, it should be like this: until the last verse [the content] should be congruous with the quality of the form and consonant with the sense of the meaning.

According to Nava'i's conception, a poem should be consistent both in form and meaning from the first line until the last. It is not surprising, then, that his rewriting of Hafez's ghazal should follow these rules.

Nava'i's and Jami's use of imagery is strictly linked to the theme in question. Rarely do they digress or introduce additional elements 'which in the ghazal of Hafiz create a more detailed context but make it seem – at least at first sight – to be more rambling and disjointed'.[46] The two Timurid poets 'have a single theme organized, line by line, into distinct semantic fields'.[47] As a result, what Losensky wrote about Jami's response poems also applies to Nava'i's imitation: 'his responses stick close to the theme of their model, regularize its structure, and elaborate on its images and topoi'.[48] The elusive structure of Hafez's ghazal is thus simplified and regularized in the Timurid responses. To sum up, and to use the expression coined by Losensky, Jami and Nava'i 'standardized' the way they responded to the first ghazal of the Shirazi poet.[49]

Hermeneutic Reorientations

Imitations are a form of metatextual poetry in that they reflect upon the text of the model. Poets such as Jami and Nava'i used poetry to talk about poetry. They used imitational poetry to analyse Hafez and to convey this analysis to the reader. The more they standardized their 'replies', the more they clarified the way they wanted Hafez's poetry to be approached by other readers.

Losensky noticed that Jami's imitations of Hafez's poetry often took the form of explicit commentary. Jami did not refrain from using words which explicitly referred to the practice of commentary. We find one of these terms in another of Jami's imitations of Hafez's opening ghazal. Here are the first (*matla'*) and the last couplets (*maqta'*) of this response poem:

A-lā yā ayyohā as-sāqī mey āmad hall-e moshkel-hā	*O cupbearer* wine is the solution to all problems
Z-e mey moshkel bud towba ader ka'san wa-nāwelhā	It is hard to repent of wine, [so] *proffer the cup and pass it around* [...]
Beh khāb az sho'la-hā-ye nur gardad gerd-e tu Jāmi	If in a dream the flames of light engulf you, o Jami
Be-shams el-rāhi 'abber-hā wa dowr el-ka'si awwel-hā[50]	*Interpret*[51] them as the sun of wine after the cup has passed from hand to hand

The use of a term like *'abber* ('interpret') leaves no other option for Jami's reader but to see wine in Hafez's poem as a mystical intoxication rather than a prosaic drunkenness.

In his various rewritings of Hafez's opening ghazals, Jami often exhibits the paraphrastic dimension of his imitational practices. First, as sometimes happens in this kind of exercise, he repeats one verse of the parent-ghazal. What is less usual, however, is that he does not refrain from commenting on it in another verse. For instance, here is the beginning of another response poem by Jami:

Sharāb-e la'l bāshad qovvat-e jān-hā qovvat-e del-hā	Ruby wine is the strength of souls and the strength of hearts
A-lā yā ayyohā as-sāqī ader ka'san wa-nāwelhā	*O cupbearer proffer the cup and pass it around*
Chu z-e avval 'eshq moshkel bud ākher ham cherā guyam	Since at first love was difficult, why in the end would I say
Keh 'eshq āsān namud avval vali oftād moshkel-hā[52]	*'For love at first appeared easy, but difficulties have occurred'?*

The insertion of rhetorical questions reveals Jami's intention to establish a dialogue with the tradition that had been built thus far on Hafez's opening ghazal. Jami questions Hafez's ghazal and the way one can interpret it, thus formulating new answers to old problems. One may imagine that, according to Jami, it was misleading to say that 'love at first appeared easy'. Love, according to his mystical conception, is never easy, and thus Jami uses Hafez's verse to reassess the nature of love. This idea that the difficulties of the lover remain because of the nature of love itself is expressed in another of his seven rewritings of Hafez's opening ghazal. Evoking one more time the difficulties of the lover (*moshkel-e 'asheq*), Jami writes that there is no point in trying to solve these difficulties with the help of the intellect (*'aql*),

Keh sad moshkel-e degar pish āyad-ash az hall-e moshkel-hā[53]	For a hundred other difficulties befall him from the solving of [these] difficulties

Jami then quotes Hafez's first verse, but at the end of his imitation, to say that only (mystical) wine can help the lover:

Chu oftad moshkeli Jāmi beh sāqi guyi chu Hāfez	When a difficulty has occurred, Jami, tell the cupbearer like Hafez
A-lā yā ayyohā as-sāqī ader ka'san wa-nāwelhā[54]	*O cupbearer proffer the cup and pass it around*

In this way, Hafez's first verse becomes the last verse in Jami's rewriting, and in doing so Jami reconfigures elements of the parent ghazal in order to give them a new significance. While Hafez asked for wine in order to bear the difficulties of love when they had come to pass, in his rewriting, Jami makes (spiritual) intoxication a permanent feature of the lover's condition.

However, it could be argued that Jami's dialogue with Hafez was conducted in a secular fashion, and that his rewriting does not entail any mystical reorientation; indeed, often the esoteric and the exoteric dimensions are intertwined in Persian classical poetry. As stated by de Bruijn,

> since poets have made more frequent uses of ghazals for the expression of mystical love [...], the fusion between the secular and the mystical in Persian ghazals has become such an essential characteristic that, in most instances, it is extremely difficult to make a proper distinction between the two, the secular and the mystical.[55]

In the case of Hafez's first ghazal, Meisami identifies three major thematic concerns: the trials of love, the celebration of love and the defence of poetry.[56] The mystical dimension is not included in this list. Accordingly, Meisami translated *rah-o rasm* (beyt 3) as customs, but she suggests that they could be identified more precisely as the traces of a ruined encampment. Following the same line of thinking, she invites the reader to interpret the 'stages' (*manzel*, beyts 3 and 4) as 'taverns' rather than as the traditional stations through which the Sufi has to pass before he reaches his final destination.[57]

If we turn to Jami's rewriting, we can see that he introduced the characters of Leyli and Majnun. This is a significant addition, since the poet was criticized at the time for introducing a narrative element not originally found in Hafez's ghazal.[58] By focusing on the condition of the lover, Jami eschewed other themes developed in the model. The introduction of Majnun, who is the archetypal intoxicated lover, might be seen as a way for Jami to illustrate the condition of all true lovers from a mystical perspective. In this way, Jami's beyt can be regarded as a paraphrase of the corresponding beyt in Hafez's poem. The elusive mention of the lovers' suffering ('what blood befell the hearts') receives here a concrete illustration, as well as a kind of commentary. If we cannot 'blame' the archetypal mystic lover even if he keeps pursuing an impossible love, it is because Majnun's longing for union (*showq-e vasl*) is precisely what animates his lifelong quest. His ever-growing ardent desire (*showq*) is what compels the Sufi traveller to go forwards along his mystical path. In the following beyt, Jami reassures his reader, by telling him that the beloved is aware of the lover's affection and longing, though she or he might not show it. It is difficult not to see the all-knowing God behind this characterization. This beyt may be regarded as an answer to the fourth beyt of the parent ghazal. There is no 'security of enjoyment', as Hafez says, but it does not mean that this is a desperate situation. In the fourth beyt, the arrival of Salma, another traditional figure of the beloved who is always about to leave, is proving the poet right. However, Salma's arrival does not change the lover's situation radically. On the contrary, the poet focuses not on the joy caused by the arrival of his beloved but on his ever-tormenting condition. Love, according to a Sufi conception, is only affliction (*bala*) and feeds on the oppression (*jafa*) of the lover, as explained by Ahmad Ghazali in his *Savaneh*, a Sufi work that Nava'i had studied with the help of Jami.[59] The mystic lover is, above all, a being who suffers; he is in constant pain and his body is always weak. The sixth beyt takes up Hafez's famous opening about the difficulties of love ('For love at first appeared easy but difficulties have occurred'). Here, again, the rewriting is more explicit, since Jami specifies the effective cause of these difficulties: separation (*hejr*) from the beloved which can be instantly solved by union. The last couplet evokes this painful cycle (*dowr-e gham-farjam*) of separation and union. Jami's trepidation about wearing out his reader with such tales is – again – a lesson of mystical love. The mystical lover cannot imagine that this sorrow is annoying, and he endeavours to accept it as a gift of the Friend. The mystic poet Sana'i wrote that no joy should be allowed to us in this world if we regard sorrow inflicted by God as a calamity.[60] Because Jami chose to focus only on one theme developed by Hafez's poem, his rewriting only answered to selected beyts of the ghazal model (beyts 1, 2 and 4). In this fashion, Jami was able to make up a poetic narrative that could also work as a didactic presentation of the mystical lover's condition. After all, in his third compilation of poems, *Khatemat al-hayat*, he proclaimed that his *Divan* consisted 'mostly of the ghazals of lovers distraught'.[61]

Nava'i's imitation appears even more explicitly to be a mystical commentary on Hafez's poem. Right from the first couplet, Nava'i gives an explanatory paraphrase: 'for the dissolved ruby of yours (i.e. wine) shows the way towards the solution of difficulties'. In terms of its wording, it is very close to the first hemistich of another of Jami's imitations that I have already quoted (*A-lā yā ayyohā s-sāqi mey āmad hall-e moshkel-hā*: 'Come o cupbearer for wine is the solution to all problems').[62] Nava'i's decision to write 'the enigma of love' (*romuz al-'eshq*) instead of simply 'love', as Hafez did in his poem, shows that he brought the discussion to a mystical level without any ambiguity, especially since the word *ramz* (plu. *romuz*) also means 'allegory'. He would not talk about carnal love, but rather of spiritual love (*'eshq-e haqiqi*), for which wordly love is only a metaphor (*'eshq-e majazi*). Wine becomes then the symbol of divine love that impregnates all things with ardent desire and spiritual intoxication (*sokr*). In the second beyt, the poet makes clear the meaning he attaches to the term *mahfel* ('gathering', beyt 6 in Hafez's poem).[63] The *mahfel*s are places where Sufis come in order to experience this spiritual intoxication that turns them from 'intellectual Sufi' (*sufiyan-e 'aql*) into 'spiritual Sufis' (*sufiyan-e ruh*). In the third beyt, Nava'i's interrogation ('I do not know whether the heat of the wine lit the fire of the heart or the fire of the heart heated up the wine') reminds the reader that the propriety of mystical wine is to strengthen love: it fills the heart with passion and ardent desire (*showq*). The following couplet (beyt 4) focuses on the rhyme word *manzel* ('stage'). By telling his reader that he 'can traverse all the stages with one step like a lightning', Nava'i clearly opts for a meaning closer to 'mystical stations' than to the 'taverns', which Meisami suggested regarding Hafez's poem. These stages are the traditional steps through which the Sufi has to pass before he reaches his final destination (*maqsad*), which is of course proximity to God. Moreover, the context in which Jami uses this rhyming phrase in one of his imitations of Hafez's first ghazal seems to confirm this reading:

Chu har manzel keh Leyli karda jā Ka'ba ast Majnun-rā	For each stop that Leyli makes is a Ka'ba for Majnun
Beh qasd-e Ka'ba Majnun-rā cheh hājat qat'-e manzel-hā[64]	When Majnun tries to seek the Ka'ba there is no need [for him] to traverse all the stages

Beyt number 5 may also be regarded as a commentary on the corresponding beyt in Hafez's poem. Before he transformed his fruitless knowledge (*'elm*) and his exoteric devotion (*zohd*) into a craving for the mystical quest, Nava'i was like these 'light-burdened ones of the shore' (*sabokbaran* in Hafez's ghazal) who know nothing about the condition of the real lover. The quest of the Sufi can only be successful if it is fuelled by wine and guided by love. The knowledge of the traveller cannot be confused with *'elm*, for Sufis know, at least since Ahmad Ghazali's *Savaneh*, that *'elm* entails the duality of an object and a subject. This duality deprives people who have this type of knowledge of union with the object of their quest.

The sixth couplet is an explicit answer to the fourth couplet of Hafez's poem. The verses of both Nava'i and Hafez talk about the sound of Leyli's camel litter (*mahmel*). The Shirazi poet evokes the bell that signals the departure of the camel-litters. However, Nava'i answers that the valley is filled by the lamentations of Majnun rather than the bells of the litters. Nava'i insists on the pain of love (*chak-e del*), and he uses the archetypal figure of Majnun, as Jami did in three of his imitations of Hafez's first ghazal.[65] As already noted above, Majnun is absent from Hafez's poem but his presence in Jami and Nava'i's rewritings enabled the two Timurid poets to give a concrete picture of the pure mystical lover in the same way that Leyli and Salma (in Jami's imitations) embodied the epiphany of the divine beauty. In two of his rewritings of Hafez's first ghazal, Jami significantly associates Leyli with the Ka'ba.[66] The fact that we do not find this association in Hafez's *Divan* reveals Jami's emphasis on 'Leyli's function'; she is first of all an epiphany of the divine beauty rather than just a mere literary figure. The romance of Leyli and Majnun is integrated into Jami's ghazal insofar as their love represents a bridge towards the love for God (*'eshq-e haqiqi*).

In the last couplet, Nava'i links the valley that hears Majnun's outcries for his beloved with the desert of annihilation (*dasht-e fana*). Here the poet alludes to the penultimate spiritual station, the stage of annihilation (*maqamat* or *manzel-e fana*), which is the end of the mystical journey. According to Islamic mysticism, *fana* refers to the extinction of the self, which in the words of a Sufi like Ahmad Ghazali allows the lover to escape separation. The lover achieves his real state of being in God, his beloved. Non-being (*fana*) leads to union, whereas the state of being only leads to separation. As long as the lover does not enter this enlightened state, he cannot obtain awareness of the intrinsic unity. Until then, he is subjected to a painful cycle of separations and unions, the same kind of which Jami speaks in his own imitation.

Unquestionably, Nava'i read the poem of Hafez as a mystical ghazal and his paraphrase should be interpreted as such. Zipoli noticed in his study that Nava'i made different uses of the rhyme words of his models.[67] In view of what has been said above, it is possible to characterize this as Nava'i's hermeneutical reorientation of the model, in which each rhyme word of the parent ghazal (*moshkel*, *mahfel*, *del*, *manzel*, etc.) becomes a key word that is glossed unambiguously according to a clear mystical framework. Even though Jami's way of proceeding is different, his focus on one theme of Hafez's ghazal, namely the hardship of the lover's condition and his didactic developments about it, show that, just like Nava'i's rewriting, the *nazira* constitutes a 'clarifying filter' of the model, to use Zipoli's words.[68] This filter helps select particular types of information of the parent ghazal according to a Sufi framework that considers worldly love only as a bridge towards 'real love' (*'eshq-e haqiqi*).

> De Bruijn remarked that
> the decision whether a given poem should be called a Sufi ghazal or a profane love song very often does not depend so much on the poem itself, but on what we know about its writer, that is the answer to the question: does the life of the poet provide us with clues of a mystical affiliation, or is the poet only known as a court poet?[69]

Admittedly, the fact that we know little about Hafez's commitment into Sufism does not help us solve the question of the religious dimension of his ghazals. The matter is nonetheless simpler with respect to Jami and Nava'i, since there is no ambiguity concerning the mystical affiliations of Jami, who was the most prominent Naqshbandi-Sufi thinker in Herat. His efforts to integrate the theosophy of mystical love of Ebn 'Arabi within the Persian literary tradition could explain his desire to frame his imitations of Hafez's ghazal according to a mystical perspective. The contents of Jami's ghazals are love lyrics that express Sufi mysticism, and there is understandably very little room for secular love in his *Divan*, as expressed in these verses:

Hast divān-e she'r-e man-e aksar	My collection of poetry for the most part
Ghazal-e 'āsheqān-e sheydā'i	Consists of ghazals of intoxicated lovers
[...]	[...]
Zekr-e downān nayābi andar vey	You will not find traces of contemptible ones
K-ān bovad naqd-e 'omr-e farsā'i[70]	For that would be a lifetime spent in vain

As for Nava'i, the preface of his Turkish *Divan* shows that he does not have much consideration for poems that do not have a religious dimension:

Yana bir bukim, gūyā ba'zī el ash'ār tahsīlidin wa dīwān takmīlidin gharaz-i majāzī husn-u jamāl tawsīfi wa maqsūd-i zāhirī khatt u khāl ta'rīfidin özgä nemä anglamay dururlar. Dīwān tapïlghaykim, anda ma'rifat-āmīz ghazal tapïlmaghay wa ghazal bolghaykim, anda maw'izat-angīz bir beyt bolmaghay. Mundaq dīwān	Another problem is that some people, after gathering poems and completing a *Divan*, show nothing but a strong inclination to describe metaphorical beauty and elegance with the purpose of extolling the down of the cheek and the mole. We find *Divan*s in which we find not one gnostic ghazal and there are ghazals in which there is not a

bitilsä, khud asru bīhūda zahmat wa zā'i' mashaqqat tartīlghan bolghay.[71]	single homiletic verse. When such a *Divan* is composed, it caused too much pain in vain and bothersome trouble.

For this reason, he tells his reader that the latter will not find a single ghazal in his *Divan* that does not include at least one or two verses adorned with the help of advice and homily (*nasihat-ara va mow'ezat-asa*).[72] Nava'i, therefore, espouses his Sufi master's conceptions. There are several ghazals in his Persian *Divan* in which he admits that Jami guided him in writing pieces that incorporated Hafez's poetry:

Beh rāh-e 'eshq agar moshkeli fetad Fāni	Fani, if difficulties arise in the path of love
Z-e ruh-e Hāfez-o ma'ni-e Jāmiesh juyam[73]	I will seek for help from the spirit of Hafez and the meaning of Jami

or

Rasad chu masti Fāni beh Hāfez-e Shirāz	When Fani's drunkenness reaches Hafez of Shiraz
Z-e jām-e Jāmi u az bād-e rahbari dānad[74]	He considers it derived from Jami's cup and the wind's guidance

Conclusion

Jami and Nava'i's imitations of Hafez's first ghazal help us identify the manner through which they preserved the poet's legacy. Their commentary-like imitations reveal that these Timurid poets contributed to the development of an evaluative and interpretive corpus surrounding the legacy of Hafez's poetry. Their metatextual poems provided a meaning that situated this heritage within a specifically Islamic context. They wanted to frame the reading of Hafez's ghazals so that his poetry could be understood as a guide to spiritual love in accordance with Ebn 'Arabi's theosophy.

We may assume that Jami and Nava'i's deep commitment to imitational poetry was to a great extent guided by their mystical agenda. One of Jami's most important intellectual contributions to the Naqshbandi order was his effort to include Ebn 'Arabi's teachings within its doctrinal corpus.[75] His rewritings of Hafez's poetry gave him another opportunity to bring the reader to an experiential level of understanding the Akbarian ideas. In *Khamsat al-motahayyerin*, a work written after Jami's death (in 1492) and dedicated to his memory, Nava'i reported that it was Jami who initiated him into the reading of the Sheykh al-Akbar.[76] Nothing then prevented him from spreading the ethos of mystical love through his imitations in the same way that his *pir* did.

Consequently, Jami and Nava'i invited their reader to contemplate Hafez's poetry and the esoteric meaning they attached to it unequivocally.

This religious dimension of their imitational poetry invites us to reconsider our idea of Persian literature at that time. While this era has long been characterized by modern scholarship as one 'marked by a cultivation of hollow rhetoric and slavish imitation',[77] it is time to approach it from a different perspective, by considering for instance the development of Sufi orders like the Naqshbandiya brotherhood and the role poetics were called on to play in the dissemination of their ideas. After all, if we regard all imitations of this period as more or less refined academic exercises, we may not grasp the real significance of some of them, which operated outside the sphere of rhetoric.

Notes:

1. Dowlatshāh Samarqandi, *Tazkerat al-sho'arā'*, pp. 302–3.
2. Priscilla Soucek, 'Hafez xii. Hafez and the visual arts', pp. 501–5.
3. Paul Losensky, *Welcoming Fighānī*, p. 145.
4. Maria-Eva Subtelny, 'A taste for the intricate', pp. 56–79.
5. See Robert Devereux's translation of *Mohakamat al-loghateyn*, 'Judgment of Two Languages', *The Muslim World* 55, no. 1, p. 37.
6. A'lākhān Afsahzād, *Lirika Abd ar-Rakhmama Dzhami*, pp. 145–52.
7. Losensky, *Welcoming Fighānī*, pp. 175–79.
8. See Abdulg'ani Mirzoev, 'Foniy va Hofiz', pp. 8-15; idem, 'Alisher Navoiyning fors-tojik tilidagi meros haqida', pp. 13–21; Rahim Vohidov, 'Xoja Hofiz Sheroziy va Alisher Navoiy', pp. 25–32.
9. Riccardo Zipoli, *The Technique of the* Ǧawāb.
10. Ibid., p. 61. Presumably due to the brevity of his book and its limited scope, the Italian scholar did not attempt to give any explanation. The question thus remains as to what prompted Navā'i's change of approach in his rewritings of Hāfez and Jāmi's ghazals.
11. Benedek Péri, 'Mīr 'Alī-Šīr Navāyī and the first ghazal of Hāfiz', p. 177.
12. Although some have acknowledged that Nava'i could have read Hafiz's first ghazal as a mystical poem and oriented his imitation in that direction (see Péri, 'Mīr 'Alī-Šīr Navāyī', p. 181).
13. Chad Lingwood, *Politics, Poetry, and Sufism in Medieval Iran*.
14. Marc Toutant, *Un empire de mots. Pouvoir, culture et soufisme à l'époque des derniers Timourides au miroir de la* Khamsa *de Mīr 'Alī Shīr Nawā'ī*.
15. See, for instance, Johannes T.P. de Bruijn, *Persian Sufi Poetry*, pp. 51–83.
16. Jāmi, *Bahārestān*, ed. Afsahzād, p. 148.
17. Subtelny, 'A taste for the intricate', p. 69.
18. Dowlatshāh uses this expression to qualify Kamāl Esmā'il's verses. See E. Bertel's, 'Literatura na persidskom jazyke v Srednej Azii', p. 211.
19. Navā'i, *Majāles al-nafāyes*, Ms. Supplément turc 965, fols. 25r–26v.
20. Devereux, 'Judgment of Two Languages', pp. 33–34.
21. Ibid.
22. Navā'i, *Mahbub al-qolub*, p. 28.
23. See the folio 3v of the manuscript that is kept at the Bibliothèque nationale de France under the name Supplément turc 317, which is a *Kolliyāt-e Navā'i* that includes this *Dibācha* among other pieces. W.M. Thackston translated this preface but he used a version based on another manuscript that seems to have lacunae; see *A Century of Princes*, pp. 363–72.
24. Jāmi, *Nafahāt al-ons*, p. 612.
25. Navā'i, *Nasā'em al-mahabba*, Ms. Supplément turc 316, fol. 149r. Dowlatshāh Samarqandi also speaks about the veneration of Qāsem al-Anvār for Hāfez's *Divān;* see *Tazkerat al-sho'arā'*, pp. 302–3.
26. This proverb is taken from Charles Caleb Colton, *Lacon: or, Many Things in Few Words*, p. 113.

27. For the seven ghazals replying to just the first poem of Hāfez, see Jāmi, *Divān*, ed. Afsahzād, vol. I, *Fātehat al-shabāb*, ghazals No. 17 (p. 194) and No. 18 (p. 195); vol. II, *Vāsetat al-ʻeqd*, ghazals No. 11 (pp. 79–80), No. 12 (p. 80), No. 13 (p. 81), and *Khātemat al-hayāt*, ghazals No. 6 (p. 468) and No. 7 (p. 469). In its final recension, prepared at the request of Navā'i, Jāmi's *Divān* is actually divided into three sections: *Fātehat al-shabāb* ('The Opening of Youth'), *Vāsetat al-ʻeqd* ('The Middle of the Necklace') and *Khātemat al-hayāt* 'The End of Life').
28. Mirza Haydar Dughlat, *Tarikh-i-Rashidi*, trans. Wheeler M. Thackston, vol. II, p. 126.
29. Devereux, 'Judgment of Two Languages', p. 37.
30. Here I refer to Rokn al-Din Homāyun Farrokh's edition, *Divān-e Amir 'Ali-Shir Navā'i 'Fāni'*.
31. Fāni, *Divān*, p. 48.
32. Ms. Supplément turc 317, fol. 2v.
33. Julie Scott Meisami regards this poem as a poetic credo containing the poet's own view on his poetic output within the literary tradition. See Meisami, 'A life in poetry', p. 179.
34. Péri, 'Mīr 'Alī-Šīr Navāyī', p. 177.
35. Hāfez, *Divān*, vol. I, p. 91.
36. Julie S. Meisami, *Structure and Meaning in Medieval Arabic and Persian Lyric Poetry*, p. 46.
37. Quoted by Meisami, *Structure and Meaning*, p. 46.
38. Zipoli, *The Technique of the* Ǧawāb, p. 24; see also Losensky, *Welcoming Fighānī*, p. 167.
39. De Bruijn, *Persian Sufi Poetry*, p. 77.
40. Michael Hillman, 'Hafez's "Turk of Shiraz" again', p. 177.
41. Jāmi, *Divān, Fātehat al-shabāb*, ghazal No. 18 (p. 195).
42. On the clarity of Jami's verses in general see Hamid Algar, *Jami*, p. 66, and for what follows.
43. Fāni, *Divān*, p. 48.
44. Navā'i, Ms. Supplément turc 317, fol. 5r.
45. I translated *jilwa/jelva* as 'splendour' but the term also means 'Presenting a bride to her husband adorned and unveiled' according to Steingass' *Persian–English Dictionary*.
46. Zipoli, *The Technique of the* Ǧawāb, p. 62.
47. Ibid., p. 47.
48. Paul Losensky, 'Jāmi i. Life and Works', pp. 469–75.
49. Losensky, *Welcoming Fighānī*.
50. Jāmi, *Divān, Khātemat al-hayāt*, ghazal No. 7 (p. 469). My emphasis.
51. My emphasis.
52. Jāmi, *Divān, Vāsetat al-ʻeqd*, ghazal No. 12 (p. 80).
53. Jāmi, *Divān, Khātemat al-hayāt*, ghazal No. 6 (p. 468).
54. Ibid.
55. De Bruijn, *Persian Sufi Poetry*, p. 55.
56. Meisami, 'A life in poetry', p. 176.
57. Ibid., pp. 169–71.
58. Algar, *Jami*, p. 69.

59. See Toutant, *Un empire de mots*, p. 491.
60. Hakim Abu'l-Majd Majdud Sanā'i, *Divān*, p. 954.
61. See Aʿlākhān Afsahzād, *Naqd o bar-rasi-ye āsār va sharh-e ahvāl-e Jāmi*, p. 327.
62. Jāmi, *Divān, Khātemat al-hayāt*, ghazal No. 7 (p. 469). Péri noticed that Navā'i's *mesraʿ* (hemistich) was also very close to the paraphrases of Kātebi and Fattāhi. According to him, the phrase *hall-e moshkel-hā* ('solution of the difficulties') had 'become an inseparable part of the *mundus significans* of the Hāfiz first ghazal network'. See Péri, 'Navāyī and the first ghazal', p. 179.
63. According to Péri, 'Navāyī and the first ghazal', p. 180, *shamʿ-e mahfel-hā* had also become an integral part of Hāfez's first ghazal paraphrase network.
64. Jāmi, *Divān, Khātemat al-hayāt*, ghazal No. 6 (p. 468).
65. See Jāmi, *Divān, Fātehat al-shabāb*, ghazal No. 18 (p. 195); *Khātemat al-hayāt*, ghazals No. 6 (p. 468) and No. 7 (p. 469).
66. Jāmi, *Divān, Khātemat al-hayāt*, ghazals No. 6 (p. 468) and No. 7 (p. 469).
67. Zipoli, *The Technique of the* Ǧawāb, p. 48.
68. Ibid., pp. 24–25.
69. De Bruijn, *Persian Sufi Poetry*, p. 55.
70. These verses are quoted by Afsahzād, *Naqd o bar-rasi-ye āsār*, p. 327.
71. Navā'i, Ms. Supplément turc 317, fol. 5r.
72. Ibid.
73. Fāni, *Divān*, p. 253.
74. Ibid., p. 148.
75. See Hamid Algar, 'Reflections of Ibn 'Arabi in early Naqshbandî tradition', pp. 45–57; idem, 'Jāmī and Ibn 'Arabī: Khātam al-shu'arā' and Khātam al-Awliyā'', pp. 138–58.
76. Alisher Navoiy, *Mukammal asarlar to'plami*, vol. XV, p. 56.
77. Mohammad Rezā Shāfiʿi-Kadkani, 'Persian literature (Belles-Lettres) from the time of Jāmi to the present day', quoted by Losensky, *Welcoming Fighānī*, p. 134.

Bibliography:

Afsahzād, Aʿlākhān, *Lirika Abd ar-Rakhmama Dzhami: problemy teksta i poetiki* (Moscow: Izdatel'stvo Nauka, 1988).

— *Naqd o bar-rasi-ye āsār va sharh-e ahvāl-e Jāmi* (Tehran: Mirās-e Maktub, 1378/1999).

Algar, Hamid, 'Reflections of Ibn 'Arabi in early Naqshbandî tradition', *Journal of the Ibn 'Arabi Society* 10 (1991), pp. 45–57.

— 'Jāmī and Ibn 'Arabī: Khātam al-shu'arā' and Khātam al-Awliyā'', *Ishraq* 3 (2012), pp. 138–58.

— *Jami* (New Delhi: Oxford University Press, 2013).

Bertel's, Evgenii, 'Literatura na persidskom jazyke v Srednej Azii', *Sovetskoe Vostokvedenie* 5 (1948), pp. 199–228.

Bruijn, Johannes T.P. de, *Persian Sufi Poetry. An Introduction to the Mystical Use of Classical Persian Poems* (Richmond: Curzon Press, 1997).

Colton, Charles Caleb, *Lacon: or, Many Things in a Few Words* (London: Longman, Orme, Brown, Green, & Longmans, 1837).

Devereux, Robert, 'Judgment of Two Languages. *Muḥākamat al-lughatain* by Mīr 'Alī Shīr Nawā'ī. Introduction, translation and notes', *The Muslim World* 54, no. 4 (1964), pp. 270–87 and *The Muslim World* 55, no. 1 (1965), pp. 28–45.

Dowlatshāh Samarqandi, *Tazkerat al-sho'arā'*, ed. E.G. Browne (Tehran: Enteshārāt-e asātir, 1382/2003).

Dughlat, Mirza Haydar, *Tarikh-i-Rashidi: A History of the Khans of Moghulistan*, trans. Wheeler M. Thackston, 2 vols (Cambridge, MA: Harvard University, 1996).

Fāni (Navā'i), *Divān*, ed. Homāyun Farrokh, *Divān-e Amir 'Ali-Shir Navā'i 'Fāni'* (Tehran: Enteshārāt-e asātir, 1375/1996).

Hāfez, Khvāja Shams al-Din Mohammad, *Divān*, ed. P. Khānlari, 2 vols (Tehran: Khvārazmi, 1362/1983).

Hillman, Michael, 'Hafez's "Turk of Shiraz" again', *Iranian Studies* 8, no. 3 (1975), pp. 164–82.

Jāmi, 'Abd al-Rahmān, *Nafahāt al-ons*, ed. M. 'Ābedi (Tehran: Ettelā'āt, 1370/1991).

— *Divān*, ed. A. Afsahzād, 2 vols (Tehran: Mirās-e Maktub, 1378/1999).

— *Bahārestān*, ed. A. Afsahzād (Tehran: Mirās-e Maktub, 1379/2000).

Lingwood, Chad, *Politics, Poetry, and Sufism in Medieval Iran: New Perspective on Jami's* Salāmān va Absāl (Leiden: Brill, 2014).

Losensky, Paul, *Welcoming Fighānī: Imitation and Poetic Individuality in Safavid-Mughal ghazals* (Costa Mesa: Mazda, 1998).

— 'Jāmi i. Life and Works', *Encyclopaedia Iranica*, vol. XIV, fasc. 5 (2008), pp. 469–75).

Meisami, Julie S., *Structure and Meaning in Medieval Arabic and Persian Lyric Poetry* (London: Routledge Curzon, 2003).

— 'A life in poetry: Hāfiz's First Ghazal', in *The Necklace of the Pleiades*, ed. F. Lewis and S. Sharma (Amsterdam: Rozenberg, and West Lafayette: Purdue University Press, 2007), pp. 163–81.

Mirzoev, Abdulg'ani, 'Foniy va Hofiz', *O'zbek Tili Adabiyoti* (1966, No. 4), pp. 8–15.

— 'Alisher Navoiyning fors-tojik tilidagi meros haqida', *O'zbek Tili Adabiyoti* (1967, No. 2), pp. 13–21.

Navā'i, Mir 'Ali-Shir, 'Kolliyāt-e Navā'i'', Paris, Bibliothèque nationale de France [BNF], Ms. Supplément turc 316–317.

— *Majāles al-nafāyes*, Paris, BNF, Ms. Supplément turc 965.

— *Mahbub al-qolub*, ed. A.N. Kononov (Moscow-Leningrad: Akademii Nauk, 1948).

Navoiy, Alisher, *Mukammal asarlar to'plami*, 20 vols (Tashkent: Fan, 1987–2003).

Péri, Benedek, 'Mīr 'Alī-Šīr, Navāyī and the first ghazal of Hāfiz', in *'Alisher Navoiy va XXI asr' mavzudagi Respublika ilmiy nazariy materiallari*, ed. S. Sirojiddinov and A. Erkinov (Tashkent: Turon-Iqbol, 2018), pp. 176–83.

Sanā'i, Hakim Abu'l-Majd Majdud, *Divān*, ed. Mohammad-Taqi Modarres-e Razavi (Tehran: Ebn Sinā, 1380/2001).

Soucek, Priscilla, 'Hafez xii. Hafez and the visual arts', *Encyclopaedia Iranica*, vol. XI, fasc. 5 (2002), pp. 501–5.

Subtelny, Maria-Eva, 'A taste for the intricate: The Persian poetry of the late Timurid period', *Zeitschrift der Deutschen Morgenländischen Gesellchaft* 36, no. 1 (1986), pp. 56–79.

Thackston, W.M., *A Century of Princes. Sources on Timurid History and Art* (Cambridge, MA: The Aga Khan Program for Islamic Architecture, 1989).

Toutant, Marc, *Un empire de mots. Pouvoir, culture et soufisme à l'époque des derniers Timourides au miroir de la* Khamsa *de Mīr 'Alī Shīr Nawā'ī* (Leuven: Peeters, 2016).

Vohidov, Rahim, 'Xoja Hofiz Sheroziy va Alisher Navoiy', *O'zbek Tili va Adabiyoti* 1991 (No. 4), pp. 25–32.

Zipoli, Riccardo, *The Technique of the* Ǧawāb. *Replies by Nawā'ī to Ḥāfiẓ and Ǧāmī* (Venice: Cafoscarina, 1995).

6

A Man of Letters: Hoseyn Va‘ez Kashefi and his Persian Project

Maria Subtelny
(University of Toronto)

The culture wars in eastern Iran during the Timurid period were fought on a number of fronts – political, religious and linguistic. On the political front, legitimation based on Islamic values promoted by the Shari‘a-minded clerical classes competed with Chinggisid principles espoused by Turko-Mongolian military elites. In the case of religion, the challenges to Hanafi Sunni orthodoxy included both conservative Shi‘ite and popular messianic and millenarian movements. On the linguistic front, Persian vied with the promotion of the Eastern Turkic literary language by Timurid dynasts and their talented Turkic protégés. As for Arabic, it retained its prestige and importance, even though it had become increasingly confined to scholastic circles and the hard sciences. What of the Persian language? Long used for historical writing, diplomatics and poetry, it held its own, but some literary-minded individuals believed it needed a boost in order to address more immediately the needs of the contemporary Persian-speaking public.

Enter the polymath, preacher (*va‘ez*) and Sufi, Kamal al-Din Hoseyn b. ‘Ali, known as Kashefi (‘the Unveiler’) (d. 910/1504–5). Securing the patronage of the Timurid ruler Soltan-Hoseyn-e Bayqara (r. 1469–1506) and influential members of his court at Herat, most notably Mir ‘Ali-Shir Nava’i, Kashefi embarked on a ‘Persian project’ in which, by his own admission, he translated, synthesized, systematized and ‘borrowed from’ an impressive range of religious, literary, ethical and esoteric works in order to make them available to a sophisticated Persian readership. A prolific author, he composed almost 40 books, virtually all in Persian, ranging from religious topics, such as commentaries on the Qur’an (*Javaher al-tafsir, Mavaheb-e ‘aliya*) and the prophetic Traditions (*al-Resala al-‘aliya fi’l-ahadis al-nabaviya*), to treatises on epistolography (*Makhzan al-ensha*), Sufism (*Lobb-e lobab-e ma‘navi*) and the occult sciences (*Asrar-e qasemi*).[1] His contemporary, the Timurid historian Khvandamir, singled out seven in his biographical entry on him: *Javaher al-tafsir, Mavaheb-e ‘aliya*, *Rowzat al-shohada’*, *Anvar-e soheyli*, *Makhzan al-ensha*, *Akhlaq-e mohseni* and *Ekhteyarat [al-nojum]* or *Lavayeh al-qamar*.[2]

Despite the immense popularity of many of his works in the medieval and early modern Persianate world, Kashefi has been under-appreciated by Western scholarship conditioned to value only 'original' compositions. At best, he has been viewed as an imitator or compiler; at worst, as a plagiarist. Truth be told, by today's standards Kashefi would, in many respects, be considered a plagiarist. His *Akhlaq-e mohseni*, a prosimetrical work on the ethics of kingship, which cites copious lines of poetry without acknowledgement and lifts entire passages from earlier prose works, is a case in point. But according to the aesthetic criteria of his time and, indeed, that of the medieval Arabo-Persian world in general, he was not, by virtue of the fact that he improved on the originals he borrowed from. Textual mis/appropriation through rewording and reorganization had been condoned by certain Greek authors, such as the fifth-century Sophist Hippias of Elis, who stated that 'after collecting the most important of these points on the same subject matter, I shall make them my own with new and complex language'.[3] A similar view was held by medieval Persian rhetoricians. The authoritative early thirteenth-century writer Shams-e Qeys, whom Kashefi cites almost verbatim in his own work on rhetorics entitled *Badaye' al-afkar fi sanaye' al-ash'ar*, stated that if a poet produced a more successful version of an idea, he was the one entitled to get credit for it:

> Experts in semantics (*arbab-e ma'ani*) have said that when an idea (*ma'ni*) occurs to a poet, and he dresses it up in infelicitious expressions and coarse wording, while another appropriates (*fara girad*) that same idea and presents it in beautiful words and pleasant expressions, then the latter is more worthy of it, and that idea belongs to him, whereas the former only has the merit of being the first [to come up with it].[4]

In this chapter, I would like to demonstrate the ways in which Kashefi pursued his project of translating, adapting and rewriting the works of his predecessors by focusing on a representative selection of the almost 40 books credited to him.[5] As more in-depth research is being conducted on individual works by Kashefi, it is becoming increasingly clear that they present a complex puzzle. Most recently, Christine van Ruymbeke has demonstrated in her analytical study of his *Anvar-e soheyli* that it was anything but an imitation of the twelfth-century Persian translation of *Kalila va Demna* by Nasrollah Monshi; it is, in fact, a complete rewriting of it.[6] As for the works that have been labelled 'compilative', these were often based on a dizzying array of sources that Kashefi reorganized into a seamless new structure. And the works that were purportedly translations from Arabic or based on Arabic works were reworked in such a way that it is difficult to call them translations, although we have to bear in mind that the medieval understanding of 'translation' (*tarjoma*) never implied faithful adherence to the original.

I will begin my overview with a discussion of several works that support my contention regarding Kashefi's Persian project and that also illustrate the complexity of his relationship to his sources, which – although he sometimes cites them – cannot always be readily identified.

A work of Kashefi's that was based largely on Arabic sources or their Persian translations was *Lavayeh al-qamar* (completed in 878/1473–74), which dealt with hemerology, or elective astrology, also known as *Ekhteyarat al-nojum* – the only book of his septet on astrology, *Sab'a-ye kashefiya*, that appears to have survived, if in fact the other volumes were ever completed.[7] Kashefi mentions over 20 books that he consulted in compiling this work.[8] Among them are the *Ekhteyarat-e 'ala'iya* (=*al-Ahkam al-'ala'iyya men al-a'lam al-sama'iyya*) of Fakhr al-Din Razi (d. 1210) and his *al-Serr al-maktum fi mokhatabat al-nojum* (The hidden secret of invocations of the stars) – originally in Arabic and translated into Persian in ca. 1236.[9] Others are *Rowdat al-monajjemin* by Shahmardan b. Abu'l-Kheyr Razi (eleventh century); *Mojmal al-osul fi ahkam al-nojum* by Kaya Kushyar (=Kushyar b. Labban b. Bashahri al-Jili), ca. 1030; *Nokat fi ma yasehhu wa ma la yasehhu men ahkam al-nojum* by Farabi (d. 950); *Kefayat al-ta'lim fi sena'at al-tanjim* by Zahir al-Din Mohammad Ghaznavi (twelfth century); *Ekhteyarat* by Mohyi al-Din al-Maghrebi (ca. 1290); *Ekhteyarat* by Abu Ja'far Mohammad b. Ayyub b. al-Hasib al-Tabari (ninth–tenth century); Nasir al-Din Tusi's (d. 1273) commentary on the *Karpos* of Ptolemy; *Jame'-e shahi* by 'Abd al-Jalil Sijzi (d. ca. 998); *al-Tafhim* by Abu Reyhan Biruni (d. 1048); and *Serr al-asrar* by Abu Bakr Mohammad b. Zakariyah Razi (d. 925). If this is a compilative work then it is, to cite Živa Vesel, 'a compilation of the highest quality, which perpetuates erudition of great breadth in an era in which Islamic science was viewed as being in decline'.[10]

Another work of Kashefi's that was purportedly based on Arabic sources is his 'Alid martyrology, *Rowzat al-shohada'* (The garden of the martyrs) (completed in 908/1502–3), thanks to which he became famously 'Shi'ite' during the Safavid period, as it served as the quasi-canonical textual basis for the commemorative practice of *rowza-khvani*. Kashefi mentions two books in the text: *Rowdat al-Eslam* by Qadi Sadid al-Din Jirufti and the *Seyar* by Imam Esma'il Khvarazmi.[11] However, neither of these sources, which most likely belonged to the *maqtal* genre that recounts the violent deaths of members of the Prophet Mohammad's family, can be identified. What is possible is that Kashefi was citing them from another unnamed and unidentified work that he used as his main source, something he was wont to do in other cases. For example, in the *Akhlaq-e mohseni*, a Mirror for Princes, he cites as his source for a particular anecdote al-Sallami's *Ta'rikh wulat Khorasan*, a tenth-century Arabic history of the governors of Khorasan. He clearly could not have consulted the original, which was long lost by his time, and not being familiar with the rules of the *Chicago Manual of Style* that strongly discourages the practice, he simply cited it from another source that cites it – the *Makarem-e akhlaq* of Nishaburi (d. 598/1201–2), who may himself have been citing it from yet another source.

Kashefi's *Asrar-e qasemi*, a short treatise on the occult sciences (completed in 907/1501–2), purports to be a translation into Persian of two Arabic works.[12] Although in the introduction Kashefi enumerates the traditional five occult sciences of *kimiya*, *limiya*, *himiya*, *simiya* and *rimiya*, the first letters of which formed an anagram that spelled out the Arabic phrase *kollohu serrun* (It is all a secret), he in fact treats only the sciences of *simiya*, or illusionism, and *rimiya*, or conjuring.[13] The two Arabic works are *'Oyun al-haqa'eq wa idah al-tara'eq* (The sources of truths and the exposition of the methods [of attaining them]) by Abu'l-Qasem Ahmad al-Simawi, and *Sehr al-'oyun* (The bewitchment of the eyes) by Abu 'Abdollah al-Maghrebi, which he says was also known as *Ketab Ebn Hallaj* (The book of Ebn Hallaj).[14] Abu'l-Qasem Ahmad al-Simawi was a well-known author of mid thirteenth-century Mamluk Egypt, who wrote principally on alchemy. As for Abu 'Abdollah al-Maghrebi, he is most probably the North African occultist Mohammad ebn al-Hajj al-Telemsani (d. 737/1336), the author of *Shomus al-anwar wa konuz al-asrar* (The suns of lights and the treasures of secrets).[15] He is not known to have composed a work entitled *Sehr al-'oyun*, but the alternate title given to his work – *Ketab Ebn Hallaj* – must be a corruption of *Ketab Ebn al-Hajj* (The book of Ebn al-Hajj [al-Telemsani]), as his *Shomus al-anwar* was popularly known.[16]

Kashefi explains that he translated al-Simawi's and al-Maghrebi's books into Persian because the Arabic terminology was too difficult to understand and hence the 'benefits' (*favayed*) of the sciences of *simiya* and *rimiya* did not reach a Persian readership.[17] However, the degree to which Kashefi actually based his translation on the two aforementioned Arabic works is difficult to gauge, as he says he supplemented them with many other, mainly Arabic, sources.[18] A further complicating factor is uncertainty about the authorship of *Sehr al-'oyun*, and whether it can be identified as al-Maghrebi's *Shomus al-anwar*. Some manuscripts of *Asrar-e qasemi* are referred to by the title *Sehr al-'oyun* and described as being a translation by Kashefi, which suggests it may have been regarded as an epitome of al-Simawi's *'Oyun al-haqa'eq*, in which case the title *Sehr al-'oyun* might be interpreted to mean 'The magic of the *'Oyun*'.[19] In the final analysis what is important for our present purposes is that, in his *Asrar-e qasemi*, Kashefi translated and synthesized a number of Arabic works in two fields of the occult sciences. Moreover, his short treatise enjoyed a long afterlife, serving as the basis of a greatly expanded work that was compiled in the early seventeenth century during the high Safavid period. Although this interpolated version added chapters on those occult sciences that Kashefi himself had not treated – chiefly *limiya*, or the science of talismans – it retained the title *Asrar-e qasemi*.[20]

Besides translating seminal texts from Arabic into Persian, Kashefi also took it upon himself to further Persianize existing Persian works. By his time, the narrative genre of choice in Persian literature had become prosimetrum, which was based on the regular alternation of prose and verse. Earlier authors, following the dictates of their period, were wont to include primarily Arabic verses with the addition of Persian ones. Kashefi picked an outstanding candidate in this respect to Persianize: Nasrollah Monshi's twelfth-century Persian translation of the Arabic *Kalila wa Demna* by Ebn al-Moqaffa', which he reorganized and rewrote as *Anvar-e soheyli* (possibly composed in 905/1499–1500), creating a new prosimetrical work of great intricacy, or, as he puts it, 'I clothed [Nasrollah Monshi's translation] in new garb (*lebas-e now*)'.[21] He proposed a Persian origin for the tales instead of the legendary Indian one, and Persianized the framework by introducing the precepts of the mythical Iranian king Hushang as the titles of the 14 chapters in lieu of the Arabic headings retained by Nasrollah Monshi.[22] Furthermore, he substituted Persian verses for the many Arabic ones cited. In the introduction to the work, he stated that he planned to confine the Arabic citations to verses of the Qur'an, prophetic traditions and well-known maxims and proverbs; otherwise, he said he would refrain from citing lines of Arabic poetry (*mota'arrez-e esbat-e abyat-e 'arabi namigardad*).[23] Instead he says 'I decorated the pages of [the book's] discourse (*sokhan*) with the gems of Persian poetic verses (*be-javaher-e ash'ar-e farsi*), which like [embedded] gold and pearls create the effect of inlay work (*sefat-e tarsi' darad*)'.[24] It is no wonder that Kashefi's rewriting of *Kalila va Demna* became more famous in the Persianate world than Nasrollah's original translation, making it one of his most widely copied works.

Likewise, Kashefi's work on poetics entitled *Badaye' al-afkar fi sanaye' al-ash'ar* (composed ca. 894/1488–89)[25] was based on two earlier Persian works – the *Hada'eq al-sehr fi daqa'eq al-she'r* by Rashid al-Din Vatvat (composed ca. 1150) and *al-Mo'jam fi ma'ayer ash'ar al-'Ajam* (composed ca. 1232–33) by Shams-e Qeys al-Razi. Although Kashefi does not explicitly name his sources, he clearly updated them, so to speak, substituting Persian poetic examples for the Arabic ones cited by the latter two writers and in fact greatly expanding the number of examples.[26] He also summarized and streamlined the organization, jettisoning the more scholarly structure of *al-Mo'jam*, which had been composed in the tradition of the Arabic literary sciences, and turning the *Badaye' al-afkar* into what Marta Simidchieva has called a 'manual for the connoisseur of poetry', designed to assist him/her in the appreciation of the poetic craft in terms of rhetorical devices and the like.[27] Elegantly concise, with copious illustrations from Persian poetry, the *Badaye' al-afkar* would have been a handy resource for the aspiring Timurid-era poet or the would-be participant in a literary salon. It was dedicated to a Timurid commander by the name of Shoja' al-Din Amir Sayyed Hoseyn, whom I have not been able to identify positively.

Kashefi's *Akhlaq-e mohseni* (completed in 907/1501–2), dedicated to the Timurid ruler Soltan-Hoseyn-e Bayqara Mirza and addressed to his wayward son, Abu'l-Mohsen Mirza, is a work in the tradition of kingly advice. It was based in part on two distinguished Persian predecessors, notably Nasir al-Din Tusi's *Akhlaq-e naseri* (composed in 633/1235) and Jalal al-Din Davani's *Akhlaq-e jalali* (composed ca. 879/1474). But unlike the latter two authors, who closely followed the tripartite Aristotelian structure of Ethics, Economics and Politics, Kashefi focused on political ethics and the moral qualities required of kings. He also turned the work into a prosimetrical composition, replete with anecdotes, which, like the *Anvar-e soheyli*, included the citation of copious lines of Persian poetry, almost invariably without attribution.

The poets Kashefi cites most frequently were the classics of a bygone age: Nezami (especially his *Makhzan al-asrar*), Amir Khosrow (especially his *Matla' al-anvar*), Sa'di (especially his *Bustan*), Rumi (usually from his *Masnavi*) and Hafez. Nezami and Amir Khosrow were greatly favoured by Timurid-era litterateurs, while Rumi was Kashefi's own preferred poet. Others he cites constitute a long list; likewise, most are pre-fifteenth century: Khaqani, 'Attar, Mo'ezzi, Ebn Yamin, Salman Savaji, Khvaju Kermani, Kamal Khojandi, Homam Tabrizi, Amir Hoseyni, Baba Afzal Kashani, Abu Sa'id-e Abu'l-Kheyr, and others. The authors Kashefi draws upon provide an insight into his literary universe, and we may assume also that of his contemporary Herati Persian audience. His grasp of the Persian poetic corpus is uncanny. He seems to have the appropriate Persian verses at his fingertips and he employs a number of stylistic strategies to integrate them into the narrative, ranging from slightly altering the originals to fit the context, to changing the sequence of lines, and even combining lines by different poets writing in the same metre.[28]

But Kashefi's borrowings were not restricted to poetic verses; they also included entire prose passages taken from the works of earlier authors. These were often lifted verbatim or almost verbatim, and rarely with attribution, from such works as the *Makarem-e akhlaq* of Nishaburi (d. 598/1201–2), 'Owfi's *Javame' al-hekayat* (composed in 625/1228), Qazvini's *al-Mo'jam fi asar moluk al-'Ajam* (composed in 684/1285), Mo'in al-Joveyni's *Negarestan* (composed in 735/1334–35) and the *Zakhirat al-moluk* of Hamadani (d. 786/1385). In some cases, the interpolated passages also contained verses, which were interpolated together with the prose text in which they were embedded. Did this constitute plagiarism? Evidently not in the minds of his contemporaries.

Judging by the praise it received in its own time and the large number of extant manuscript copies, Kashefi's most popular work was his Qur'an commentary *Mavaheb-e 'aliya* (completed in 899/1494). It presents a moderately esoteric interpretation of the scriptural text which is illustrated by means of citations from Persian mystical poets like 'Abdollah Ansari, Sana'i, 'Attar, Jami and especially Rumi. Although Kashefi was not the first person to use poetry to comment on the meaning of a Qur'anic verse, to quote Kristin Sands, who wrote a pioneering article on the *Mavaheb-e 'aliya*, '[he] took the incorporation of poetry to a new level, rarely writing more than a page … without citing a few lines'.[29] More importantly, he translates the Qur'anic verses he is commenting on into Persian without citing the Arabic original.

To provide a random example, in his commentary on Surah 7 (*al-A'raf*), verse 54, Kashefi provides a loosely literal Persian translation of the Arabic, which begins with the statement that God created the heavens and earth in six days. He cites the opinion, supposedly expressed in *al-Tebyan*,[30] that for God each of these 24-hour periods was the equivalent of a thousand years (Q 22:47) and he explains that, despite his great power, God created the universe 'in stages' (*be-tadrij*) without haste, as epitomized by the Arabic proverb 'Haste is from the devil and deliberateness from the Merciful' (*al-'ajala men al-sheytan wa'l-ta'anni men al-Rahman*).[31] He supports this rather novel interpretation (which turns out to be Rumi's) with verses from the *Masnavi* that contain an allusion to the aforementioned Qur'anic verse:

> The devil may be all hurry and haste
> But patience and calculation are [from] the grace of God.
>
> Creation issued from God with deliberateness (*ta'anni*)
> Until in six days the earth and celestial spheres [appeared].
>
> Otherwise He would have been able, with the command 'Be and it is'
> To bring a hundred earths and heavens into existence.
>
> This deliberateness (*ta'anni*) is for the sake of instructing you.
> Be patient, take your time (*dir ay*) with anything you do, and stay focused![32]

Few readers will have noticed that these verses are not only not all sequential but are taken from different books of the *Masnavi* – the first from book 5, line 2572 and the second and third from book 3, lines 3500–501. As for the last line, the two hemistiches are themselves taken from different books of the *Masnavi* – the first from book 3, line 3506 and the second from book 2, line 3145.[33] Moreover, the second hemistich has been altered by Kashefi to provide a more contextually appropriate motivational message for his readers: instead of Rumi's *sabr kon kan-ast tasbih-e dorost* ('Be patient for that is the true glorification [of God]'), we have *sabr kon dar kar dir ay va dorost* ('Be patient, take your time with anything you do, and stay focused!').

Likewise, in his commentary on 40 prophetic Traditions, entitled *al-Resala al-'aliya fi'l-ahadis al-nabaviya* (his very first dated work, completed in 875/1470–71), although he provides the Arabic of a given prophetic tradition, he translates it into Persian, explaining its meaning and illustrating it by means of poetic verses, maxims and anecdotes, almost always in Persian.

In the conclusion to *al-Resala al-'aliya*, Kashefi explains his modus operandi by comparing his work to a dervish cloak (*moraqqa'*) that he says he has stitched together from patches taken from everywhere with what he refers to as 'the thread of appropriateness' (*be-reshta-ye monasabat*).[34] The metaphor is apt, as it alludes to Kashefi's Sufi proclivities as well as to his ability to weave together passages taken from the works of others. In verses following this telling statement, he calls himself a *tarjoman* – a term that can mean both translator and interpreter – a function that he says he has performed 'in all honestly' (*az sar-e rasti*):

As for how we have fashioned this fresh garland (*nakhl-e tar*),[35]
Do not imagine that we have done it all by ourselves.

We have taken provisions from every corner,
And gleaned kernels from every harvest.

We have picked fruits from every garden,
And begged at every treasury.

In assembling the words of the wise of heart (*saheb-delan*)
We have become an honest interpreter (*tarjoman*).

Whatever they have said thanks to their inspiration, we have repeated
Whatever pearls [of meaning] they presented us with, we have strung together.[36]

In the last verse, Kashefi deploys the stock trope of the pearl which symbolizes the ideas or images (*ma'ani*) developed by others, whom he refers to as *saheb-delan*, or 'the wise of heart' – oftentimes a designation for Sufis – whose poetical mastery he attributes to inspiration from the Unseen world (*gheyb*). Extending the metaphor, he states that his own contribution has been to string these pearls together – a pearl necklace is implied – which is of his own fashioning even though the individual pearls are not. True to form, Kashefi borrowed the second line, 'We have taken provisions from every corner/And gleaned kernels from every harvest', from Sa'di's *Bustan*, which he adapted slightly to suit the present context.[37]

The foregoing should not be interpreted to mean that Kashefi was unoriginal or that he was a plagiarist in the modern sense. His is anything but a copy-and-paste technique. In fact, he believed that he was adding value to the works of others by reassembling them into a coherent structure. In several of his works he cites a verse that illustrates his appreciation of the nature of his particular contribution. In the *Akhlaq-e mohseni* he cites the verse to introduce a long citation from Hamadani's *Zakhirat al-moluk*:

When a bouquet of flowers is tied together with straw
The beauty of its components is enhanced.[38]

And in the introduction to the *Anvar-e soheyli* he cites a variant of the same first hemistich to introduce his citation of so many anecdotes, maxims and proverbs in this work:

Even a bouquet of flowers is tied together with straw.[39]

The implication is that Kashefi's own literary contribution is tantamount to the strand of straw that is used to bind together a bouquet, the flowers of which would severally not have the same visual impact. By the same token, Kashefi is making a show of humility before his literary predecessors, whose works are so many flowers whose beauty he enhances by bundling them together, so to speak. There is no doubt from the foregoing that Kashefi was fully aware of his synthesizing skill and at the same time mindful of the literary appropriation in which he was engaging.

Why is Kashefi, this Persian man of letters, important? I maintain that he succeeded in reviving, renewing and updating an entire range of works in both Persian and Arabic that might otherwise have gone out of circulation in the eastern Islamic world by the late fifteenth century. Most of his identifiable sources date from the thirteenth to fourteenth centuries and had become either too difficult for a contemporary Persian reader, too Arabic or simply too old-fashioned to suit the tastes of a Timurid-era public. Kashefi repackaged these in a way that made them accessible without dumbing them down, to use a vernacular expression. He knew that by refashioning and reorganizing the works of his predecessors, he was enhancing their usefulness to a Persian readership. In fact, he often reiterates the idea of the 'benefits' that accrue to his audience from his culling from the works of others. In the introduction to the *Badaye' al-afkar* he states:

> I have been a gleaner of kernels (*khusha-chin*)[40] from the harvest of the most learned and a borrower (*moqtabes*)[41] of rays of knowledge from the most accomplished litterateurs and erudite scholars, and to the best of my ability I have helped myself to all sorts of benefits (*anva'-e favayed*) from the fruits of their bountiful tables.[42]

And it will be recalled that he composed his *Asrar-e qasemi*, supposedly as a translation from Arabic works, so that 'every sincere seeker and confidant of the secrets of spiritual subtleties will be able to derive benefit (*fayeda*) in accordance with his aptitude (*este'dad*) and degree of spiritual realization (*estehqaq*)'.[43] Thanks to his ability to synthesize his sources, his literary flair and prodigious memory, he managed to rework, transform and, in most cases, surpass the originals on which he drew. Almost all of Kashefi's works made a lasting impression on the culture of the Safavid period and beyond, including the Persianate cultures of Central Asia, Mughal India and even Ottoman Turkey.

Notes:

1. For a list of his works in chronological order of composition, see my entry in *The Encyclopaedia of Islam, Three (Online)*, s.v. 'Ḥusayn Vā'iẓ Kāshifī', as well as an earlier entry in *Encyclopaedia Iranica*, s.v. 'Kāšefi, Kamāl-al-Din Ḥosayn Wā'eẓ', where his works are listed in alphabetical order.
2. Gheyās al-Din Khvāndamir, *Tārikh-i Habib al-seyar fi akhbār afrād-e bashar*, vol. IV, p. 345.
3. Marianina Olcott, 'Ancient and modern notions of plagiarism', p. 1048.
4. Shams al-Din Mohammad b. Qeys al-Rāzi, *al-Mo'jam fi ma'āyer ash'ār al-'Ajam*, p. 403. Kamāl al-Din Hoseyn b. 'Ali, Vā'ez Kāshefi, *Badāye' al-afkār fi sanāye' al-ash'ār*, pp. 167–68; cited by Marta Simidchieva, 'Imitation and innovation in Timurid poetics', p. 519, no. 41.
5. For a listing, see Maria Eva Subtelny, 'Husain Va'iz-i Kashifi: Polymath, popularizer, and preserver', pp. 464–65.
6. See Christine van Ruymbeke, *Kāshefi's Anvār-e sohayli.*
7. See Sergei Tourkin and Živa Vesel, 'The contribution of Husayn Va'iz-i Kashifi to the transmission of astrological texts', pp. 589–99. It was composed for the Timurid vizier Majd al-Din Mohammad Khvāfi (d. 899/1494).
8. According to Tourkin and Vesel, 'Contribution of Husayn Va'iz-i Kāshifī', pp. 592–96 and Živa Vesel, 'Le *Lavâ'eḥ al-qamar:* Un traité d'astrologie de Ḥoseyn Vâ'eẓ Kâšefi', pp. 712–15.
9. Živa Vesel, 'The Persian translation of Fakhr al-Din Rāzi's *al-Sirr al-maktūm*', pp. 14–16.
10. 'une compilation de grande qualité, représentative d'une époque qui voit la science islamique sur le déclin, mais qui perpetue l'érudition de grande envergure'. Vesel, '*Lavâ'eḥ al-qamar*', p. 714. The work was very popular; abridgements of it and translations into Chaghatay Turkish and Ottoman were made in the eighteenth century – see Tourkin and Vesel, 'Contribution of Husayn Va'iz-i Kāshifī', p. 596.
11. Kamāl al-Din Hoseyn b. 'Ali, Vā'ez Kāshefi, *Rowzat al-shohadā'.*
12. I have consulted two manuscript copies of *Asrār-e qāsemi* in the Majles Library in Tehran, because the Bombay lithograph editions represent a later expanded version of the work: Mss. 12559/2, p. 55 and 12568, p. 6. For a detailed discussion, see my forthcoming article 'The occult sciences and confessional ambiguity in Late Timurid Iran: Kāshifī's *Asrār-i qāsimī* and its Safavid afterlife'.
13. Kāshefi, *Asrār-e qāsemi*, Ketābkhāna-ye majles-e shurā-ye eslāmi, Mss. 12559/2, p. 55 and 12568, p. 6.
14. Kāshefi, *Asrār-e qāsemi*, 12559/2, p. 54 and 12568, p. 5.
15. For these two authors, see Manfred Ullmann, *Die Natur- und Geheimwissenschaften im Islam*, pp. 391–92 and pp. 235–36.
16. For a full discussion, see my forthcoming 'Occult sciences and confessional ambiguity'.
17. Kāshefi, *Asrār-e qāsemi*, 12559/2, p. 54 and 12568, p. 5.
18. Kāshefi, *Asrār-e qāsemi*, 12559/2, p. 55 and 12568, p. 6.
19. As in one of the manuscripts under discussion – see Kāshefi, *Asrār-e qāsemi*, 12568, p. 6.
20. This expanded version is represented by the Bombay lithograph edition: Kāshefī, *Asrār-e qāsemi* (Bombay, 1302/1885).

21. Kamāl al-Din Hoseyn b. 'Ali, Vā'ez Kāshefi, *Anvār-e soheyli yā Kalila va Demna-ye Kāshefi*, p. 8.
22. See van Ruymbeke, *Kāshefi's Anvār-e sohayli,* pp. 333–34 and pp. 59–60.
23. This is not entirely accurate, but certainly the number of lines of Arabic poetry was reduced to a minimum.
24. Kāshefi, *Anvār-e soheyli*, p. 10. My translation differs from van Ruymbeke, *Kāshefi's Anvār-e sohayli*, p. 43.
25. As the exact date is not known, this is the date of the earliest extant manuscript copy.
26. Simidchieva, 'Imitation and innovation', p. 518.
27. Ibid., pp. 519–20.
28. This topic will be covered in my forthcoming edition and translation of the *Akhlāq-e mohseni.*
29. Kristin Zahra Sands, 'On the popularity of Husayn Va'iz-i Kashifi's *Mavāhib-i 'aliyya*', p. 471.
30. The reference could not be located.
31. Kamāl al-Din Hoseyn b. 'Ali, Vā'ez Kāshefi, *Mavāheb-e 'aliya yā Tafsir-e hoseyni (be-fārsi)*, vol. I, pp. 449–50.
32. Ibid., p. 450.
33. Jalāl al-Din Mohammad Rumi, *Masnavi-ye ma'navi.*
34. Kamāl al-Din Hoseyn b. 'Ali, Vā'ez Kāshefi, *al-Resāla al-'aliya fi'l-ahādis al-nabaviya*, p. 372.
35. The definition of *nakhlband* provided in Zenker, *Türkisch-arabisch-persisches Handwörterbuch*, as 'garland' or 'festoon, a decoration' fits the present context.
36. Kāshefi, *al-Resāla al-'aliya*, p. 373.

    Bedin guna kin nakhl-e tar basta im
    Mapendār kaz khvish bar basta im.
    Za har gusha'i tusha'i borda im
    Za har khermani khusha'i borda im
    Za har bāgh yak miva āvarda im
    Gadā'i za har makhzani karda im
    Be-jam'-e sokhan-hā-ye sāheb-delān
    Shodim za sar-e rāsti tarjomān
    Za gheybat āncheh goftand ān gofta im
    Dorri-rā keh dādand ān softa im.

37. Sa'di, *Bustān*, p. 11, line 4: *Tamatto' za har gusha'i yāftam/Za har khermani khusha'i yāftam*. Kashifi's statement is reminiscent of Nezāmi's exposition of his own method, as he states in his *Sharafnāma*:

    I have chosen the best from every book
    And extracted the kernel from every rind/volume.
    Words upon words, I have amassed a treasure,
    And from all of that I have made an epitome (*sar-jomla*).

    See Nezāmi Ganja'i, *Sharafnāma*, p. 106, lines 21–22. Cited in Christine van Ruymbeke, 'Nezami's giant brain tackles Eskandar's *Sharafnameh*', p. 71, with a slightly different reading.

38. Kamāl al-Din Hoseyn b. ʻAli, Vāʻez Kāshefi, *Akhlāq-e mohseni*, Berlin, Staatsbibliothek, Ms. Diez A quart. 77, fol. 107r: *dasta-ye gol chu bar geyā bandand/zivari-ye digarash beyafzāyand*. The verse is unidentified.
39. Kāshefi, *Anvār-e soheyli*, p. 10: *bar dasta-ye gol niz bebandand geyā-rā.*
40. Interestingly enough, *khusha-chin* can also mean a plagiarist!
41. *Moqtabes* can also mean a person who cites from the literary works of others.
42. Kāshefi, *Badāyeʻ al-afkār*, p. 69.
43. Kāshefi, *Asrār-e qāsemi*, 12559/2, p. 54 and 12568, p. 5.

Bibliography:

Kāshefi, Kamāl al-Din Hoseyn b. 'Ali, Vā'ez, *Akhlāq-e mohseni*, Berlin, Staatsbibliothek, Ms. Diez A quart. 77.

— *Asrār-e qāsemi*, Tehran, Ketābkhāna-ye majles-e shurā-ye eslāmi, Mss. 12559/2 and 12568.

— *Mavāheb-e 'aliya yā Tafsīr-e hoseyni (be-fārsi)*, ed. Mohammad Rezā Jalāli Nāyeni, 4 vols (Tehran: Eqbāl, 1317–29/1938–50).

— *al-Resāla al-'aliya fi al-ahādis al-nabaviya*, ed. Sayyed Jalāl al-Din Mohaddes (Tehran: Bongāh-e tarjoma va nashr-e ketāb, 1344/1965).

— *Anvār-e soheyli yā Kalila va Demna-ye Kāshefi* (Tehran: Amir Kabir, 1362/1983).

— *Badāye' al-afkār fi sanāye' al-ash'ār*, ed. Mir Jalāl al-Din Kazzāzi (Tehran: Nashr-e markaz, 1369/1990).

— *Rowzat al-shohadā'*, ed. Āyatollāh Hājj Sheykh Abu'l-Hasan Sha'rāni, Reprinted edn (Tehran: Enteshārāt-e eslāmiya, 1379/2000–2001).

Khvāndamir, Gheyās al-Din b. Homām al-Din al-Hoseyni, *Tārikh-e Habīb al-seyar fi akhbār afrād-e bashar*, ed. Jalāl al-Din Homā'i, 4 vols (Tehran: Khayyām, 1333/1954-55; 3rd reprint, 1362/1984).

Nezāmi Ganja'i, *Sharafnāma*, ed. Behruz Sarvatiyān (Tehran: Amir Kabir, 1386/2007).

Olcott, Marianina, 'Ancient and modern notions of plagiarism: A study of concepts of intellectual property in classical Greece', *Journal of the Copyright Society of the U.S.A.* 49, no. 2 (2002), pp. 1047–52.

Rumi, Jalāl al-Din Mohammad, *Masnavi-ye ma'navi*, ed. and trans. Reynold A. Nicholson, six books in eight volumes (London: Luzac, 1925–40; reprinted edn vols 1–6, 1985).

van Ruymbeke, Christine, *Kāshefi's Anvār-e sohayli: Rewriting Kalila and Dimna in Timurid Herat* (Leiden: Brill, 2016).

— 'Nezami's giant brain tackles Eskandar's *Sharafnameh:* The authorial voice of the poet-scholar-rewriter', in *The Coming of the Mongols: The Idea of Iran*, vol. 7, ed. David O. Morgan and Sarah Stewart (London: I.B. Tauris, 2018), pp. 69–94.

Sa'di, *Bustān*, ed. Nurollāh Irānparast (Tehran: Dānesh, 1352/1973).

Sands, Kristin Zahra, 'On the popularity of Husayn Va'iz-i Kashifi's *Mavāhib-i 'aliyya*: A Persian commentary on the Qur'an', *Iranian Studies* 36, no. 4 (2003), pp. 469–83.

Shams al-Din Mohammad b. Qeys al-Rāzi, *al-Mo'jam fi ma'āyer ash'ār al-'Ajam*, ed. Sirus Shamisā (Tehran: Enteshārāt-e ferdows, 1373/1994–95).

Simidchieva, Marta, 'Imitation and innovation in Timurid poetics: Kashifi's *Badāyi' al-afkār* and its precedessors, *al-Mu'jam* and *Ḥadā'iq al-siḥr*', *Iranian Studies* 36, no. 4 (2003), pp. 509–30.

Subtelny, Maria Eva, 'Husain Va'iz-i Kashifi: Polymath, popularizer, and preserver', *Iranian Studies* 36, no. 4 (2003), pp. 463–67.

— 'A late medieval Persian *summa* on ethics: Kashifi's *Akhlāq-i muhsinī*', *Iranian Studies* 36, no. 4 (2003), pp. 601–14.

— 'Kāšefi, Kamāl-al-Din Ḥosayn Wā'eẓ', *Encyclopaedia Iranica*, vol. XV, fasc. 6 (2012), pp. 658–61. Online at http://www.iranicaonline.org/articles/kasefi_kamal [accessed 7 April 2019].

— 'Ḥusayn Vā'iẓ Kāshifī', *The Encyclopaedia of Islam, Three (Online)*. Online at https://referenceworks.brillonline.com/entries/encyclopaedia-of-islam-3/husayn-vaiz-kashifi-COM_30585?s.num=0&s.f.s2_parent=s.f.book.encyclopaedia-of-islam-3&s.q=Kashefi [accessed 7 April 2019].

— 'The occult sciences and confessional ambiguity in late Timurid Iran: Kāshifī's *Asrār-i qāsimī* and its Safavid afterlife' (forthcoming).

Tourkin, Sergei, and Živa Vesel, 'The contribution of Husayn Va'iz-i Kashifi to the transmission of astrological texts', *Iranian Studies* 36, no. 4 (2003), pp. 589–99.

Ullmann, Manfred, *Die Natur- und Geheimwissenschaften im Islam, Handbuch der Orientalistik*, Abteilung 1, Ergänzungsband 6, Abschnitt 2 (Leiden: Brill, 1972).

Vesel, Živa, 'Le *Lavâ'eḥ al-qamar:* Un traité d'astrologie de Ḥoseyn Vâ'eẓ Kâšefi', in *Proceedings of the Second European Conference of Iranian Studies held in Bamberg, 30th September to 4th October 1991, by the Societas Iranologica Europaea*, ed. Bert G. Fragner et al. (Rome: Istituto Italiano per Il Medio ed Estremo Oriente, 1995), pp. 711–18.

— 'The Persian translation of Fakhr al-Din Rāzi's *al-Sirr al-maktūm* ('The occult secret') for Iltutmish', in *Confluence of Cultures: French Contributions to Indo-Persian Studies*, ed. Françoise 'Nalini' Delvoye (New Delhi: Manohar Centre for Human Sciences; Tehran: Institut Français de Recherche en Iran, 1994), pp. 14–22.

7

The Timurid Book: *golshan-e naqsh-o tazhib* A Garden of Painting and Illumination

Eleanor Sims

In memory of Ernst, as always and without whom...

I have been toiling in the Timurid garden for a significant number of decades. That this is so is entirely due to my late and much-missed spouse, for it was he who first suggested that I step eastward from my study of Franco-Flemish illuminated manuscripts of the fourteenth and fifteenth century and look, instead, at the arts of the Eastern book: enter the Timurid garden, so to speak. I did direct myself eastward; and it is only recently that I have begun to look back, to consider how the Eastern and Western gardens might share some of their most distinguishing features.[1]

Primary is that the Timurid garden, like all living things, requires continuous tending. For it has grown since 1967 – not uncontrollably but very greatly: much work has been done since that date, and many different issues now animate our study, within the broader confines of the fifteenth century in the history of Iran. The Timurid book, inside which most Timurid painting is actually found, offers a special example of the visual arts in this Eastern world.

None would dispute that, at its finest, it is a supreme example of 'the taste for the intricate', as Maria Subtelny so well expressed it, more than three decades ago.[2] But it is also a dual exemplar of an art: fine fifteenth-century Eastern volumes virtually always function together with another paramount Timurid art, texts of all kinds, especially of *belles-lettres*. This is in some contradistinction to so many other small, intricately patterned Timurid objects, for instance, Ologh Beg's beautiful little wooden casket,[3] its finely carved ornament clearly emanating from the pen-drawn designs made in contemporary workshops for so many potential purposes,[4] starting with the non-pictorial aspects of the finest volumes in this period. Indeed, it is difficult to separate the literary arts from those that went into the making of a good Timurid volume containing such literature. These include paper and the writing transcribed upon on it; the painted and gilded ornament that adorns so many pages of these manuscripts; their bindings; and the illustrations that have been the means – for so long, almost the sole feature – by which the history of this art has been established.

My brief, for the 'Idea of Iran' in November of 2017, was to discuss the 'reflection of the Timurid era' in the manuscripts made in that era. For all the obvious reasons, especially space and time, it seemed right then – as still it does, in transforming my verbal presentation into print – to limit my focus to some of the finest examples, since their 'look' in good part really does define one aspect of 'The Idea of Timurid Iran'. Thus, the remarks that follow should largely be understood as pertaining only to the finest, and the most carefully conceived and executed, examples of the arts of the illustrated book in the fifteenth-century world in which Iranian material culture was the model.

Digging fairly deeply, now, into the Timurid garden reveals how the shape of the garden has changed in the last half-century. One reason is, naturally, the passage of time and our accumulated knowledge of the material.[5] Another is the growing appreciation of fifteenth-century painting styles other than the 'classical', a taste I shared with my *maître*, B.W. Robinson.[6] A third is the identification, and the subsequently revised estimation, of the manuscripts created under the patronage of – for and by – the Turkmen dynasties, the Qoyunlu, both 'Qara' and 'Aq'. By the later 1960s, Robinson, acknowledging the assistance of colleagues – Priscilla P. Soucek and, in the Topkapi Sarayi Library especially, Filiz Çağman and Zeren Tanındı[7] – had come to appreciate the extraordinary quality of the court-sponsored manuscripts made for these princes. He was also readying us to reconsider the extensive commercial book-making 'industry' in later fifteenth-century Shiraz, one of whose essential features was the adoption of the Turkmen illustrative mode at its simplest.[8]

A fourth is the somewhat belated recognition that the arts of the book in the fifteenth century, in Iranian lands, really do embrace far more than their illustrations – their 'miniatures', in earlier parlance.[9] The latter attitude is now quite out of date but, it was quite characteristic of the study of this art from the first years of the twentieth century, to well past mid-century.[10] For one thing, it accounts for the close trimming (or framing) of folios removed from their parent manuscripts, a practice that created immense obstacles, and required much later work, to identify and reconstruct them. Indeed, the notion is inherent, still, in the titles of all of Ivan Stchoukine's pioneering systematic surveys, published between 1928 and 1977: *Les peintures des manuscrits ...*,[11] while Robinson's invaluable volumes are essentially lists of illustrations in the Persian manuscripts in three significant British libraries.

But it is now more than evident that the illumination of these fine volumes, along with their bindings and even their paper, all count towards the character of a fifteenth-century Iranian manuscript. One example is Turkmen illumination: it is astonishing, and quite differently beautiful from what we think we know of 'Timurid' illumination. I dare to quote myself, in a conversation in the later 1970s in Robert Skelton's office in the Victoria and

Albert Museum, to the effect that illumination would surely provide a key to unlocking some of our problems in understanding the development of Persian book-painting. Elaine Wright has helped us focus on all the non-illustrative components of these fine manuscripts: her *Look of the Book*, of 2012, has made us all truly aware that, henceforth, we must always take into account the non-pictorial features of the arts of the Eastern manuscript.[12] And a fifth reason is simply the entry, into the Timurid garden, of so many younger, better equipped and better trained scholars. Their passion, their careful thinking, and their sheer hard work, along with the passage of time, all combine to alter the way we now examine, evaluate, interpret the stuff of our study from what had seemed important as late as, say, 1991.

One more fundamental change in our thinking is embodied in the very nomenclature of the period – as well as the title of the thirteenth 'Idea of Iran'. Just as, today, we may not ignore the significant Turkmen component of fifteenth-century history in Iran by speaking only of the 'Timurid' century, so we may no longer ignore the significant Turkmen components in the arts of the fifteenth-century Eastern book, even if there still seems some imbalance in the way we recognize them – or fail, as yet, adequately to have done so. For which reason, 'Timurid', in the following pages, should be understood as referring to the manuscripts sponsored by both the descendants of Timur and their Turkmen rivals.

My original plan for this chapter had been to demonstrate the theme by looking briefly at the components of ten superb manuscripts, dated (or datable), made throughout the century, and thus spanning it. Having essentially abandoned the idea, let me nonetheless briefly touch upon certain aspects of the volumes that figured in it, since their 'look' in good part really does define one aspect of the 'Idea of Timurid Iran'. My list spanned the century. It began with the celebrated late fourteenth-century copy of several *masnavi*s of the poet known as Khvaju Kermani, made not for a Timurid or Turkmen patron but for Soltan Ahmad Jalayer:[13] Turko-Mongol by descent and one of the most sophisticated bibliophiles of the age, ruling – serially – from Ardabil, Tabriz and then Baghdad, from 1382 to his death in 1410. It ended close to the end of the century, with a copy of the celebrated work of the mystic poet Farid al-Din 'Attar, an equally celebrated volume begun in Herat, in the circle of the court of the last Timurid ruler, Soltan-Hoseyn-e Bayqara but left, still, unfinished for more than a century.[14]

My list, necessarily, had lacunae. Missing, for instance, was the manuscript from which came the beautiful image used on the announcement and the programme from which this volume arises: it comes from a celebrated *Khamsa* of Nezami, one painting bearing the hejri date of 900/1494–95, and having a number of illustrations considered to be the work of Kamal al-Din Behzad.[15] Another was the later-Timurid *Zafarnama* made for Soltan-Hoseyn-e

Bayqara.[16] ‘Choices, choices’, as my father used to lament. All represent, in all of the essential ways, all the arts of the fifteenth-century Eastern book. Thus, the characteristics shared by the manuscripts on that list, along with any of the others also named in this ‘stroll through the Timurid garden’, elicit some preliminary observations.

They were virtually all made at the behest of princely patrons: Jalayerid, Timurid, Turkmen; sponsored, commissioned, ordered: all connected, in one way or another, with a person of rank and means, well-educated and with exacting standards, who all shared that Timurid ‘taste for the intricate’. They were made in different but significant centres spanning the Iranian world of the fifteenth century: the majority in Herat, in Khorasan, but also elsewhere: in Jalayerid-controlled Baghdad, in Timurid-ruled Shiraz, Sharvanshahi Shemakha and Turkmen Tabriz. They contain works composed in Arabic – the classical language of Islam; in Eastern Turkish – the mother-tongue of many of the princes of fifteenth-century Iran; and in Persian, the language of the educated class to which they belonged – by birth, by education, by both. These manuscripts were transcribed in both Arabic and Uighur scripts, by some of the finest calligraphers anywhere in the Muslim world, at a time when a fine calligraphic hand was a cultural desideratum and – for instance, when demonstrated by the Timurid princes Baysonghor and his brother Ebrahim-Soltan – called forth notable comments of approbation by contemporary observers.[17]

In content, they are both religious and secular; in literary genre they are both prose and poetry. One volume on my original list is a splendid Qur’an:[18] the revelation transmitted by the Prophet Muhammad to all who would submit to this revelation; another is an extraordinary copy of an Eastern Turkish religious work, prose of great simplicity but with a fervently proselytizing purpose.[19] There are volumes of the most important, and most beloved, works of Persian poetry: Ferdowsi – and Nezami, Khvaju Kermani and Sa‘di, ‘Attar and Jami; Amir Khosrow Dehlavi and Hafez. One poet who did not figure in this list, but should have, is ‘Ali-Shir Nava’i: a picture identified as an idealized meeting, of the Timurid poet ‘Abd al-Rahman Jami and ‘Ali-Shir with the shade of Nezami, is found within one of the volumes of his own *Khamsa*.[20]

Finally, most of the manuscripts, both on my original list and those encountered elsewhere in this chapter are illustrated. This is one overriding source of their fame. Moreover, all are gorgeously ornamented and would, originally, have been splendidly bound, although bindings are among the most potentially fragile components of a fine eastern volume – ‘fragile’ in the sense of their physical connection to the text-block they surround – and tend not to have survived still enclosing the volume for which they were originally commissioned.

These characteristics – patron, place, and content; language and script and ornament of all kinds, both abstract and pictorial – go some considerable way towards defining the look of the 'Timurid' book, if primarily at its highest level of production (and again, I stress that the following comments really only pertain to the finest of the manuscripts made in princely courts). Perhaps the best known of such courts is Baysonghor's, in Herat in the later 1420s and early 1430s, whose activities are so evocatively described in the famous *'arza-dasht*, a workshop-document describing the progress made in some short space of time on a great variety of projects being executed for this prince.[21] An obvious corollary is that quality – of both materials and the skills of those who executed the work – must be added to the 'cast' of defining characteristics of the arts of the Eastern book in the fifteenth century in Iran; for although means usually assure quality, such is not always the case. I suggest, then, that a different set of features, in conjunction with the superior quality of materials and the superb skills of the craftsman, might also serve to help define the 'look of the Timurid book': these would be size and scale, shape and proportion. Of course, these features are hardly unique to the characteristics of a fine 'Timurid' volume: they also define architecture, especially in the fifteenth century: how differently proportioned, for instance, are the three buildings on the Registan in Samarqand, Ologh Beg's madrasa of 1417–21[22] and the two seventeenth-century buildings, the Shir Dar madrasa (1619–36) and the Tilla Kari, begun a decade later;[23] and how different are the impressions one derives from walking into, and through, each of the three.

One particular aspect of the 'look of the book' in the fifteenth century in Iran is that, even closed, many actually *do* have a specific look. When one unfolds the flap (should it still survive), turns back the cover (of whatever date and style) and opens the volume, what is immediately clear from even a single page of a good fifteenth-century book is its proportional layout and composition, one that is essentially characteristic of this period. To be specific, in good and classical 'Timurid' volumes, the height of the ruling – the *jadval* – enclosing the rectangle of the written surface has a numerical relationship to the width of the unmargined folio, in its original size. The measured numbers may not be precisely the same number but, when they are manipulated – reduced successively by factors of 10, and then by 5 – the measurements reveal a discernibly proportional relationship of folio size to written surface, one that may be expressed as a simple ratio. I list some of them, in an appendix in my doctoral dissertation of 1973.[24] There, I noted that Shahrokh's large *Kolliyat-e tarikhi*, B. 282 in the Topkapi Sarayi Library, with a folio size of 42.2 × 31.5 cm and various dates, 818–19/1415–16 and 820/1417–18,[25] displays a ratio – of the original folio size to written surface – of 4:3. This is exactly the same ratio as that of the few original pages, the first and the last, of the very small Garrett *Zafarnama* of 872/1467–68.[26] Note that these two original folios measure only 21.5 × 12.6 cm, smaller by almost half – at least in height – than the *Kolliyat-e tarikhi*, made over half a century earlier. I suggest that, notwithstanding the differences in size, these two Timurid volumes share the same aesthetic of proportion, and I continue to think that this is neither coincidental nor an isolated instance.

I would further suggest that, with some experience, one can often tell much about a good 'Timurid' volume even 'from its cover', irrespective of its size and the number of its folios. The 26 examples I had collected, and listed, by 1973, date from between 1425 and 1560, and they come from all the centres of fine manuscript-making that are noted above. I have not studied many of the finer – the princely, or courtly – Turkmen volumes from this point of view and would here venture only a single further comment on one that was on that list of 1973, the Chester Beatty *Tarikhnama* of Tabari, dated 874/1469, and considered an Aq Qoyunlu production: its ratio was 4:4.[27] But I have also observed that, regardless of the actual size of a commercial Turkmen volume, its shape and proportions are different (if sometimes only subtly) from fine contemporary 'Timurid' volumes.[28] Eventually, this feature also goes far towards defining the shape of the classical Shiraz sixteenth-century volume, with or without illustrations: its ratio of folio to written surface I had long ago found to be 5:3.[29]

Of course, many other features in addition to the written surface and the original size of a page comprise such proportionality. Even in 'Timurid' manuscripts of little pretension and modest materials, it starts with calligraphy: the proportional features of the script then also ordain the width of a column of poetic text.[30] Proportional relationships may even determine aspects of the illuminated ornament and, as well, extend to the width of the rulings. And it goes without saying that the notion of a proportional relationship of all parts to the whole is hardly limited to manuscripts of the fifteenth century, fine or rather less than: Chahriyar Adle systematically examined all of these features in an early seventeenth-century copy of Seyaqi-Nezam's *Fotohat-e Homayun*, made in Shiraz, and reported a similarly interlocking, proportional structure.[31] A student of mine, in the later 1970s, was fascinated with these inherent possibilities and started to examine a far finer and, also, more interesting manuscript – the Cairo *Bustan* – from this point of view; ultimately, the law, rather than the history of a highly specialized art, claimed his time and interests. Thus, the extent to which these physical characteristics always define the fifteenth-century volume in the East – of whatever text and quality – is still open to further examination. I can only say that, in my experience, it appears to hold true for some of the finer fifteenth-century 'Timurid' volumes: historical as well as *belles-lettres*, illustrated or not, large or small.

A different observation concerns the actual works enclosed within the covers of the fine fifteenth-century Eastern manuscript. Needless to reiterate that texts – of all kinds – were composed and copied, and sometimes intensely discussed, throughout this period, as our symposium and the accompanying publication so well attest. But a certain intellectual fashion, at least in the choice of texts to be illustrated, also seems to have operated throughout the later period in Herat, discernible, if but dimly. Again, let me focus only on the finer volumes of history and literature, especially of poetry and with illustrations: my working example is Ferdowsi's epic, the *Shahnama*. Some years ago, I had examined the three princely Timurid illustrated volumes of Ferdowsi: great Timurid copies of this treasure, all masterpieces of the early Timurid book, if in varying ways.[32] Apart from one volume of the *Shahnama*, with related post-*Shahnama* epics, copied in Shiraz in 1398, it then took several generations for Timurid princes – grandsons of Timur and, all of them, sons of Shahrokh – to commission their own copies of the *Shahnama*. I find the reasons self-evident, but the manifestations are still striking.

To review: Baysonghor's was completed in 833/1430, in Herat, in Khorasan. It is a magnificent manuscript: large, the text rigorously edited with a 'new' preface; gorgeously illuminated and impressively illustrated, even if its pictorial programme, 21 paintings only, is notably restricted.[33] That of the youngest brother, Mohammad Juki, is the latest of the three, a work of the early 1440s and also made in Herat, with 31 surviving paintings and exquisite illumination; it is probably the illustrated Timurid volume that most perfectly embodies the fairy-tale quality of fifteenth-century Persian painting.[34] Ebrahim-Soltan's, made in Shiraz early in the decade of the 1430s, is sumptuously illuminated and has over twice as many pictures, but most are only half-page in size and are, moreover, painted in a style that is anything but classically 'Timurid' – or at least, classically Baysonghori.[35]

Given the apparent rarity of illustrated early Timurid *Shahnama* copies, princely or otherwise, what then occurred (after Ebrahim's death in 1435) is also astonishing: illustrated copies of Ferdowsi's epic poem seem to have been made in remarkably large numbers (in company, of course, with numbers of illustrated copies of all Persian classical poets). In the middle 1990s, I had compiled a list of 19, comprising only those volumes made in Shiraz between 1435 and 1450; since then, two more complete manuscripts have been added to my master-copy.[36] Far greater in number – close to 50 – are those on a list of all fifteenth-century illustrated copies of the *Shahnama* (assembled as an appendix to a slightly earlier study).[37] Already incomplete when it was published in 1992, this is also constantly being annotated, as more examples, both complete volumes and single folios, come to light.

It is therefore relevant to note that many of the latter – all of them fifteenth-century illustrated copies of *Shahnama* – were produced in the commercial workshops of Turkmen-dominated Shiraz. Moreover, while five illustrated *Shahnama* volumes, dating in the decade between about 1450 and 1460, appear on Robbie's master list of 17 Qara Qoyunlu 'court-style' manuscripts,[38] all five are in decidedly 'mixed' pictorial styles: combining 'Herat-Turkmen' or 'Shiraz-Timurid' manners of painting with the commercial Turkmen style, if at different levels of achievement (sometimes within the same manuscript). But no illustrated *Shahnama* volumes – stylistically mixed or otherwise – appear on his list of 13 princely Aq Qoyunlu manuscripts.[39] One asks, again, if rhetorically: why this might be and is it of significance?

Nor does the *Shahnama* figure among the finest of later-Herat illustrated volumes: instead, these include Sharaf al-Din's *Zafarnama*; there are works of Nezami and Sa'di and Amir Khosrow Dehlavi; and, of course, Jami and 'Ali-Shir Nava'i and Hatefi, and still others.[40] But, at least to the best of my knowledge, Ferdowsi's 'title deeds of the Persian nation's nobility' – as Mirza Mohammad 'Ali Forughi had long ago described the *Shahnama*, in a letter to E.G. Browne[41] – did not seem a desideratum to the circle of Soltan-Hoseyn-e Bayqara in the last decades of the century.

Such matters as the patron – or sponsor or commissioner: choose your word – and the place of a manuscript's making, the many components contributing to the 'look of the entire book' and comments on its contents, may all go some way towards defining some of the essential qualities of the 'Turko-Timurid' manuscript. But might we look at those other qualities – size and scale, shape and proportion – and explore another way in which one or another of them – or all of them taken together – also contributes to the essence of the 'Timurid' book?

To address this matter, I turn now to one of the most beautiful, as well as most celebrated, of Timurid paintings anywhere (see Plate V).[42] It is a single folio removed from an illustrated manuscript and mounted, as if for an album: an image whose precise date, and original context, remain still uncertain, but whose subject is evident and whose magical quality is unsurpassed. It comes from another copy of Khvaju Kermani's *masnavi*s and illustrates a moment in the story of *Homay-o Homayun*, the dream in which Homay meets Homayun in a beautiful garden.

That it comes from such a work is evident from the text – three *beyt*s – at the upper right, and a section heading now placed just below the painting, as well as the nine illuminated chapter headings pasted onto the folio at top, right and bottom.[43] Beautiful as they are, they also alter the shape and size of the picture, albeit much about the parent manuscript, of which it appears to be the sole surviving folio, might be deduced from the composition and the placement of the four figures.

Homay and Homayun stand in a verdant enclosed garden under a star-spangled dark night sky with a crescent moon at the top left; the conventions of this art, of course, permit us to see them perfectly. He has just entered the garden and stands, hands crossed at his breast, at the lower right; she stands a bit above and to the left, facing him; two attendants stand beside her, a youth above her, towards the centre of the painting, and a maiden below her, at the left of the painting. The pale ground on which they all stand is thick with blossoming shrubs and watered by a silver stream (now dark with tarnish); it dips, in and out of the picture in the foreground, circling back into the middle ground behind the figures, its edges fringed with grass, orange lilies and purple iris, and flowering trees. In the background, the garden is walled: reddish panels with trilobed arches surrounded with red frames are set on a foundation of pale-green dressed stone blocks; the wall turns downward at the upper left, just where the stream in the background appears to loop upward, catching the water from a lion-headed spout in a rectangular stone basin whose sides are carved with floral sprays.

The recomposed image now measures 29.4 ×18 cm.[44] The painting itself is surely wider than the width of the written surface of its parent manuscript: this is evident on the right side (between the illuminated rubrics). I once analysed it by quantifying, and multiplying, the width of a column of text; this exercise yielded the precise placement of the vertical text-ruling on the other side of the folio. On the illustrated side, it also ordains the placement of the angle of the wall and the upward turn of the stream: just at the implicit vertical ruling. This exercise also suggested the painting's original dimensions. In abstract terms, it is 9 implicit units in height and 6 in width. Its width is also the height, *not* of the horizon, but the boundary of the garden: the base of the green foundation-stones of the wall are placed at about 6 implicit units of height – two-thirds of the height of the painting. Such a placement can be seen in other mature Timurid paintings, in which figures of substantial size operate within landscapes and architectural settings of an acceptably 'realistic' scale.[45]

As do these four. Moreover, each is placed 'within' one of the four columns of text written on the reverse of this folio. Better, perhaps, to say 'more or less' placed within these vertical rulings, since each figure is set faintly to one or the other side of the implicit column on the reverse; perhaps achieved by means of an impression from the *mastar*, which may have been still palpable when the picture was painted. Indeed, every aspect of this beautiful painting reveals the subtle manipulation of all its compositional elements. The broad, shallow, irregularly curving line of the figures, carefully placed on a set of implied vertical axes, is not echoed by the curves of the silver stream, even though each figure is 'comfortably' accommodated in the resulting spaces between it. The painting, even as mounted now, as a construct, is an example – here meticulously executed – of the Timurid aim of proportionality, between all the parts of a manuscript and the entire entity. This also holds true, of course, for the architecture of the 'Timurid' period (although such is a feature of fifteenth-century architecture more generally, whether in Florence or Ming China).

Other features in this magical image offer further defining characteristics, both of the 'Idea' of the Timurid illustration, as well as the entire manuscript for which it was prepared. Perhaps the greater significance applies to the latter feature: it appears to be a new composition for a subject rarely, if ever, illustrated. At the moment of writing, no other known versions of the subject come to mind and none (insofar as I am aware) have ever been recorded. This is quite in line with A.T. Adamova's observations, developed in two important articles in the last years of the twentieth century: that in 'princely fifteenth-century illustrated manuscripts ... each [would have] contained ... some miniatures ... copied from works created earlier ...; several variations on well-known compositions ...; several unexpected *hors-de-tradition* compositions [of] "classical" subjects ...; and unfailingly, one – or more – miniatures depicting subjects that had not heretofore been executed ....'[46] I would suggest that this painting, illustrating the dream in which Homay actually encounters Homayun – whose picture he had seen and, immediately, fallen in love with – removed from a superb but no longer extant Timurid manuscript, is just that: a new composition for a new subject.

Another defining characteristic displayed by this painting is that all the compositional elements are densely, but evenly, spread throughout it. The palette is beautifully balanced, the strong blue of the night sky and the bright red of the elaborate wall in its upper part, beyond the silver stream in the background, echoed, less forthrightly, in the lower half, where garments of lavender, saffron-orange and a purplish-brown vary the repeated red 'punctuation' of the flowers but with no sense that they are merely formulaic. Gold, too, is equally seen throughout the painting (and its compound mount), used not only for architectural elements and vessels, for headdresses and the small-scale ornament on garments, but also in the illuminated cartouches, either as golden arabesque-scrolls over which rubrics are written, or for the calligraphy itself, gold against scrolls of chestnut, silver or green. Salvaged, saved and now pasted around the top, right and bottom edges of the picture but never intended to be placed where they are, nonetheless they frame the painting and create an even, gold-touched rectangle out of a composition of many corners. Their beauty, their colouristic variety, the fine calligraphy of the rubrics and the exquisitely fine execution are extraordinary. In the lamentable absence of the entire manuscript, they offer yet another glimpse of the superb quality of this lost volume and all of its constituent elements, epitomizing the standards to which Timurid artists might aspire, even if few Timurid paintings are quite so magical.

As to how such a painting may truly convey an idea of Iran, I fall back on an art-historical point, the variety of its pictorial sources: they exemplify a feature that is, I would suggest, fundamental to the 'Idea of Iran'. I see this painting, one having the subtlest of designs and an extraordinarily fine level of execution, as the product of an equally accomplished, subtle and sophisticated milieu: with virtual certainty, this is Herat, in Khorasan, uncontested Timurid capital from about 1410 to the death of Shahrokh in 1447 (after which it was greatly contested by both Timurid and Turkmen princes until 1469, when again it came under Timurid control that lasted until virtually the end of the century). Yet 'Timurid' painting – within which I also include Turkmen illustrative painting, but only at its best, probably really only Aq Qoyunlu – is an art of many and varying sources; and some do not come from the classical Iranian heartland but from the broader Iranian world, or even beyond its borders. In this case, surely the residual stiffness of the two ladies, at the left, comes from Soltan Ahmad's western milieu – Tabriz, but also Baghdad. From Samarqand, but deriving from Buddhist lands still farther east, surely come the fluttering, rippling sleeves, scarves and sashes.[47] They are notable in 'Abd al-Hayy's wondrous painting intended for Soltan Ahmad's earlier Khvaju Kermani, of 1396,[48] but – so I am convinced – actually executed in Timur's Samarqand; equally notable is that these Buddhist accoutrements are largely absent from the other images in Soltan Ahmad's manuscript.[49] But Iran could always absorb the foreign: influences of religion; architectural practice and the materials of revêtment; styles and techniques, forms and materials of sculpture and painting; fashions of dress and accoutrement. For millennia, it has been able to transmute the foreign, make it its own, turn it into something immediately recognizable as Iranian. This supernally beautiful image, breathtaking and magical, sole survivor of a volume that must have been one of the finest creations of a culture in which the finest of manuscripts was the norm, offers many ideas of Iran.

One last 'Idea of Iran' inherent in this painting lies in its garden setting: the garden is not only enclosed, but also encircled, by a flowing stream of water. By this date – in the ninth hejri century – the *topos* of the Iranian garden was watered by two streams: that of the pre-Islamic tradition, documented as early as the sixth-century BC garden-pavilion of Cyrus the Great at Pasargadae,[50] and that of the Muslim tradition, the Islamic paradise-garden, visited by the Prophet Mohammad on his *me'raj* and in which every devout Muslim hopes to awaken. It would be hard to imagine a more breathtakingly beautiful presentation of an Iranian garden, one 'Idea of Iran' that could hardly have been more evocatively, magically realized. Indeed, this celebrated dream of a night-time encounter, when Homay sees Homayun in an enclosed garden, is the perfect paradigm for an Idea of Iran: subtle, *recherché*, but removed from a specifically stated place or date; an idea – an ideal – as expressed in one of the finest of all Iranian book illustrations of all time.

Acknowledgements

I am indebted, and most grateful, to Judith Lerner, Manijeh Bayani and Wheeler Thackston, for assistance in the final stages of preparing this text.

Appendix One: bibliographical note

Among the most frequently consulted works (and still of great use), in chronological order, are: F.R. Martin, *The Miniature Painting and Painters of Persia* (1912); Georges Marteau and Henri Vever, *Miniatures Persanes* (1913); Ph. Walter Schulz, *Die persisch-islamische Miniaturmalerei* (1914); Ananda K. Coomaraswamy, *Les Miniatures Orientales de la Collection Goloubew* (1929); A. Sakisian, *La Miniature Persan* (1929); Laurence Binyon, J.V.S. Wilkinson and Basil Gray, *Persian Miniature Painting* (1933, hereafter BWG); Ernst Kühnel, 'History of miniature painting and drawing' (1938–39); Eric Schroeder, *Persian Miniatures in the Fogg Museum* (1942); A.J. Arberry et al., *The Chester Beatty Library* (1959–62); Ernst J. Grube, *Muslim Miniature Paintings from the XIII to XIX Century* (1962); B.W. Robinson, *Persian Miniature Painting from Collections in the British Isles* (1967, hereafter Robinson, *British*). A decade later, the word 'miniature' was still in use: Norah Titley, *Miniatures from Persian Manuscripts* ([1977], hereafter Titley *MPM*).

In another sense, this focus on pictures – whatever word is used – within texts has also animated a number of important studies and collaborative projects whose aim was to list the illustrations, or illustrated text-points, in manuscripts of classical Persian literature (from all periods, albeit that the fifteenth century occupies a major role within them all). Many derive from research conducted in pursuit of a doctoral degree, starting with those devoted to Nezami's *Khamsa*. They are the subject of both Larissa Dodkhudoeva's *Poemy Nizami v srednevekovoy miniaturnoy zhivopisi* (1985) and Priscilla P. Soucek's 'Illustrated Manuscripts of Nizami's Khamseh: 1386–1482' (1971). The two efforts dedicated to the illustrations of Ferdowsi's *Shahnama* are different in genesis but, together, quite strikingly bracket technological advances in the second half of the twentieth century: Jill Norgren and Edward Davis' *Preliminary Index of Shah-Nameh Illustrations*, keyed to the French translation of Jules Mohl, was distributed as an unpublished typescript in 1969 and, unfortunately, has no page numbers; while by 2005 a collaborative electronic version, the Cambridge *Shahnama* Database, was well under way. As this ambitious project was being developed, the notion of the 'break-line' – the precise point in a Persian text at which an illustration was inserted – was being set forth by Farhad Mehran, 'The break-line verse', pp. 151–69; but this and a further study, 'Mapping illustrated folios of *Shahnama* manuscripts', pp. 238–66, were limited to Ferdowsi alone. A very different, if necessarily brief, approach to the same issue is by Jerome W. Clinton, 'Ferdowsi and the illustration of the *Shahnameh*'; he focuses on the fundamental differences between the aesthetic arenas in which the verbal and visual arts 'competed'. Studies of the manuscripts of two other classical poets, and the text-points or subjects therein illustrated, also derive from doctoral research; the first is the *Khamsa* of Amir Khosrow Dehlavi, by Barbara Brend, *Perspectives on Persian Painting*, who includes fifteenth-century Ottoman copies, as well as Mughal Indian copies up to the period of Jahangir; Amir Khosrow was of much interest to the three eldest sons of Shahrokh, see Wheeler M. Thackston, *A Century of Princes: Sources on Timurid History and Art*, pp. 23–24; also Eleanor Sims, 'The hundred and one paintings', pp. 119–27, especially p. 120 (and illustrations pp. 104–10). The second is Farid al-Din 'Attar's *Manteq al-teyr*, studied by Ilse Sturkenboom, 'The Imagery of the *Mantiq al-Tayr*', in her doctoral thesis (Bamberg, 2016).

Notes:

1. Eleanor Sims, 'Riflessioni sulle arti del libro nell'Oriente islamico del XV secolo', pp. 91–95, and 'I "principi bibliofili" del XV secolo e le arti del libro', pp. 280–326.
2. Maria Subtelny, 'A taste for the intricate', pp. 56–79.
3. Ernst J. Grube, 'Notes on the decorative arts of the Timurid period', pp. 233–79, esp. figs 144–45; Thomas W. Lentz and Glenn D. Lowry, *Timur and the Princely Vision*, Cat. 49, pp. 142, 207–8 (hereafter Lentz & Lowry).
4. Ernst J. Grube, 'Notes on the decorative arts of the Timurid period. II', esp. pp. 178–80, and figs 21–38; adumbrated earlier by Grube (as in note 2 above), pp. 255, 258–59, and figs 115–16, 124–27; for more drawings, Lentz & Lowry, pp. 182, 192–98, Cats. 90–98, and 100, and pp. 347–49; also pp. 218–19, Cats. 115, 118, pp. 352–53.
5. Starting in 1969, from the UNESCO-sponsored symposium on Timurid art held in Samarqand and the accompanying exhibition, *Catalogue of the All-Union Exhibition*, included 78 Timurid manuscripts, both illustrated and only illuminated, pp. 26–35 (Russian), pp. 47–57 (English). For the arts of the book, one 'immediate' result is *The Arts of the Book in Central Asia* (hereafter *ABCA*); a decade later came the important loan exhibition staged in both the Freer/Sackler Gallery in Washington DC and the Los Angeles County Museum of Art, whose catalogue (Lentz & Lowry) remains an immensely useful reference tool. Even before that date, Lentz had written 'Painting at Herat under Baysunghur ibn Shahrukh', in 1985. The fifteenth-century materials in four celebrated albums kept in the Topkapi Saray Library in Istanbul (H. 2152, 2153, 2154 and 2160), were also added to the bibliographical pool in this period: see *Islamic Art*, I, 1981. Fifteen years later came David. J. Roxburgh's doctoral dissertation (hereafter Roxburgh, 'Our works'). In addition to those already named above, a useful bibliography of fifteenth-century Persian painting would now include books and articles by not only B.W. Robinson, Ivan Stchoukine, Norah Titley (usually in the *Journal of the British Library*), A.T. Adamova, Priscilla P. Soucek, Filiz Çağman, Zeren Akalay/Tanındı, Barbara Brend, Karin Rührdanz and the present writer, but also those of the 'next generation', Elaine Wright, Lâle Uluç, Christiane Gruber, Yael Rice, Simon Rettig, Emily Shovelton, Ilse Sturkenboom, James White and Giti Norouzian.
6. Exemplified, for instance, by B.W. Robinson's 'The Dunimarle Shāhnāma', pp. 207–18.
7. Key studies would include: B.W. Robinson, 'Turkman court painting: A preliminary survey', an unpublished (and undated) typescript, datable some time between 1969 and the publication of 'The Turkman School to 1503', in *ABCA* (hereafter, Robinson, *ABCA*), pp. 215–47; Priscilla P. Soucek, 'The New York Public Library "Makhzan al-asrār"', pp. 1–37; B.W. Robinson, *Fifteenth Century Persian Painting*, Chapter 2: The Turkmans, pp. 21–34; Priscilla P. Soucek, 'The Ann Arbor *Shahnama*', pp. 267–81; and Simon Rettig, 'La production manuscrite à Chiraz sous les Aq Qoyyunlu entre 1467 et 1503'.
8. Eleanor Sims, *The Tale and the Image*, and also in a contribution to a forthcoming volume on the Bernard Berenson Persian paintings at Villa I Tatti. Norihito Hayashi, 'The Turkman commercial style of painting', pp. 169–87, is unfortunately notable for its misunderstanding of the usually accepted defining terminology of period and patronage.

9. The word 'miniature' derives from the vocabulary of European manuscript illumination, in which minium – an orange-red lead compound, lead tetroxide, Pb_3O_4 – was much used; words built from the past participle of the Latin verb *miniare*, such as the English *miniate* and, also, *miniature* (with variations in most European languages) have come to mean both the act (and the person performing the act) of painting, as well as the size of what is so painted, the latter in use from roughly the later fifteenth century. Even though the scale of 'Timurid' painting is usually small, I have come to feel that words derived from minium, especially 'miniature', are not applicable to 'Eastern' works on paper and try to avoid their usage altogether. Daniel V. Thompson, *The Materials of Medieval Painting*, pp. 101–2, sums up the linguistic aspect clearly and concisely; sections in Stella Panayotova, ed., *Colour: The Art and Science of Illuminated Manuscripts*, pp. 27–28, 193–95, 382, are also relevant.
10. For a bibliographical note on this topic, including titles not otherwise referred to in this chapter, see Appendix One.
11. Ivan Stchoukine, *La peinture indienne à l'époque des Grands Moghols* (Paris, 1929); *La peinture iranienne sous les derniers 'Abbâsides et les Îl-Khâns* (Bruges, 1936); *Les peintures des manuscrits Tîmûrides* (hereafter Stchoukine, *MT*); *Les peintures des manuscrits Safavis de 1502 à 1587* (Paris, 1959); *Les peintures des manuscrits de Shah 'Abbas Ier à la fin des Safavis* (Paris, 1964); and *Les peintures des manuscrits de la "Khamseh" de Nizâmî.*
12. Elaine Wright, *The Look of the Book* (hereafter Wright, *LoB*); still another reworking of a doctoral dissertation, prepared for the University of Oxford and awarded in 1997, she refines earlier thinking about the non-pictorial aspects of the Eastern book in the Ilkhanid and Timurid periods: codicology, calligraphy, bindings and illumination, in addition to illustration; several decades later, David Roxburgh addresses selected examples of these aspects in 'The aesthetics of aggregation', esp. pp. 119–22; he also illustrates a more recent study uniquely with fifteenth-century illumination: 'Many a wish has turned to dust', pp. 175–221.
13. London, British Library (formerly Museum), Ms. Add. 18113: Charles Rieu, *Catalogue of the Persian Manuscripts*, vol. II, pp. 620–22; Stchoukine, *MT*, Ms. VI, pp. 33–35, Pls. IV–VIII; Robinson, *British*, p. 40, Cat. 8, with all references up to 1967; Titley, *MPM*, p. 117, no. 251; Teresa Fitzherbert, 'Khwājū Kirmānī', esp. pp. 137–39, 142–43. Digitally: www.bl.uk/manuscripts/FullDisplay.aspx?ref=Add_MS_18113 [accessed 24 March 2019].
    blogs: Ursula Sims-Williams (1 August 2013), 'An illustrated 14th century Khamsah by Khvaju Kirmani' https://blogs.bl.uk/asian-and-african/2013/07/an-illustrated-14th-century-khamsah-by-khvaju-kirmani.html [accessed 7 April 2019]; also Sheila Blair (16 June 2015), 'The archaeology of a manuscript: the Khamsah of Khvaju Kirmani' https://blogs.bl.uk/asian-and-african/2015/06/the-archaeology-of-a-manuscript-the-khamsah-of-khvaju-kirmani.html [accessed 24 March 2019].
14. New York City, The Metropolitan Museum, 63.210: Ernst J. Grube, 'The fifteenth century miniatures', pp. 317–38; Assadullah Souren Melikian-Chirvani, 'Kh^{w}āje Mīrak Naqqāsh', pp. 97–146; Yumiko Kamada, 'A taste for intricacy', pp. 129–76; Lentz & Lowry, pp. 279–80, 290, Cats. 153–54, pp. 360–61; Sturkenboom, '*Mantiq al-Tayr*', pp. xiii–xiv, 334–41.

15. London, British Library, Ms. Or. 6810: much illustrated, in addition to F.R. Martin and Thomas Arnold, *The Nizami MS. Illluminated by Bihzad, Mirak and Qasim Ali …*; Ivan Stchoukine, 'Les peintures de la Khamseh de Nizami du British Museum (Or. 6810)', pp. 301–13; Stchoukine, *MT*, Ms. LXXXI, pp. 78–81; G.M. Meredith-Owens, *Handlist of Persian Manuscripts*, p. 66; Robinson, *British*, p. 51, Cat. 29, with references up to 1967; Titley, *MPM*, p. 141, no. 319; Lentz & Lowry, pp. 274–77, 282–83, 288, 291, Cat. 140, pp, 357–58.
16. Baltimore, Johns Hopkins University, John Work Garrett Collection: Thomas Arnold, *Bihzād and his Paintings in the Zafar-Nāmah MS.*; Stchoukine, *MT*, Ms. LXXXII, pp. 81–83, 138–40; Eleanor Sims, 'The Garrett Manuscript of the Zafar-Name' (hereafter Sims, Garrett); eadem, 'Sultan Husayn Bayqara's Zafar-Namah and its Miniatures', pp. 299–311; Lentz & Lowry, pp. 262, 264–67, 289, Cat. 147, p. 359.
17. For instance, the inscription he designed, and signed, for the entrance *ivān* of his mother's mosque in the Shrine of Imam Reza in Mashhad, dated 821/1418; Lisa Golombek and Donald Wilber, *The Timurid Architecture of Iran and Turan* (hereafter Golombek & Wilber), vol. I, pp. 328–31, 368; Lentz & Lowry, pp. 81–84, fig. 25; illustrated completely and in good colour by Mahdi Sahragard, *Masterpieces of Āstān-e Quds-e Razavi*, pp. 56–63; see also Dowlatshāh Samarqandi, *Tadhkerat al-sho'arā*, as translated by Thackston, *A Century of Princes*, for Bāysonghor's calligraphic interests, pp. 22–24; for Ebrāhim-Soltān, pp. 33–34: he transcribed at least six copies of the Qur'an, and designed at least half a dozen building-inscriptions that still survive, Lentz & Lowry, pp. 84, 370.
18. Detroit, USA, Detroit Institute of Arts, 30.323: Lentz & Lowry, Cat. 20, pp. 78–79, 332 there described and dated ca. 1425–50.
19. Paris, Bibliothèque Nationale de France, Ms. Supplément turc 190, usually called the *Me'rājnāma*: Stchoukine, *MT*, Ms. XXXVII, pp. 54–55; Marie-Rose Séguy, *The Miraculous Journey of Mahomet*; Francis Richard, *Splendeurs persanes*, Cat. 41, p. 77; Christiane J. Gruber: *El "Libro de la Ascension" (Mi'rajnama) Timurid.* Digitally: Gallica, website of the Bibliothèque Nationale de France: 'Deux livres en turc-oriental, écrit en caractères mongols, dits ouïghours' https://gallica.bnf.fr/ark:/12148/btv1b8427195m.image [accessed 24 March 2019].
20. On fol. 95v, in Ms. Elliott 339 in the Bodleian Library, Oxford, the *Sadd-e Eskandar*, one volume of 'Ali-Shir Nava'i's *Khamsa* of 890/1485: Susan Scollay, ed., *Love & Devotion*, fig. 14.12, p. 197; see also B.W. Robinson, *A Descriptive Catalogue of the Persian Paintings in the Bodleian Library* (hereafter Robinson, *Bodl.*), no. 616, p. 66.
21. In Istanbul, Topkapi Saray, H. 2153, fol. 98r: noted by Zeki Velidi Togan as early as 1948, it was first discussed at some length by M. Kemal Özergin in 1976: 'Temürlü Sanatma âit Eski bir Belge', pp. 471–518; English trans. by Thackston, in Lentz & Lowry, pp. 364–65 (also in Thackston, *Century of Princes*, pp. 323–27); Sergei Tourkin offers a somewhat variant reading, with careful emendations: 'Returning to the "Petition" by Ja'far Bāysonghori', pp. 34–38.
22. Golombek & Wilber, vol. I, Cat. 30, pp. 263–65, and passim; vol. II, Pls. 88–95, Pl. VIIa, figs. 28–29.

23. Edgar Knobloch, *Turkestan*, pp. 168–73, with a plan on p. 171; Vitaly Naumkin, ed., *Caught in Time*, pp. 15–16, figs 69–79 – as they were in the late nineteenth century; Lentz & Lowry, pp. 90–95, and for a restored, later twentieth-century view of the entire Registan, pp. 92–93.
24. Sims, Garrett, Appendix I, pp. 379–82; note that measurements therein are recorded in millimetres.
25. Eleanor Sims, 'The illustrations of Baghdad 282 in the Topkapi Sarayi Library', pp. 222–27; on its dates, Lentz & Lowry, Cat. 46, pp. 338–39, the latter date – 820/1417–18 – noted, and communicated, by Ilse Sturkenboom in 2018.
26. Arnold, *Zafar-Nāmah*, illustrated facing pp. 1 and 22.
27. Dublin, Chester Beatty Library, Ms. Per. 144: see BWG, p. 80, Cat. 71; Stchoukine, *MT*, Ms. LXIX, p. 68; A.J. Arberry et al., *Chester Beatty*, vol. I, pp. 79–80; note, however, that the measurements there cited were taken from the published catalogue and, being perhaps inexact, should be used with caution.
28. As could be appreciated by simply looking at the illustrations in Roxburgh, 'Many a wish'.
29. Sims, Garrett, pp. 381–81; compare Grace Dunham Guest, *Shiraz Painting in the Sixteenth Century*, esp. Chapter I and pp. 28–29, and fig. 8, facing p. 32; Lâle Uluç, *Turkman Governors, Shiraz Artisans, and Ottoman Collectors*, does not discuss this feature at any length but her volume is densely illustrated with such sixteenth-century Shiraz paintings.
30. Priscilla P. Soucek, 'The arts of calligraphy', in *ABCA*, pp. 7–34, esp. pp. 8, 10 and 21 (Pl. III); Wright, *LoB*, pp. 231, 254.
31. Paris, Bibliothèque Nationale de France, Ms. Supplément persan 226: Chahriyar Adle, 'Recherche sur le module et le tracé correcteur', pp. 81–105.
32. Eleanor Sims, 'The illustrated manuscripts of Firdausi's *Shahnama* Commissioned by Princes of the House of Timur', pp. 34-68 (hereafter Sims, 'House of Timur').
33. Tehran, Gulistan Palace Library, Reg. No. 761 (formerly Ms. 61), the date of completion 833/1430: widely published since it was first exhibited in London in 1931: BWG, p. 56, Cat. 49, pp. 69–71, and pls. XLIII–L; a facsimile was produced in 1971, on the occasion of the '2500th anniversary of the founding of the Iranian monarchy': *Shāhnāma-ye Ferdowsi az ru-ye nuskha-ye khatti-ye Bāysonghori keh dar ketābkhāna-ye saltanati negāhdāri mishavad* (*Shāhnāma* of Ferdowsi, Facsimile of the Baysunghuri Manuscript Kept in the Royal Library), illustrated not photographically but by watercolour copies; good illustrations of illumination and paintings in Mohammad-Hasan Semsar, *Golestan Palace Library*, pp. (unnumbered 86)–109.
34. London, Royal Asiatic Society, Ms. Morley 239, undated but attributed to the 1440s: also widely published, starting with J.V.S. Wilkinson, *The Shāh-nāmah of Firdausī*; BWG, Cat. 67, pp. 78–79, 93, and pl. LVIII; Barbara Brend, *Muhammad Juki's Shahnamah of Firdausi*. Now on long-term loan to the Cambridge University Library and digitized: https://cudl.lib.cam.ac.uk/collections/ras/1
35. Oxford, Bodleian Library, Ms. Ouseley Add. 176, also undated but datable to the years between about 1430 and 1432: Robinson, *Bodl.*, pp. 16–22; Sims, 'The hundred and one paintings', pp. 120–22; the Ms. is now also available digitally: 'The Shāhnāmah of Ibrāhīm Sulṭān, Online from Digital.Bodleian:

https://digital.bodleian.ox.ac.uk/inquire/Discover/Search/#/?p=c+0,t+,rsrs+0,rsps+10,fa+,so+ox%3Asort%5Easc,scids+,pid+bcbfd832-086b-4874-80f8-87500e0de704,vi+1bb1bc76-7abd-444f-97b0-771847072561

36. Eleanor Sims, 'Towards a study of Šīrazī illustrated manuscripts of the "Interim" period', Appendix, pp. 620–23; surely more exist, eventually to be added.
37. Sims, 'House of Timur', Appendix B, section 3, pp. 67–68. One important addition is the ex-Jeuniette *Shahnama* of 890–91/1485–86, now in the N.D. Khalili Collection, MSS713, discussed in the forthcoming catalogue by this writer.
38. Robinson, *ABCA*, pp. 245–46.
39. Ibid., pp. 246–47.
40. Marie Lukens Swietochowski, 'The School of Herat from 1450 to 1506', in *ABCA*, pp. 179–214, remains a discursive and thorough overview, to be supplemented by later, and more specific, studies; Lentz & Lowry offers numbers of very good colour illustrations.
41. Quoted by A. J. Arberry, *Classical Persian Literature*, p. 47.
42. Paris, Musée des arts decoratifs 3727, on long-term loan to the Musée du Louvre since 2006, purchased from Nicolas-Alexis Jaroszinski in May 1887: also much published: BWG, p. 68, Cat. 47, pl. XLI and reprint-cover; Lentz & Lowry, Cat. 34, ill. p. 117, and again on the cover; Eleanor Sims et al., *Peerless Images*, p. 168, no. 82; Remy Labrousse, ed., *Purs Decors?*, Cat. 68, p. 122; Sophie Makariou, ed. *Islamic Art at the Musée du Louvre*, pp. 417-18.
43. Fitzherbert, 'Khwājū', pp. 137, 145; she confirms that she has checked all the rubrics against an edited Persian version.
44. Information kindly supplied by Charlotte Maury, Département des arts de l'Islam, Musée du Louvre (a scant difference from '29.5 × 18', as published in *Purs decors*, p. 122). She also identifies another cartouche from the original manuscript, pasted underneath the portrait of Soltān-Hoseyn-e Bāyqarā, formerly in the Topkapi Palace Library and now in the Harvard University Art Museums, 1958.59; illustrated in colour, in Sims et al., *Peerless Images*, p. 270, no. 186; see also Roxburgh, 'Our works', pp. 787–88. On 17 October 2018 (in the period since this text was worked up for publication), Maury delivered a lecture on the painting, following a thorough scientific examination in the laboratories of the Louvre; it was entitled 'Nouveau regard sur un chef d'œuvre de la peinture persane: "Humay et Humayun" ou la Vision Inspirée du Rêve d'un Prince' and is also available online: https://www.louvre.fr/conferences-en-ligne/l-oeuvre-en-scene
45. Such as 'The Games of Backgammon and Chess', from Bāysonghor's anthology of 830/1426–27, also illustrated in colour in Sims et al., *Peerless Images*, p. 215, no. 126.
46. A[da] Adamova, 'Repetition of compositions in manuscripts', pp. 67–75; and eadem, 'The Hermitage Museum manuscript of Nizami's *Khamseh*, dated 835/1431', pp. 76–77.
47. Alexander C. Soper, 'Northern Liang and Northern Wei in Kansu', pp. 132–33, figs 7, 13; Annette Juliano and Judith A. Lerner, *Monks and Merchants*, p. 132, fig. 11.
48. Istanbul, Topkapi Sarayi Library, Ms. H. 2154, fol. 20v: first identified by Verna Prentice, 'A detached miniature', pp. 60–66; she was uncertain of the attribution to 'Abd al-Hayy, but I am inclined to accept it, as was also Roxburgh, 'Our works', p. 821; illustrated in colour in Sims et al., *Peerless Images*, p. 263, no. 179.

49. Homay, in the wedding-scene (on fol. 45v), wears a very simplified version of the fluttering scarf: illustrated in colour in the British Library Blog by Ursula Sims-Williams, 1 August 2013: 'An illustrated 14th century Khamsah by Khvaju Kirmani': https://blogs.bl.uk/asian-and-african/2013/07/an-illustrated-14th-century-khamsah-by-khvaju-kirmani.html; the rippling, bicoloured sashes worn by the footless angels in the spandrels of the painting on fol. 91r (Sims, et al., *Peerless Images*, p. 192, no. 105) are more similar to those in 'Abd al-Hayy's picture; they also occur in other paintings and drawings in the Istanbul albums, H. 2153 and H. 2160: figs 51, 53, 91–94, and fig. 104, in *Islamic Art* I.
50. David Stronach and Hilary Gopnik, 'Pasargadae', *Encyclopaedia Iranica*, online edition, 2009, in addition to specific studies by Stronach noted therein: 1978, 1989, 1997.

Bibliography:

Adamova, A., 'Repetition of compositions in manuscripts: The *Khamsa* of Nizami in Leningrad,' in *Timurid Art and Culture: Iran and Central Asia in the Fifteenth Century*, ed. Lisa Golombek and Maria Subtelny, *Studies in Islamic Art and Architecture*. Supplements to *Muqarnas*, vol. 6 (Leiden: Brill, 1992), pp. 67–75.

— 'The Hermitage Museum manuscript of Nizami's *Khamseh*, dated 835/1431', *Islamic Art* 5 (2001), pp. 53–132.

Adle, Chahriyar, 'Recherche sur le module et le tracé correcteur dans la miniature orientale: I. la mise en évidence à partir d'un example', *Le monde iranien et l'islam, sociétés et cultures* 3 (1975), pp. 81–105.

Arberry, A.J., *Classical Persian Literature* (London: G. Allen & Unwin, 1958).

Arberry, A.J., Edgard Blochet, Mujtaba Minovi, B.W. Robinson and J.V.S. Wilkinson, *The Chester Beatty Library: A Catalogue of the Persian Manuscripts and Miniatures*, 3 vols (Dublin: Hodges, Figgis & Co., 1959–62).

Arnold, Thomas, *Bihzād and his Paintings in the Zafar-Nāmah MS.* (London: Quaritch, 1930).

Binyon, Laurence, J.V.S. Wilkinson and Basil Gray, *Persian Miniature Painting* (London: Oxford University Press, 1933). (BWG).

Brend, Barbara, *Perspectives on Persian Painting: Illustrations to Amīr Khusrau's Khamsah* (London: RoutledgeCurzon, 2003).

— Muhammad *Juki's Shahnamah of Firdausi* (London: Royal Asiatic Society & Philip Wilson, 2010).

Catalogue of the All-Union Exhibition on the Arts of the Timurid Period (Tashkent, 1969).

Clinton, Jerome W., 'Ferdowsi and the illustration of the *Shahnameh*', in *Islamic Art and Literature*, ed. Oleg Grabar and Cynthia Robinson (Princeton: Markus Wiener, 2001), pp. 57–78.

Coomaraswamy, Ananda K., *Les Miniatures Orientales de la Collection Goloubew au Museum of Fine Arts de Boston. Ars Asiatica* 13 (Paris; Bruxelles: Van Oest, 1929).

Dodkhudoeva, Larissa, *Poemy Nizami v srednevekovoy miniaturnoy zhivopisi ('The Poems of Nizami in Mediaeval Miniature Painting')* (Moscow: Nauka, Glavnaya redaktsiya vostochnoy literatury, 1985).

Fitzherbert, Teresa, 'Khwājū Kirmānī (689-753-1290-1352)', *Iran* 29 (1991), pp. 137–51.

Golombek, Lisa and Donald Wilber, *The Timurid Architecture of Iran and Turan*, 2 vols (Princeton: University Press, 1988). (Golombek & Wilber).

Gray, Basil, ed., *The Arts of the Book in Central Asia* (Paris: UNESCO, 1979). (*ABCA).*

Grube, Ernst J., *Muslim Miniature Paintings from the XIII to XIX Century from Collections in the United States and Canada*, exhibition catalogue (Venice and New York: N. Pozza, 1962).

— 'The fifteenth century miniatures', *Bulletin of the Metropolitan Museum of Art*, NS 25, no. 9 (May 1967) (and separate reprint, *The Language of the Birds*), pp. 317–38.

— 'Notes on the decorative arts of the Timurid period', in *Gururajamanjarika: Studi in onore di Giuseppe Tucci* (Naples: Istituto Universitario Orientale, 1974), vol. I, pp. 233–79.

— 'Notes on the decorative arts of the Timurid period. II', *Islamic Art* 3 (1989), pp. 175–208.

Grube, Ernst J. and Eleanor Sims, eds. *Between China and Iran*, Colloquies on Art and Archaeology in Asia, no. 10 (London: SOAS and the Percival David Foundation, 1981). (*Islamic Art* I).

Gruber, Christiane J., *El "Libro de la Ascension" (Mi'rajnama) Timurid: Estudio de textos e imagenes et un contexto panasiatico/The Timurid "Book of Ascension" (Mi'rajnama): A Study of Text and Image in a Pan-Asian Context* (Valencia: Ediciones Patrimonio, 2008), text in Spanish, pp. 5–240 and English, pp. 249–432.

Guest, Grace Dunham, *Shiraz Painting in the Sixteenth Century* (Washington, DC: Freer Gallery of Art, 1949).

Hayashi, Norihito, 'The Turkman commercial style of painting: Origins and developments reconsidered', *Orient* 47 (2012), pp. 169–87.

Hillenbrand, R., ed., *Persian Painting from the Mongols to the Qajars* (London and New York: I.B. Tauris, 2000). (*Robinson Festschrift*).

Juliano, Annette and Judith A. Lerner, *Monks and Merchants: Silk Road Treasures from Northwest China, Gansu and Ningxia 4th–7th Century* (New York: Abrams, 2001).

Kamada, Yumiko, 'A taste for intricacy: An illustrated manuscript of *Mantiq al-Tayr* in the Metropolitan Museum of Art', *Orient* 15 (2010), pp. 129–76.

Knobloch, Edgar, *Turkestan* (Munich: Prestel, 1973).

Kühnel, Ernst, 'History of miniature painting and drawing', *Survey of Persian Art*, vol. III, pp. 1829–97, vol. V, pls. 815–918 (Oxford: University Press, 1938–39).

Labrousse, Remy, *Purs Decors? Arts de l'Islam, regards du XIXe siècle*, exhibition catalogue (Paris: Les Arts Décoratifs, 2008).

Lentz, Thomas W., 'Painting at Herat under Baysunghur ibn Shahrukh', doctoral dissertation (Harvard University, 1985).

Lentz, Thomas W. and Glenn D. Lowry, *Timur and the Princely Vision, Persian Art and Culture in the Fifteenth Century* (Los Angeles: County Museum of Art; Washington: Sackler Gallery, 1989). (Lentz & Lowry).

Makariou, Sophie, ed., *Islamic Art at the Musée du Louvre*, exhibition catalogue (Paris: Musée du Louvre, 2012).

Marteau, Georges and Henri Vever, *Miniatures Persanes exposées au Musée des Arts Décoratifs (Juin–Octobre 1912)*, 2 vols (Paris: Bibliothèque d'Art et d'Archéologie, 1913).
Martin, F.R., *The Miniature Painting and Painters of Persia, India and Turkey from the 8th to the 19th Century*, 2 vols (London: Quaritch, 1912, reprinted in 1 volume: Holland Press, 1971).
Martin, F.R. and Thomas Arnold, *The Nizami MS. Illluminated by Bihzad, Mirak and Qasim Ali …* (Vienna: privately printed, 1926).
Mehran, Farhad, 'The break-line verse: The link between text and image in the "First Small" *Shahnama*', in *Shahnama Studies I*, ed. Charles Melville (Cambridge: Centre of Middle Eastern Studies, 2006), pp. 151–69.
— 'Mapping illustrated folios of *Shahnama* manuscripts: The concept and its uses', in *Shahnama Studies II*, ed. Charles Melville and Gabrielle van den Berg (Leiden: Brill, 2012), pp. 238–66.
Melikian-Chirvani, Assadullah Souren, 'Khwāje Mīrak Naqqāsh', *Journal Asiatique* 276, nos. 1–2 (1988), pp. 97–146.
Meredith-Owens, G.M., *Handlist of Persian Manuscripts, 1895–1966* (London: British Museum, 1966).
Naumkin, Vitaly, ed., *Caught in Time: Samarkand* (Reading: Garnet, 1992).
Norgren, Jill and Edward Davis, *Preliminary Index of Shah-Nameh Illustrations* (Ann Arbor: Centre for Near Eastern and North African Studies, 1969).
Özergin, M. Kemal, 'Temürlü Sanatma âit Eski bir Belge: Tebrizli Ca'fer'in Bir Arzi', *Sanat Tarihi Yilligi* 6 (1976), pp. 471–518.
Panayotova, Stella, ed., *Colour: The Art and Science of Illuminated Manuscripts*, exhibition catalogue (London: Harvey Miller, 2016).
Prentice, Verna, 'A detached miniature from the Masnavis of Khwaju Kermani', *Oriental Art*, NS 17 (1981), pp. 60–66.
Rettig, Simon, 'La production manuscrite à Chiraz sous les Aq Qoyyunlu entre 1467 et 1503', doctoral dissertation (Université Aix-Marseille I, Université de Provence, 2011).
Richard, Francis, *Splendeurs persanes: Manuscrits du XIIe au XVIIe siècle*, exhibition catalogue (Paris: Bibliothèque Nationale de France, 1997).
Rieu, Charles, *Catalogue of the Persian Manuscripts in the British Museum*, 3 vols (London: British Museum, 1879–95).
Robinson, B.W., *A Descriptive Catalogue of the Persian Paintings in the Bodleian Library* (Oxford: University Press, 1958). (Robinson, *Bodl.*).
— 'The Dunimarle Shāhnāma: A Timurid manuscript from Mazandaran', in *Aus der Welt der islamischen Kunst: Festschrift für Ernst Kühnel zum 75. Geburtstag am 26.10.1957*, ed. R. Ettinghausen (Berlin: Gebr. Mann, 1959), pp. 207–18.

— *Persian Miniature Painting from Collections in the British Isles*, exhibition catalogue (London: Victoria and Albert Museum, 1967). (Robinson, *British*).
— 'The Turkman School to 1503', in *ABCA*, pp. 215–47. (Robinson, *ABCA*).
— *Fifteenth Century Persian Painting: Problems and Issues* (New York: University Press, 1991).
Roxburgh, David. J., '"Our Works Point to Us": Album Making, Collecting, and Art (1427–1565) under the Timurids and Safavids', doctoral dissertation, 2 vols (Harvard University, 1996).
— 'The aesthetics of aggregation: Persian anthologies of the fifteenth century', in *Islamic Art and Literature*, ed. Oleg Grabar and Cynthia Robinson (Princeton: Markus Wiener, 2001), pp. 119–42.
— 'Many a wish has turned to dust: Pir Budaq and the formation of Turkmen arts of the book', in *Envisioning Islamic Art and Architecture: Essays in Honor of Renata Holod*, ed. by David J. Roxburgh (Leiden and Boston: Brill, 2014), pp. 175–221.
Sahragard, Mahdi, *Masterpieces of Āstān-e Quds-e Razavi: Inscriptions of Goharshād Mosque* (Mashhad: Āstān-e Quds-e Razavi, 2013) (in Persian).
Sakisian, Armenag, *La Miniature Persan du XIIeme au XVIIeme siècle* (Paris and Bruxelles: Van Oest, 1929).
Schroeder, Eric, *Persian Miniatures in the Fogg Museum* (Cambridge, MA: Harvard University Press, 1942).
Schulz, Ph. Walter, *Die persisch-islamische Miniaturmalerei*, 2 vols (Leipzig: Hiersemann, 1914).
Scollay, Susan, ed., *Love & Devotion: From Persia and Beyond*, exhibition catalogue (Oxford: Bodleian Library/Macmillan Art Publishing, 2012).
Séguy, Marie-Rose, *The Miraculous Journey of Mahomet: Miraj Nameh: Bibliothèque Nationale, Paris (Manuscrit supplément turc 190)*, introduction and commentaries (New York: George Braziller, 1977).
Semsar, Mohammad-Hasan, *Golestan Palace Library: Portfolio of Miniature Paintings and Calligraphy* (Tehran: Zarrin & Simin Books, 2000) (in Persian and English).
Shāhnāma-ye Ferdowsi az ru-ye nuskheh-ye khatti-ye Bāysonghori keh dar ketāb-khāneh-ye saltanati negāhdāri mishavad, 1350 *sh.* (*Shahnama* of Ferdowsi, Facsimile of the Baysunghuri Manuscript Kept in the Royal Library ([Tehran], 1350/1971).
Sims, Eleanor, 'The Garrett Manuscript of the Zafar-Name: A Study in Fifteenth-century Timurid Patronage', doctoral dissertation (New York University, 1973). (Sims, Garrett).
— 'Sultan Husayn Bayqara's Zafar-Namah and its miniatures', in *VIth International Congress of Iranian Art & Archaeology, Oxford, September 11–16th 1972* (Tehran: Iranian Centre for Archaeological Research, 1976), pp. 299–311.

— 'The illustrated manuscripts of Firdausi's *Shahnama* commissioned by Princes of the House of Timur', *Ars Orientalis* 22 (1992), pp. 34–68.

— 'Towards a study of Šīrazī illustrated manuscripts of the "Interim" period', *Oriente Moderno* NS Anno XV, 76, no. 2 (1996 [1998]), pp. 611–25.

— 'The hundred and one paintings of Ibrahim-Sultan', in R. Hillenbrand, ed., *Robinson Festschrift*, pp. 119–27, and illustrations pp. 104–10.

— 'The illustrations of Baghdad 282 in the Topkapi Sarayi Library in Istanbul', with a contribution by Tim Stanley, in *Cairo to Kabul: Afghan and Islamic Studies Presented to Ralph Pinder-Wilson*, ed. Warwick Ball and Leonard Harrow (London: Melisende, 2002), pp. 222–27.

— 'Riflessioni sulle arti del libro nell'Oriente islamico del XV secolo', pp. 91–95, and 'I "principi bibliofili" del XV secolo e le arti del libro', pp. 280–326, in *Il Montefeltro e L'oriente Islamico: Urbino, 1430–1550, Il Palazzo Ducale tra Occidente e Oriente*, ed. Alessandro Bruschettini (Genoa: Sagep editori, 2018).

— *The Tale and the Image: History and Epic Paintings from Iran and Turkey*, Part 1 (London, forthcoming).

Sims, Eleanor (and Boris Marshak, with a contribution by Ernst J. Grube), *Peerless Images: Persian Painting and its Sources* (New Haven and London: Yale University Press, 2002).

Soper, Alexander C., 'Northern Kiang and Northern Wei in Kansu', *Artibus Asiae* 21, no. 2 (1958), pp. 131–64.

Soucek, Priscilla P., 'Illustrated Manuscripts of Nizami's Khamseh: 1386–1482', doctoral dissertation, 2 vols (New York University, 1971).

— 'The arts of calligraphy', in *ABCA*, pp. 7–34.

— 'The New York Public Library "Makhzan al-asrār" and its importance', *Ars Orientalis* 18 (1988), pp. 1–37.

— 'The Ann Arbor *Shahnama* and its importance', in R. Hillenbrand, ed., *Robinson Festschrift*, pp. 267–81.

Stchoukine, Ivan, 'Un Gulistan illustré par des artistes tîmûrides', *RAA* 10 (1936), pp. 92–96.

— 'Les peintures de la Khamseh de Nizami du British Museum (Or. 6810)', *Syria* 27 (1950), pp. 301–13.

— *Les peintures des manuscrits Tîmûrides* (Paris: Geuthner, 1954). (Stchoukine, *MT*).

— 'La peinture à Baghdād sous Sultān Pīr Būdāq Qārā-Qoyūnlū', *Arts Asiatiques* 25 (1972), pp. 3–18.

— *Les peintures des manuscrits de la "Khamseh" de Nizami au Topkapi Sarayi Müzesi d'Istanbul* (Paris: Guethner, 1977).

Stronach, David and Hilary Gopnik, 'Pasargadae', *Encyclopaedia Iranica*, online at www.iranicaonline.org/articles/pasargadae (2009) [accessed 24 March 2019].

Sturkenboom, Ilse, 'The Imagery of the *Mantiq al-Tayr:* A Fifteenth-century History of Illustrated Manuscripts Incorporating "Attār's *Conference of the Birds*"', doctoral dissertation, 2 vols (Otto-Friedrich University, Bamberg, 2016).

Subtelny, Maria, 'A taste for the intricate: The Persian poetry of the late Timurid period', *Zeitschrift der Deutschen Morgenländischen Gesellschaft* 136, no. 1 (1986), pp. 56–79.

Swietochowski, Marie Lukens, 'The School of Herat from 1450 to 1506', in *ABCA*, pp. 179–214.

Thackston, Wheeler M., *A Century of Princes: Sources on Timurid History and Art* (Cambridge, MA: Aga Khan Program for Islamic Architecture, 1989).

Thompson, Daniel V., *The Materials of Medieval Painting* (London: G. Allen & Unwin, 1936).

Titley, Norah, *Miniatures from Persian Manuscripts: Catalogue and Subject Index of Paintings ... in the British Library and the British Museum* (London: British Library, [1977]). (Titley, *MPM*).

Tourkin, Sergei, 'Returning to the "Petition" by Ja'far Bāysonghori addressed to his patron, Bāysonghor b. Šāhrokh', *Manuscripta Orientalia: International Journal for Oriental Manuscript Research* 9, no. 3 (September 2003), pp. 34–38. (Also in Russian, in *Peterburgskoe vostokovedenie* 10 (2002), pp. 335–41).

Uluç, Lâle, *Turkman Governors, Shiraz Artisans, and Ottoman Collectors: Sixteenth Century Shiraz Manuscripts* (Istanbul: Türkiye Bankası, 2006).

Wilkinson, J.V.S., *The Shāh-nāmah of Firdausī: With 24 Illustrations from a Fifteenth-century Manuscript ... now in the Possession of the Royal Asiatic Society ...* (London: India Society, 1931).

Wright, Elaine, *The Look of the Book: Manuscript Production in Shiraz, 1303–1452* (Washington, DC: Freer Gallery of Art, 2012). (Wright, *LoB*).

Digital sources [All accessed 25 March 2019.]

Bibliothèque Nationale de France, 'Deux livres en turc-oriental, écrit en caractères mongols, dits ouïghours:

https://gallica.bnf.fr/ark:/12148/btv1b8427195m.image.

BL. Ms. Add. 18113:

www.bl.uk/manuscripts/FullDisplay.aspx?ref=Add_MS_18113

Blog: Ursula Sims-Williams (1 August 2013), 'An illustrated 14th century Khamsah by Khvaju Kirmani'

https://blogs.bl.uk/asian-and-african/2013/07/an-illustrated-14th-century-khamsah-by-khvaju-kirmani.html

Blog: Sheila Blair (16 June 2015), 'The archaeology of a manuscript: the Khamsah of Khvaju Kirmani':
https://blogs.bl.uk/asian-and-african/2015/06/the-archaeology-of-a-manuscript-the-khamsah-of-khvaju-kirmani.html
Cambridge University Library:
https://cudl.lib.cam.ac.uk/collections/ras/1
Louvre Museum, Paris:
https://www.louvre.fr/conferences-en-ligne/l-oeuvre-en-scene
Oxford Bodleian Ms. Ouseley Add. 176:
https://digital.bodleian.ox.ac.uk/inquire/Discover/Search/#/?p=c+0,t+,rsrs+0,rsps+10,fa+,so+ox%3Asort%5Easc,scids+,pid+bcbfd832-086b-4874-80f8-87500e0de704,vi+1bb1bc76-7abd-444f-97b0-771847072561

8

From Maragha to Samarqand and Beyond: Revisiting a Quartet of Scientific Traditions in Greater Persia (ca. 1300s–1500s)[1]

Elaheh Kheirandish
(Harvard University)

This chapter concerns four scientific traditions whose developments must be re-evaluated in the light of historical sources introduced and contextualized here, mostly for the first time. These sources, which represent the state of these sciences during post-Mongol times and in 'Greater-Persian' lands, do so according to historical pieces drawn directly from specific times and places, in line with the concept of the 'Idea of Iran',[2] one reflecting historical as well as modern perceptions of the Persian past. Sources accordingly referred to here as 'period pieces' do more than change the picture long painted of scientific activity during the late Islamic Middle Ages; they literally invert images often held of their underexposed 'dark chambers', to use imagery from 'camera obscura',[3] an entity with its own developments in Islamic lands much earlier than in Europe.

What follows extends the discussion of four Persian scientific traditions: optics, astronomy, mechanics and geometry, from the early middle ages (ca. 1000) addressed by the present author elsewhere, to the later middle ages (ca. 1300s–1500s), where the expression 'Persian' continues to represent specific features identifiable within the respective scientific traditions, from linguistic expressions and ethnic associations, to geographical locations and sites of transmission. A study of these four scientific traditions in the earlier period after ca. 1000 was part of an event titled 'Persian Culture as a World Culture',[4] where geometry, astronomy, mechanics and optics were presented in that order as 'prime players in the quartet of world science' and featured in a companion 'documentary short'.[5] The present 'revisiting' of the same scientific traditions in different times and places is not limited to extending their historical and geographical boundaries to periods after AD 1000 and areas beyond Persian lands of the Islamic Middle Ages. The historical evidence that follows in the atypical form of a Preface, a Letter, a Postscript, an Introduction and other excerpts from texts in both Arabic and Persian, provides successive period pieces which offer, through their respective contexts, a picture of the various states of these sciences. They may be contrasted sharply with those views long held of a single entity called 'science' and of a blanket scientific 'decline' applied to it collectively.[6] The distinct pieces selected here rather represent a greater Persia, not just in temporal and spatial terms, but in the literal sense of a Persia (historically, *Fars*), that is 'greater' both regionally and intellectually in terms of developments within the four subjects that follow, and their respective transmissions, institutions, traditions and associations.

The post-Mongol period pieces selected for each of the four disciplines from the 1300s to 1500s, are presented here in an order and context different from my earlier discussion of the previous centuries post-ca. 1000, as they are analysed not only with reference to primary sources that include geographical locators such as 'Persian' lands (Fars); the pieces also represent various genres from successive centuries that are rarely exposed or treated from the present angle and, in a few published attempts, require revisions in translation or interpretation. Featured in chronological order and historical context are the following cases, discussed with reference to the relevant primary and secondary sources, and supplied with original transcriptions of selected passages in an Appendix (P.I – P.VI): in each selection, the key statements are numbered in correspondence with those in English translation or paraphrase within the body of the present text for the successive cases under discussion (e.g. P.I: 1–10).

First, on optics, is a *Preface* by Kamal al-Din Faresi (d. ca. 718/1318) in his commentary, composed ca. 704/1304, on the Book of *Optics* of Ebn al-Heytham (d. after ca. 432/1040–41), *Ketab al-manazer*, composed ca. 411–21/1020–30.[7] This reports an otherwise unknown transmission of the latter work throughout 'Persian lands' (Fars) (P.I): an excerpt from Faresi's preface is selected for recording the limited transmission of that important work in Islamic lands in great contrast to the much wider European transmission of its seven books. Second, is a *Letter* by Gheyas al-Din Jamshid Kashani, better known as Kashi or al-Kashi (d. ca. 832/1429), sent to his father from Samarqand to Kashan (composed after ca. 824/1421).[8] This covers little-known aspects of the astronomy of the time in the Samarqand school and observatory sponsored by the Timurid Prince, Ologh Beg (r. independently 851–53/1447–49): an excerpt from the letter of Kashani (hereafter Kashi) is selected for including an atypically detailed report on the state of the sciences in Fars (P.II). Third, is a *Postscript* on practical geometry by the much less-known Abu Eshaq Kubanani (d. after ca. 888/1483),[9] an understudied author with other unpublished works and letters, often signed with dates, places and names of patrons from Sari and Yazd to Kerman and Jarun (Hormoz). An excerpt from Kubanani's postscript is selected for revealing important information about his contemporaries and the state of mathematical sciences in his own time (P.III). Fourth, is an *Introduction* by Mohammad Hafez Esfahani to a mechanical work (composed after ca. 918/1512),[10] naming the involvement of Timurid rulers and viziers in his commissioned construction of a European-style mechanical clock. An excerpt from Hafez Esfahani's introduction is selected for the details it provides on his self-proclaimed novelty, which the author discusses with reference to specific figures and sites within greater Persia (P.IV). Returning to optics at a later period, there is an anonymous Persian text datable to the early 1500s, naming the Ottoman sultan Selim I (r. 918–28/1512–20),[11] with an unparalleled account of European 'mirrors' sent to scholars in Khorasan for 'experiment and testing' (P.V). An excerpt from this text, which survives in a shorter Arabic version (P.VI) naming the same sultan,[12] though not datable as a report on a past event in either of the two known versions, is selected here for its striking content. The reported east to west transmission of optics at this early modern period not only challenges the expected direction of the transfer of knowledge but it also presents a useful contrast to contemporary sciences such as mechanics, where an instrument like a mechanical clock is given an explicit European prototype.

Optics

The first period piece (P.I) concerns optics (*manazer* in Arabic and Persian) through the *Preface* of Faresi's commentary on Ebn al-Heytham's *Optics*, both composed in Arabic. The latter enjoyed a much wider impact in Europe than in Islamic lands, in contrast to Faresi's commentary, composed in the early 700s/1300s, probably in Tabriz in northwest Iran, a work so far considered to have been transmitted only internally. Faresi's preface to that commentary, composed as a *Revision* (*Tanqih*) of the *Optics* of Ebn al-Heytham from over two centuries earlier, contains a key passage with unexpected revelations about the state of that science in that specific time and place, with direct reference to 'Persian' identifiers. We find in the unfolding sentences of that preface (P.I: 1–10) various pieces of historical information, all otherwise unknown: the first few capture the state of the sciences in the Persian lands of the Islamic Middle Ages, and the unexpected prominence of scientific observation. Faresi remarks that he saw in the statements of more than one 'leading thinker' (P.I: 1) – a likely reference to Nasir al-Din Tusi (d. ca. 672/1274), the teacher of his own teacher Qotb al-Din Shirazi (d. ca. 711/1311)[13] – a 'puzzling' premise about 'four equal angles' produced when light encounters a medium denser than air, making the angle of refraction equal to those of incidence and reflection (P.I: 2); Faresi continues that 'he was perplexed at where these rules came from' (P.I: 3); and these being, significantly, contrary to experience (P.I: 4), his puzzlement increased (P.I: 5); that he related the whole story to his mentor, Shirazi (P.I: 6), reminding him of the similarly larger appearance of objects near the horizon (P.I: 7). Here is where Faresi adds a few critical statements about scientific transmission, with a focus on Persian lands: he relates that Shirazi, 'then remembered that he had seen in his youth in one of the libraries in Fars' (either his native province of Fars or 'Persia'), 'a book on optics attributed to Ebn al-Heytham in two large volumes' (P.I: 8); that 'he said he would obtain it for him', however hard (P.I: 9), and that with the firm determination of Faresi's mentor, the book eventually 'arrived from distant lands' (P.I: 10).[14]

This part of the report documents, in graphic detail, not only the previously rare presence of the important *Optics* of Ebn al-Heytham in Persian lands, whatever the term 'Fars' is taken to designate in terms of an exact location; but also a culture of active scientific engagement and mentorship at a time and place often considered, if not on the brink of scientific decline, as having been largely dormant at the very least.

It must be noted that Faresi's *Revision* of Ebn al-Heytham's *Optics*, a work that took its important prototype in new directions by supplying it with additional supplementary sections and explicit statements about expanding the disciplinary domain of the field, survives in many more manuscripts worldwide compared with the few known copies of Ebn al-Heytham's *Optics* itself, with which it is occasionally confused.[15] In contrast to both sources, the period pieces representing the subjects of astronomy, mechanics and geometry, as well as optics of a later period, are all known through single manuscripts (App. P.II – P.VI).

Astronomy

The case of astronomy is of great interest for various reasons, one with a different development and context altogether. About two centuries after the establishment of a school and observatory in Maragha, where scholars like Nasir al-Din Tusi and his student, Qotb al-Din Shirazi, worked just before the latter's student Kamal al-Din Faresi was active in nearby Tabriz, we have the case of a similar institutional complex in the early 800s/1400s in Samarqand, a city to the far east of Maragha, representing a still more outstanding case of the sciences in the much-expanded lands of Persia.[16] The case of Samarqand is especially well documented by revealing period pieces, including not one but two letters written by the scholar resident Gheyas al-Din Jamshid Kashi, who provides specific documentation for the unexpectedly rich case of the sciences, especially astronomy, thriving in a 'greater Persia' in both geographical and intellectual terms. In what is published as the first letter of Kashi to his father, discovered long after his second letter to him was published,[17] there is a key passage with many specifics about the state of the sciences, especially the institutions advancing them in that particular time and place.

The first letter of Kashi on the riches of the Samarqand of his own time (P.II: 1) starts by reporting that the Timurid prince Ologh Beg, founder of, and active participant in, the Samarqand school complex, had donated a 'charitable gift', here specified as 30,000 *kopaki* dinars, of which as much as 10,000 were ordered to be given to deserving students (P.II: 2). To begin with, such amounts of educational aid are substantial, especially with the author's pricing of elaborate architectural structures as 200 *kopaki* tomans in his much lesser known notes on the 'rarities of Samarqand'.[18] Kashi then offers a number of other unexpected statistics, reporting roughly 10,000 students qualifying for aid, steadily engaged in studying and learning (P.II: 3), and the same number with the privilege of doing so in their own homes among the notables and their offspring (P.II: 4). He even records 500 of these as having begun to study mathematics (P.II: 5).

In addition, Kashi's letter reports that the 'World-conqueror' student prince, Ologh Beg, had himself been studying 'this art', namely mathematics, for 12 years (P.II: 6), that students are inclined to it and working hard at it (P.II: 7); that the art itself was taught at 20 places (not 12, as wrongly published) (P.II: 8); and, above all, that the state of teaching and learning mathematics in Samarqand has 'no parallel in Fars and Iraq' (P.II: 9). Here, 'Fars' is likely meant as greater Persia, not 'Persia in the Southern province of Iran' as given in its published English version; so is *'Erāq*, meant as a non-Arab (*'Ajam*) region including the author's own native city of Kashan at the time. The passage then extends its quantitative measure beyond mathematics, specifying some of the 24 number calculators as being astronomers (P.II: 10).[19]

There are many more specific details in Kashi's letters about the impressive Samarqand school and observatory complex: the physical and social structure of that institution, the profile and relation of its community, the nature and level of their problem solving and the features and components of their instruments. But the piece selected here is enough to demonstrate an active scientific community no less productive than those in the Europe of the time; an unexpectedly secular institutional setting with rich scientific activities often assumed to have been limited, or limited to religious matters.

The period pieces selected for the two remaining subjects, mechanics and geometry, are not only similarly composed in Persian, as opposed to the case of optics composed in Arabic by a Persian native called Faresi; they are both directed to the practical aspects of mechanics and geometry, in contrast to the earlier selections.

Geometry

The next piece to be discussed in chronological order concerns the science of geometry: this is in the form of a rich postscript to a late ninth/fifteenth-century Persian translation of an Arabic work on practical geometry by Abu'l-Wafa' Buzjani (d. ca. 388/998), a work translated as *Geometrical Constructions* after its short title, *A'mal-e handasiya*, and with a strong tradition in Persian throughout at least four centuries.[20] The noticeably Persian weight of this tradition, in terms of the language of composition, ethnic associations and geographic location, starts with the successive Persian translations of Buzjani's *Geometrical Constructions*, from the latest of which a key passage is selected. This late translation, carrying the name, Abu Eshaq Kubanani Yazdi (d. after ca. 888/1483) as the figure 'completing that translation', has an uncommon postscript, which acts as a good source for projecting an informed picture of the state of a science such as geometry, from its theoretical and practical traditions to those developed in both Arabic and Persian.[21]

In that long and detailed period piece, presented as a postscript to the text's colophon, Kubanani provides an exceptionally rich context for a largely Persian scientific tradition, one that is surprisingly specific and explicit for its time and place. After announcing the end of the book (P.III: 1), and the typical naming of God Almighty, in this case 'giving him power to solve the problems of the geometrical propositions of Buzjani's wondrous book' (P.III: 2), Kubanani goes on to name people involved in his completed project, from an enquirer named Shams al-Din (P.III: 4–6), to an initiator, called Najm al-Din … (P.III: 7), the former requesting the reconstruction of the latter's unfinished book, 'without losing any time, during the course of two months' (P.III: 8). Kubanani ends his postscript with statements that suggest an active community of scholars around him, something also emerging from his unpublished letters.[22] He first asks the 'sages of the time, in places of slips [and] defects, not to refrain from rejecting his reasoning … and to give their opinions about invalidities and complexities' (P.III: 9); he then explicitly states 'how far human capacity has reached in earthly matters' in his own time (P.III: 10).

Despite problems of interpretation posed by certain lines of Kubanani's postscript, from the exact relation of the requester and initiator of his 'reconstruction' project, to his own involvement in the completion of a translation started by someone whom he calls his 'dearest brother' – whether literally or figuratively – this postscript is particularly important for addressing various historical questions, including dating. Critical among these is a close relation between Kubanani and an anonymous Persian *Compendium*, one recently published and of increasing historical significance.[23] In the same manuscript volume of Kubanani's 'completion of the Persian translation' of Buzjani's *Geometrical Construction*, there is an anonymous and undated Persian text entitled *On the Interlock of Figures*, which offers many more clues on the state and location of activities in geometry that are particularly important for understanding the evolving state of that subject, and the relation between its theoretical and practical traditions, especially in Persian lands.[24]

For example, one of the 61 patterns of the *Interlock of Figures* has been identified on a wall of Esfahan's *Jame'* mosque, one that carries the same exact patterns through superimposition,[25] though the exact relationship between the demonstrated and constructed patterns, as well as the dating of these and other texts and structures within this Persian tradition, remain subjects of much further study.

Mechanics

This brings us to the case of mechanics, the last of the four scientific subjects under discussion, where the period piece selected is a little-known work in Persian from a slightly later period, namely the early tenth/sixteenth century.

The key passage selected here is in the form of an 'Introduction' (*moqaddema*) to the first of three treatises titled *Natijat al-dowla*, composed by Mohammad Hafez Esfahani, a text surviving in a unique manuscript, probably the autograph, published in a Persian edition.[26] The three treatises concern his inventions of a weight-driven mechanical clock, a hydraulic oil press and a special water mill.[27] Before reproducing some critical lines from Hafez Esfahani's 'Introduction' to his treatise on clocks, it is important to cite the few pieces of information available about the author, his work under discussion and its estimated dates of composition in secondary works.

In an encyclopedia entry on this figure, the little-known author is introduced as a *mokhtare'* (inventor), where his 'timekeeper' is described as 'the first weight-driven mechanical alarm clock ever made, not only in the Islamic world, but in the whole Orient':

> Ḥāfeẓ Eṣfahānī relates that in order to save the high esteem of Islam, the Ottoman Sultan, Bāyazid II (886/1481–918/1512), whose engineers and artisans had failed to reproduce an essentially European type of mechanical clock, sent one of these clocks to Iran to be constructed there. The European clock reached Tabriz and then Herat, but nobody seems to have managed to work out how it operated. The Timurid court then asked Ḥāfeẓ Eṣfahānī to fulfill this task, and not only did he solve the puzzle and describe it in his treaty[sic], but he also made both a portable and a fixed kind of the originally European clock.[28].

Concerning Hafez Esfahani's patrons, while it is stated by the same modern author that he 'was not attached to any particular royal court', he is associated with the Timurid court of Soltan-Hoseyn-e Bayqara [r. 873–911/1469–1506], and his 'clock-making operation' is said to have been carried out under the patronage of the vizier 'Ali-Shir Nava'i [d. 906/1501]. The same source also refers to the *Zinat al-majales*,[29] written in 1004/1595, to add that 'one of Hafez Esfahani's reproductions was fixed in the tower of a hospital in Kashan'. From these and other details it may be implied that his work on the clock was carried out some time between 886/1481 and 906/1501, within the reign of Bayezid and the lifetime of Nava'i.[30] Different contextual information, including names and dates, is given by the editor of the *Natijat al-dowla*,[31] whose introductory notes refer to the author's early patrons, the Timurid brothers, Ahmad and Mahmud Gurkani (Güregeni; d. 899/1493–94 and 900/1494–95 respectively);[32] they were based in Samarqand, where Hafez Esfahani was summoned to make an oil press, as he describes in the second *Resala*.[33] The author himself notes that this was his third invention, the invitation to Samarqand presumably following his success with the European clock, suggesting that its arrival in Herat may have occurred first, i.e. before ca. 899/1494 and the death of Ahmad Gurkani.[34]

The date of composition of the *Natijat al-dowla* is uncertain, though it may be approximated from the relevant primary sources. The text's editor suggests a date after 928/1521–22, due to the author's reference to a certain Amir Khosrowshah, who supposedly died that year, as someone deceased.[35] However, this argument is problematic, because the intended Amir Khosrowshah died in 910/1505, which would have anchored the events recorded in the very last years of Timurid rule in Khorasan, and brings the *terminus post quem* forward.[36] It is important to note that the Iranian king is also mentioned as deceased (*maghfur*, *marhum*) and there can be little doubt that the ruler is, as generally accepted, Soltan-Hoseyn-e Bayqara; not least because of the splendour of the court in Herat in his time, but also because 'Ali-Shir Nava'i is reported to have been the sponsor of one of the unsuccessful scientists who was given the job ahead of Hafez Esfahani.[37] This is consistent with Hafez Esfahani's own writings, for example, concerning a paper smoother that he dates to 912/1506, i.e. shortly after the death of Soltan-Hoseyn-e Bayqara.[38]

It seems probable that the author left Khorasan after the collapse of the Timurids and returned to western Iran, as suggested by the fact that he evidently dedicated the book to Gheyas al-Din Mansur Dashtaki (ca. 866–67/1461 to 948/1541–42), from Shiraz, who was an influential figure and briefly held the office of Sadr under Shah Tahmasp.[39] Hafez Esfahani probably died before Dashtaki – mentioned as being very much alive and in Tabriz at the time the envoy passed through – and evidently left the work unfinished. A date of composition as late as 949–50/1542–43, i.e. after Dashtaki's death, is clearly implausible.[40]

Given the available evidence, while Hafez Esfahani's work on the clock may be dated between ca. 886/1481 and 906/1501, the composition date of his *Resala* describing its construction may safely be assumed to be after the death of Bayazid II (ca. 918/1512) and before that of Dashtaki (ca. 948/1541), based on the author's reference to them as deceased and living respectively.

Despite outstanding questions of date, patron and production, however, a reading of the author's own introduction, presented here as our fourth period piece, reveals many of the activities and motives involved, as do accounts of both earlier and later clocks with other functions, including more than one reported in Kashan.[41]

Hafez Esfahani begins his introduction to clocks by reporting something noteworthy, however problematic its exact meaning as transmitted in the published text:[42] he relays that it was heard from the envoy bringing a gift to Khorasan [from the Ottoman sultan Bayezid, named later[43]] that if this [gift of a] time [piece]/clock (*vaqt-o sa'at*)], which had been assembled by Greek sages and existed in the Frankish lands and was particular to them, was to be sought (*talab*) as a gift and souvenir for the prosperous emperor (*khaqan-e sa'id*) – an apparent reference to the Timurid Soltan-Hoseyn-e Bayqara – it would be outstanding and dearly valued (P.IV: 1). The saintly king (*hazrat padshah*) [that is, Soltan Bayazid II], 'to whom this idea appeared to be right and good, sent a messenger to Europe seeking the abovementioned time [piece] and clock' (P.IV: 2). After several initially unsuccessful attempts, reportedly due to the ancestral habits of Europeans to keep such devices to themselves and not let them be taken to Islamic territory, the Ottoman sultan was able to acquire the remarkable device. Given his expressed intention that 'this marvelous souvenir and wondrous gift should become commonplace and normal among the Muslims', and exasperated by the excuses and incapability admitted by native scholars, the Ottoman sultan sent 2,000 *tanka* (tangas) to the envoy bringing the timepiece and clock to Khorasan (P.IV: 3). The author elaborates that the envoy in the course of his long journeys and passages from one major city to another, was ordered, 'once he arrived at any city, to announce this to the inhabitants and learned, and people of refinement and expertise and tempt them with this fund' (P.IV: 4); and that 'If anyone was disposed to making that timepiece and clock, he [the envoy] should stop there for a while and, after ensuring it was complete without any defects', give the mentioned fund and the device to whoever performed that construction (P.IV: 5). The purpose of this was that this novel (*badi'*) invention [i.e. the mechanical clock] should become commonplace in Islamic lands (P.IV: 6). The author adds that [after the failure of two Khorasani scholars to make the clock work], the king and refuge of Islam summoned him with infinite kindness and generosity and said that, 'from the beginning, we knew this delicate matter should be left exclusively to you, and no one else can handle this major task' (P.IV: 7); 'since the lofty desire and concern of that holy one was that this most lowly speck of dust should be the one to demonstrate its construction', I accepted, 'even though I did not see myself worthy.' (P.IV: 8). Then 'this sincere one understood the matter with the initial help and concern of the sultan, and invented instruments and tools without which this work would have been impossible' (P.IV: 9).

The author's detailed account of the work includes something about post-production processes of scientific validation and compensation: first, the king arranged a gathering and made all the notable scholars of insight and discernment attend and recorded it all with his own signature and stamps, that so-and-so had pursued this rare and remarkable matter to completion. He then prepared a report for Bayezid [II], and dispatched the envoy to return with gifts and presents and ordered honours and rewards 'for this nobody in the most perfect manner' (P.IV: 10).

Such reports are not only largely unknown or otherwise unexpected; however isolated the cases they represent, they change some long-held assumptions about an uninformed and unmotivated age, as well as an inactive and ineffective system of support, for both the practical and theoretical sides of a science such as mechanics. The introductory lines above paint a picture of the early tenth/sixteenth century as an age far from scientific dormancy and indifference: that the scholars and patrons of the time were scientifically informed and motivated is indicated by their knowledge of a novel subject such as a clock, from its age-old forms in ancient Greece to its much more advanced stage in early modern Europe; that the figures involved were active and effective in supporting developments in areas such as a mechanical clock is documented through more than one case. In the case of our author, being not only one selected from among a few candidates, but capable of 'inventing instruments and tools' for such challenging work; and in the case of the patron of that work, not only having stated a desire 'to advance such novelties in Islamic lands', but to have allocated funds, made arrangements and taken credit for such undertakings.

What stands out most in the case of mechanics at this late period, as compared with the earlier cases of optics, astronomy and geometry, is the associations with Europe. At least in the branch of the field involving the production of mechanical clocks, references to Europe are not only unprecedented but also explicit: from statements about mechanical 'clocks being particular to European lands' and the expressed wish that this novelty 'becomes commonplace in Islamic regions', to the envoys sent to Europe seeking it, and in-house scholars producing and adjusting it.

It is worth noting that despite the strong scientific tradition in Tabriz, following the foundation of the observatory in Maragha under Tusi's directorship in the thirteenth century, there was no one there who could figure out, let alone construct, such a clock. On his way to Khorasan, the envoy is reported to have arrived in Tabriz where he presented the clock and Gheyas al-Din Mansur [Dashtaki] discussed the matter with the (now deceased) Mowlana Mohibb al-Din Monajjem;[44] but the scholars there could not devise the instruments needed to reproduce it. The envoy therefore assumed that no one could construct one like it even in Herat, where, however, the fortunate blessed (and deceased) king, 'the sultan and shadow of God over the earth', i.e. Soltan-Hoseyn-e Bayqara, had taken up the challenge, and where Hafez Esfahani succeeded in constructing the clock and its mechanisms. The scientific centre had clearly moved eastwards to Herat and Khorasan, although it is worth remembering that two Khorasani scientists had also failed before Esfahani succeeded.

To end this study with the comparative case of optics at this later period, there are parallels with practical mechanics when it comes to explicit references to Europe. But the period piece representing optics at a slightly later period, while confirming exchanges with Europe, presents a puzzle in suggesting an opposite direction for the transfer of knowledge. Striking details come from an anonymous optical text in Persian from a slightly later period, a text only dateable approximately through its reference to the Ottoman sultan Selim I (r. 918–27/1512–20), the son of Bayezid II.[45] The anonymous optical text survives in a short Arabic version, this time naming, in addition to the same patron,

Selim Shah, son of Bayezid, also Sa'dollah b. 'Isa (= Sa'd-e Çelebi: d. ca. 945/1538–39) as the transcriber of the Arabic excerpt (P.VI). The text gives an eye-opening account of the state of the sciences during a period long considered isolated, in a key passage reporting on a 'late' transmission in a direction other than that expected, without the exact time and place reported in either of its two versions. To start with the Persian version, in the words of the author, 'there was a time when scholars (*hokama*) from Europe (*Farangestan*) constructed a high-standing mirror and sent it for experiment (*tajrebi*) and testing (*emtehan*) to the learned (*'olama*) in Khorasan to explain its rationale (*hekmat*)' (P.V. 6).

Unpacking such a striking passage requires a close look at the wording of the above sentence, as well as the successive statements in both the surviving versions. The author of the Persian text, referring to himself as 'insignificant and distressed', first states that he saw in some cities in Khorasan and India a mirror in the hands of some travellers (P.V: 1), one that, if held close to one's face, the face would appear in its natural state (P.V: 2); if held further away, it would appear as 'reflected or inverted' (P.V: 3); and if in the middle position, would not appear at all (P.V: 4). He then goes on to say that 'some practitioners and proponents of wonders and marvels' who would [test] these matters, and seek the knowledge of its rationale and reason (P.V: 5), would refer to 'a time when scholars from Europe' would send such mirrors 'for experiment and testing to the learned in Khorasan to explain their rationale' (P.V: 6); adding that at that time, none of the distinguished scholars could take charge of this matter (P.V: 7), and the few words written on it, were defective and incomplete (P.V: 8). The author then explains that since he 'had pursued the science of optics and catoptrics to the extent of his ability and power', he was asked for the 'explanation of the rationale of that marvellous and wondrous story' (of the mirror), in the 'best and most complete manner', and 'most firm and solid way' (P.V: 9); and significantly, 'after he brought it to the attention of its requesters, they accepted it' (P.V: 10).

The text's anonymous author, while using a modest form of self-address, as customary at the time, must be sought among those specialized enough, not only to have carried out much investigation in optics and catoptrics according to his own words, but to have had the confidence to 'reject the words' (*daf'-e kalam*) of Fadel-e Qushji, whom he calls the 'most distinguished of the later scholars' (*afzal al-mota'akherin*) elsewhere in the text.[46] A possible candidate to consider as author is Miram Çelebi (ca. 880–932/1475–1525), who, besides being a direct descendant of 'Ali Qushji (d. ca. 879/1474), has various overlaps with both the anonymous authors of the bilingual optical text under discussion, from the dates and places of his life to his scientific writings in both Arabic and Persian. An encyclopedia article on 'Mīram Čelebī',[47] which introduces him as the great grandson of 'Ali Qushji,[48] as well as another distinguished figure in Samarqand, Qadizada al-Rumi (d. ca. 844/1440), describes Miram Çelebi as 'becoming the most prominent figure of his time in the mathematical sciences', one asked by Soltan Bayezid II to be his teacher and appointed during the reign of his son, Selim I, as a high official. The fact that Miram Çelebi is credited in the same modern article, in addition to 'works on optics', with 'an important work on hunting' is consistent with the colophon of the Arabic version of the optical treatise as written in a hunting ground with Soltan Selim I in 919/1513 (P.VI: 4–5). Another factor in favour of the above hypothesis is the attribution by the modern author of the same article, of an optical work to Miram Çelebi, titled 'The Rainbow and Halo', subjects considered to be part of optics by that time.[49]

There are other matters to note in the consideration of the latter text, as well as at least one of the bilingual texts under discussion as a work by Miram Çelebi, while some historical facts await further documentation and explanation. First is the fact that the anonymous author specifies, in the Persian version, that he had travelled to 'cities in Khorasan and India', where he observed mirrors which he describes in the hands of some travellers; but the extant Arabic passage does not include either the places of travel or the reference to Europe (*Farangestan*) found in the Persian passage (P.V–VI). Miram Çelebi's reported pilgrimage to Mecca does not place Khorasan and India on his route. But it is also possible that either Çelebi's other travels are not identifiable, or the two versions are not by the same author, including the case that one may be a translation of the other. Second, an anonymous Arabic treatise entitled '*On the Science of Optics*' is catalogued in the inventory of Bayezid II's Royal Library, completed ca. 909/1503–4, one that carries a title closely comparable with the Arabic optical treatise under discussion.[50] If these are the same work, this means the latter was also composed during the reign of Bayezid II and only copied in 919/1513 during the reign of the succeeding sultan, Selim I, when the Persian treatise was supposedly composed as well. This possibility can be supported by the extra words of the Persian passage (P.V: 1, 6), which may be explained either as later additions to the Persian or omissions from the Arabic (P.VI: 1–5).[51]

Whatever the author(s), date(s) of composition, or 'time'(s) of the reported transmissions, what can be concluded from the latest passage under discussion is the existence of a scholarly community with the spirit of inquiry and persistence, as well as communication and validation: the closing lines of both the Arabic and Persian versions refer explicitly to distinguished scholars at the time, whether those who could not fully explain the rationale of some 'wonders' and 'marvels' and requesting it from the text's author, or those for whom the latter's explanation was to be produced stripped from defects and points of contention (P.V–VI: 7–10).

Conclusion

This study started and ended with optics, a subject called 'the best and most perfect of demonstrative sciences' by an author as early as Qusta b. Luqa from the third/ninth century.[52] The sources presented here on the status of optics, confirm that optics had risen above other sciences in at least the two periods from the early eighth/fourteenth to the tenth/sixteenth centuries, on the evidence of key passages datable to those periods (P.I, P.V–VI). In terms of the 'Idea of Iran' as highlighted in this volume, these and other selections in the present chapter do not merely show the flourishing of scientific activities in Persian lands of the time in each case; they are also notable for expressing contemporary awareness of such activities, as indicated by the selections in astronomy and geometry (P.II–III), where the unparalleled nature of mathematics education, and high reach of human capacity in earthly matters, are respectively underscored, not just in 'Persian' lands, but in the Persian language. The final selections of the present chapter, including that on mechanics (P.IV), are notable for yet other indications: they further show that the flourishing of scientific activity was recognized as such by both the neighbouring Ottomans and more distant Europeans; that there was also internal awareness of developments elsewhere; and, above all, that there were explicitly expressed wishes for scientific activities of this slightly later period to become common and continuous in Islamic lands at large.

It will require much more work to advance the subjects and periods covered in the present study not only of optics, but of astronomy, mechanics and geometry, from around the 1300s to the 1500s, and from Maragha to Samarqand and beyond. Given the evidence that, of the 10,000-plus scientific manuscripts documented in Islamic languages, most of them significantly date from the 'late' period, namely 'after the most creative period of Islamic science',[53] selective studies and publications of more period pieces would further illuminate the state of the sciences in the lands of the late Islamic Middle ages in general, and of 'greater Persia' in the Timurid era of this volume, in particular.

Appendix

In this Appendix, my additions and omissions appear within square [ ] and angled < > brackets respectively.

P.I: Preface (Arabic)

كمال الدين فارسى، تنقيح المناظر لذوى الابصار و البصائر

Kamal al-Din Fāresi (d. ca. 718/1318), *Tanqih al-manāzer li-dhowi al-ebsār wa'l-basā'er* (composed ca. 704/130): *Revision of Optics* ...

[1] ... رأيت فى كلام بعض أئمّة الحكمة غير واحد منهم [2] أنّ ...زوايا الاستقامة والانعكاس والنفوذ و الانعطاف كلّها متساوية ... [3] فتحيرت فى هذه الأحكام من أين يأخذها، [4] وبنيت على هذه المقدمة وتفرغت اليها مدة فتفرغت عنها أحكام فى الرؤية بالانعطاف جلّها يخلاف المحسوس، [5] فزادت حيرتى، [6] فراجعت الحضرة وحكيت القصّة [7] وذكرت أيضا زعمهم أنّ رؤيه الكواكب عند الافق أعظم منها فى وسط السماء إنما هى بسبب الانعطاف ... [8] ففكّر ساعة و ثمّ تذكر أنه كان قد رأى فى أوان صباه... فى بعض خزائن الكتب بفارس كتاباً منسوباً الى ابن الهيثم فى المناظر مجلدين كبيرين [9] فقال لعل طلبتک ثم ، وعلى تناوله ولو منوطاً بالثريا... [10] و حصل الكتاب <بخط ابن الهيثم> من أقصى البلاد...

Arabic edition: M. Hejāzi and M. Mokhtār, *Tanqih al-manāzer* ..., pp. 39–51, from pp. 43–45; English translation: A.I. Sabra, 'The Commentary that saved the text', pp. 131–32.

P.II: Letter (Persian)

غياث الدين جمشيد كاشانى، نامه

Gheyās al-Din Jamshid Kāshāni (d. ca. 832/1429), *Nāma* (*Letter*).

[1] ... در بلده سمرقند صانها الله عن الحدثان [2] بندگى حضرت سلطنت پناهى امثال سى هزار دينار كپكى صدقه فرموده بود و فرموده بود كه از آنجمله ده هزار دينار بطلبه دهند.[3] قلمى كردند ده هزار و كسرى طلبه كه مستحق صدقه باشند بقلم آمد كه دايماً بدرس و تحصيل مشغول اند [4] وهمين مقدار در خانهاى خود باشند از بزرگان و بزرگ زادگان [5] و از آنجمله پانصد كس باشند كه ايشانرا در رياضيات شروع است [6] واكنون دوازده سال است كه بندگى حضرت سلطنت پناهى كشور گشايى خلد الله ملكه بدين فن مشغول است [7] هرآينه طلبه هم در آن مايل و ساعى اند وهرچند ميتوانند كوشيد ميكوشند درآن [8] و در بيست موضع درس اين فن ميگويند كه ادنى است از مدرسان اين فن [9] چنانست كه امروز در فارس و عراق مثل او نيست [10] وبيست و چهار مستخرج هستند كه بعضى از آنان هيوى وبعضى نى و بعضى از اقليدس هم شروعى دارند.

Persian transcription: Mohammad Bagheri, *Nāma-hā*, p. 38 (Ms. page, p. 130); English translation: Mohammad Bagheri, 'A newly found letter of al-Kāshī', p. 243.

[2] ... نوبتى ميرزا الغ بيگ امثال سى هزار دينار كپكى صدقه فرموده بودند كه از آنجمله ده هزار [دينار] به طلبه دهند. [3] اسامى طلبه را قلمى كردند، ده هزار و كسرى بود [طلبه] كه بدرس و تدريس مشغول اند [4] وهمين مقدار در خانهاى خود هستند از بزرگان و اولاد ايشان كه محتاج به وظيفه نيستند [5] واز آنجمله پانصد كس برياضيات مشغولند [8] و در بيست وپنج موضع درس اين

فن میگویند [9] ادنای ایشان در فارس و عراق نظیر ندارد [10] و بیست و چهار مستخرجند که بعضی هیوی اند.

Persian transcription of letter excerpts: Mohammad Bagheri, *Nāma-hā*, p. 94 (Ms. pages, pp. 134–35).

P.III: Postscript (Persian)

ابواسحاق کوبنانی، ترجمه کتاب ابي الوفاء محمد بن محمد البوزجاني در اعمال هندسية

Abu Eshāq ebn ʻAbdollāh Kubanāni Yazdi (d. after ca. 888/1483), *Tarjoma-ye Ketāb-e Abi'l-Wafā' Mohammad ebn Mohammad al-Buzjāni Dar Aʻmāl-e handasiya* (composed before ca. 888/1483): *Translation of Abu'l-Wafā' Buzjāni's Geometrical Constructions.*

[1] تم [2] خدای سبحانه وتعالی بنده ضعیف فانی ابواسحاق بن عبدالله کوبنانی یزدی را قوه داد که تیسیر عبر[3] وحل اشکال اشکال این کتاب عجاب [4] بر حسب التماس استاد بشر ویگانه بر هنر که در کارخانه قضا و قدر... مؤثرات افلاک چنان استادی مهندس برسطح کره خاک ندیده بلکه طایر تیز فهم اقلیدس بر شرفات بدایع اعمال او... [5] در شاگردی ودستیاری او انگشت فرمانبری بر دیدگان نهاد [6] الموفق من عندالله شمس الدین ابوبکر شاه بن [7] استاد کامل عالم عامل دانا نجم الدین محمود شاه بن زمح الحاج والمعتمرین حاجی تاج الدین کدوک [8] الی البناء لا سلب مداه در عرض دو ماه تحریر گردد... [9] والتماس از فضلاء روزگار میرود که در مواقع زلل [و] خلل ز سد و رد علل دریغ ندارند و در مداحض غوامض امعان بصر وانعام نظر فرمایند [10] که قابلیت بشر در کارهای زمین تا کجا رسیده...

Persian facsimile reproduction and English translation: Elaheh Kheirandish, 'An early tradition in practical geometry,' pp. 107–10 (Ms. page, p.109).

P.IV: Introduction (Persian)

محمد حافظ اصفهانی، نتیجة الدوله

Mohammad Hāfez Esfahāni (fl. after ca. 880/1475), *Natijat al-dowla* (composed after ca. 918/1512).

مقدمه : در ابداع واختراع این امر بدیع غریب عجیب ... [1] از ایلچی ای که این تحفه را به جانب خراسان آورده بود مسموع گشته ... که این وقت وساعت که تدوین حکمای یونان است و در دیار فرنگ میباشد و مخصوص به ایشان است اگر آن را طلب فرموده هدیه و تحفه خاقان سعید مشارالیه نموده شود بسیار نمایان وعزیز القدر خواهد بود. [2] حضرت پادشاه را این رای صواب و مستحسن نموده رسولی به جانب فرنگ فرستاده جهت طلب داشتن وقت و ساعت مذکور ایشان [3] بنا بر تأکید وصیت آبا واجداد ومبالغه درآن که این امرغریب عجیب را به جانب اسلام نبرند و ایشان نبینند و مخصوص دیار فرنگ باشد ایلچی محروم با دست خالی باز گشته ... چون این امر غریب به جانب روم رسیده حضرت پادشاه اعیان علما و متفطنان اذکیاء زمان را طلب فرموده ... که اهل اسلام به تشریف این علم دقیق و عمل به آن مشرف گردند تا منحصر بدیشان نماند...ایشان...معترف به عجز گشته اند. حضرت پادشاه از مبالغه عذر وعجز علما بسیار متآثر گشته وچون همت وعزیمت آن حضرت این بوده که این تحفه عجیب و هدیه غریب در میان اهل اسلام معمول ومرتب گردد مبلغ دو هزار تنکه به ایلچی که حامل آن بوده به جانب خراسان داده [4] و فرموده که در این مسافت بعید عبور و مرور[که] به شهر های معظم می افتد به هر شهر که رسی اهالی و افاضل و اهل دقت و

خبرت را اعلام نما وایشان را تطمیع کن به این وجه مذکور [5] و اگر کسی در معرض ساختن آن در آید چند وقتی توقف نما بعد از تمام کردن که مسلم گردد وقصوری نداشته باشد وجه مذکور را به او بده و ساخته نیز به او باشد، [6] مقصود آنکه در دیار اسلام این امر بدیع معمول گردد ... [7] دیگر بار حضرت پادشاه اسلام پناه این مخلص را طلب فرمود والتفات وعنایات بی غایت نمود [و] فرمود که در اول حال این امر دقیق را به تو منحصر دانسته بودیم واحدی از عهده این عمده بیرون نمی آید [8] چون همت عالی نهمت آن حضرت بر این بود که این ذره احقر مظهر ساختن آن گردد اگر چه خود را قابل نمی دید اما نظر اکسیر اثر کیمیا ثمر آن حضرت کار کرد... [9] این مخلص به استعانت فاتحه حضرت سلطان وهمت ایشان متوجه این امر گشت وآلات وادواتی چند از سوهان و غیر آن اختراع نمود که این کار بی آن ادوات میسر نمیگردد ... [10] بعد از آن حضرت پادشاه اجلاس عالی فرمود و تمام علمای اعیان واهل بصیرت وامعان حاضر ساخته تذکره و محضری فرمودند و اشراف از جهت وثوق و اعتماد همه موشح به خط و مهر شریف خود فرمودند در آن که فلانی این امر بدیع غریب را تتبع نمود... وحضرت پادشاه مکتوبی نوشت به حضرت پادشاه مبرور <الدرم> بایزید [الثانی] وایلچی را باتحف و هدایا بدان جانب فرستادند وتشریفات وانعامات بر وجه اکمل به این حقیر فرمودند...

Persian edition: Taqi Binesh, *Seh resāla dar ekhterā'āt-i san'ati*, from pp. 11–19.

P.V: Chapter (Persian)

رسالة فی سبب رؤیة الاشیاء وبیان المذاهب فیه وبیان رؤیة الاشیاء فی المرایا المصنوعة
مقالة ثالثة در بیان أحوال بعض مرایا و بیان أسباب آن بنا برمذاهب ثلثة مذکور ...

Anonymous, *Resāla fi sabab ru'yat al-ashyā' wa bayān al-madhāheb fihi wa bayān ru'yat al-ashyā fi'l-marāyā al-masnu'a* (composed ca. 918–927/1512–20). *Treatise on the Cause of the Vision of Objects and the Explanation of Traditions [on Vision] and the Vision of Objects in Constructed Mirrors ... Third Chapter: On the Explanation of the states of some mirrors and the explanation of their causes according to the aforementioned three traditions* (names al-Soltān ebn al-Soltān ebn Selim ebn al-Soltān Bāyazid Khān ebn Mohammad Khān: Selim I).

بر رأی مشکل گشای عقلاء روزگاروضمیر گیتی نمای فضلاء نامدار مخفی نماند که این کمینه پریشان در بعض بلاد خراسان [1] وهندوستان در دست بعض از مسافران زمان آیینه مشاهده کرد که [2] اگر نزدیک روی میداشتند ویرا بوضع طبیعی مینمود [3] واگر دور از روی میشد بوجه انتکاس وانعکاس مینمود [4] واگر در مقام توسط می بود أصلا نمی نمود . [5] و بعضی از أصحاب و احباب استعجاب و استغراب این امر مینمودند و در پی دانستن حکمت و علت وی میشدند [6] ومیگفتند که زمانی از زمان حکما فرنگستان این مرآت عظیم الشأنرا ساخته بر سبیل تجربه و امتحان به نظر علما خراسان فرستاده بودند که تا حکمت آن بیان کرده و به پیش ایشان ارسال فرمایند. [7] ودر آن زمان هیچ کس از فضلاء متصدی این امرنتوانستند گشت [8] وبعد از آن یکی از علمای ذوی الابصار در وجه این ابصار کلمه ای چند سودمند بقلم آورده اما از قصور وناتمامی خالی و عاری نیست [9] و چون این فقیر بینوا در علم مناظر و مرایا بحسب وسع و اقتدار تتبع بسیار کرده بود بطریق ابرام و الحاق التماس و اقتراح نمودند که تا حکمت این قصّه غریبه و <قصه> عجیبه بر وجه اکمل و احسن و بطریق محکم و متعن تحقیق و تنقیح تبیین و توضیح کرده شود [10] پس بنابرآن این شکسته پریشان در بیان حکمت آن کلمه ای چند...بنظر ایشان رسانید وهمه آن فحول تلقی به قبول نمودند...

Persian transcription: Elaheh Kheirandish (unpublished).

P.VI: Chapter (Arabic)

رسالة فى علم المناظر<ة>
المقالة ثالثة فى بيان أحوال بعض المرايا و بيان أسبابها بناء على مذاهب الثلثة المذكورة

Anonymous, *Resāla fi ‘elm al-manāzer. Treatise on the Science of Optics: Third Chapter: On the Explanation of the states of some mirrors and the explanation of their causes according to the aforementioned three traditions.*

[1] اعلم أنّا قد لقينا فى سفرنا بعض المسافرين ورأينا عندهم مرآتا [2] اذا اخدناها قريباً من وجوهنا و رأيناها على الوضع الطبيعى [3] واذا اخذناها بعيدًا عنها رأينا ها على وجه الانعكاس [4] واذا وقعت بين المرآتين المذكورتين لايكون الوجوه فى هذه الحالة مرئية فيها اصلاً [5] ولما شاهدناها كذلك استغرب عنها بعض الاصحاب واستعجب من حكمتها اولوا الالباب [6] وقالوا سمعنا أنّ بعض الحكما صنعوا مثل هذه المرأة و ارسلوا على سبيل التجربه و الامتحان الى العلما والعظام من خراسان لتبيّن لميّتها وتعيين علّتها وحكمتها [7] وفى ذلك الزمان لم يكن واحد من الفضلا متصدّيا الى حلّ ذلك الأمر العظيم [8] و بعد ذلك حرّر واحد من الحكماء فى حلّه كلمات غير خالية الى الفايدة لكن لقصورها عن افادة حقيقتها ما كانت من حيز القبول عند اجلّة الفحول [9] فكتبت بالتماس بعض الاخوان [10] ... فكان بتوفيق الله الاعلى الاجلّ خالياً عن المواضع الخلل و موانع الزلل... [11] تمّت الرسالة على يد الفقير سعد الله بن عيسى غفر الله له و والديه [12] فى ٢١ شهر رجب سنه ٩١٩ [13] بالموضع المسمى بطوكدرمة اداسى من توابع ديمتوقة [14] و هو كان اذ ذاک مخيماً للسطان المظفر سلمشاه بن بايزيد خان [؟ = ثان] خلد الله ملكه [15] أقام فيه ايّاماً لأجل الاصطياد...

Arabic transcription: Elaheh Kheirandish (unpublished).

Notes:

1. The title, 'From Maragha to Samarqand' is adopted from an 'Early Science' exhibit that I curated at Harvard University's Houghton Library in 2008, where two other display cases labelled 'From Alexandria to Baghdad' and 'From Baghdad to Isfahan' reflected the opening titles of two related courses I had offered at the Departments of Classics and Near Eastern Languages and Civilization: Elaheh Kheirandish, 'Windows into Early Science', pp. 66–74. The article includes images and an exhibit write-up, with an excerpt at: http://news.harvard.edu/gazette/story/2008/04/houghton-exhibit-features-islamic-sciences/. The present subtitle, 'Revisiting a Quartet of Scientific Traditions' acts as a sequel to my presentation at London SOAS in 2011 on the occasion of the tenth anniversary of the Soudavar Memorial Foundation: it extends the coverage of the period from ca. 1000 to the 1300s–1500s; see also note 4.
2. The distinction between the historical accounts of the times and places under discussion, as opposed to modern studies, was emphasized by Charles Melville in the introduction to the presentations in the 'Idea of Iran' conference behind this volume.
3. On some early treatments of the 'camera obscura' in the form of '*beyt al-mazlum*' (dark chambers) in the *Book of Optics (Ketāb al-Manāzer)* of Ebn al-Heytham, and the *Revision of Optics (Tanqih al-manāzer)* of Kamāl al-Din Fāresi, see A.I. Sabra, *The Optics of Ibn al-Haytham*, vol. II, pp. li–lii and n. 72; and Elaheh Kheirandish, 'The mixed mathematical sciences', p. 102 and n. 68.
4. Elaheh Kheirandish, 'A quartet of Persian scientific traditions'; see note 1 above.
5. Elaheh Kheirandish with Maera Siddiqi, 'An early science quartet', https://vimeo.com/51476052 [accessed 25 March 2019].
6. Willy Hartner, 'When and how did the impetus of science in Islam come to an end?', pp. 99–120; J.J. Saunders, 'The problem of Islamic decadence', pp. 701–20; A. I. Sabra, 'The appropriation and subsequent naturalization of Greek science in Medieval Islam', pp. 223–43: 'Problem of decline'.
7. On Fāresi, see Roshdi Rashed, 'Kamāl al-Dīn Al-Fārisī', pp. 212–19 (the death date of Fāresi as given by his student in a manuscript copy is 718/1318); Fāresi's Commentary, *Tanqih al-manāzer*, a 'Revision' (*Tanqih*) of Ebn al-Heytham's *Optics*, similarly composed in Arabic, is published in two poor editions in Hyderabad and Cairo. A key passage in the important preface of that work is discussed in Sabra, *The Optics of Ibn al-Haytham*, vol. II, pp. lxxi–lxxii, nn. 112–14; and translated by idem, 'The Commentary that saved the text', pp. 131–33. On the published editions and translations of Ebn al-Heytham's *Optics*, see Ebn al-Heytham, *Ketāb al-manāzer*, Books I–III: On direct vision; Books IV–V: On reflection, and images seen by reflection; Sabra, *The Optics of Ibn al-Haytham*: Books I–III on direct vision; see also Elaheh Kheirandish, 'Light and dark: The checkered history of early optics', pp. 73, 84, n. 9; most of the above sources refer to the book's European transmissions via Latin and Italian translations and a printed edition.
8. Mohammad Bagheri, ed. *Nāma-hā-ye Gheyās al-Din Jamshid Kāshāni beh pedarash*; trans. in 'A newly found letter of al-Kāshī on scientific life in Samarqand', pp. 241–56.

9. On the author and work, see: Elaheh Kheirandish, 'An early tradition in practical geometry', pp. 107–14, and p. 117 for the author's death date as after 888/1483, based on a manuscript that places it later than thought.
10. On the author, see Parviz Mohebbi, 'Ḥāfeẓ Eṣfahāni'. On the work, see Mohammad Hāfez Esfahāni, *Natijat al-dowla*, discussed below.
11. Anonymous treatise in Persian with an Arabic title, *Resāla fi sabab ru'yat al-ashyā' wa bayān al-madhāheb fihi* ..., see Fehmi Edhem Karatay, *Topkapı Sarayı Müzesi kütüphanesi Arapça Yazmalar Kataloğu*, p. 321. On the Persian text, see Elaheh Kheirandish, *The Arabic Version of Euclid's Optics*, vol. I, pt. 1, p. lviii and n. 37; Elaheh Kheirandish, 'Footprints of "experiment" in early Arabic optics', pp. 79–104; and eadem, 'Optics', *Encyclopaedia Iranica*. The Persian text names the Ottoman sultan Selim I (r. 918–27/1512–20) as the son of Bayezid II (r. 886–918/1481–1512), as does a shorter Arabic version also surviving in a unique manuscript in Istanbul (see the note below).
12. The short Arabic treatise, surviving in two folios, is titled *Resāla fi 'elm al-manāzer (Treatise on the Science of Optics)*, not '*al-monāzera*' as transcribed there. The colophon names include sultan Selim I, as the son of Bayezid II, similarly mentioned without his exact relation to the text; the copyist, as well as Sa'dollāh ebn 'Isā (Sa'd ebn 'Isā in the preceding text); Sa'di Çelebi, mentioned on the cover page, is identifiable as the mufti and book collector of Constantinople, d. ca. 945/1538–39). See A. Tashköprüzāde, *Shaqā'eq al- no'māniyya fi 'olamā' al-dowlat al-'othmāniyya*, no. 379. Initial information by Himmet Taşkömür.
13. Sabra, *The Optics of Ibn al-Haytham*, vol. I, p. lxxi; Sabra, 'The Commentary that saved the text', p. 120.
14. Sabra, *The Optics of Ibn al-Haytham*, vol. II, pp. lxx–lxxi, nn. 111–12 (includes the conjecture that Nasir al-Din Tusi was among the 'leading thinkers' mentioned); Sabra, 'The Commentary that saved the text', pp. 131–33, p. 132, translates 'Fārs' as 'Persia'.
15. Sabra, *The Optics of Ibn al-Haytham*, vol. II, p. lxxii, n. 115, includes a list of 12 Arabic manuscripts of Fāresi's *Tanqih al-manāzer*, in addition to the much fewer known or complete copies of Ebn al-Heytham's *Ketāb al-manāzer*, ibid., pp. lxxx–lxxxi; Mostafā Derāyati, *Fehrestvāra-ye dastnevesht-hā-ye Irān (Dinā)*, pp. 374–75, adds six manuscripts in the Libraries of Iran. The same catalogue reports a manuscript in Tehran's Melli Library as 'Ibn al-Haytham's Kitāb al-Manāẓir', vol. 10, p. 36, which my personal examination showed to be yet another copy of Fāresi's *Tanqih al-manāzer*.
16. Aydın Sayılı, *The Observatory in Islam*; Parviz Varjāvand, *Kāvesh-e rasadkhāna-ye Marāgha*.
17. E.S. Kennedy, 'A letter of Jamshīd al-Kāshī', pp. 191–213. This apparently 'second letter' is published more than once: Mohit Tabātabā'i, in *Āmuzesh va Parvaresh*, pp. 9–16 and p. 57 (Persian text); Aydın Sayılı, *Ghiath al-Dīn al-Kāshī's Letter on Ulugh Bey* (Persian text, English and Turkish translation). Bagheri, *Nāmeh-hā-ye Gheyās al-Din Jamshid*, pp. 28–31 (Persian text, pp. 61–74, Ms. pages, pp. 131–33; details and translations in Arabic, Russian and German, pp. 28–31).
18. Bagheri, 'A newly found letter of Al-Kāshī', p. 243; p. 251, n. 5, and Bagheri, *Nāma-hā-ye Gheyās al-Din Jamshid*, p. 51, n. 3, describe the kopaki dinar and toman as common units of money during the Mongol, Timurid and Safavid periods.

The latter, pp. 87–92 includes the Persian text of 'Rarities of Samarqand', attached to one of Kāshi's *Letters*, where the editor refers to an earlier publication in Persian so titled by Mohit Tabātabā'i in *Āmuzesh va Parvaresh*, pp. 55–60, and where, on p. 89, the cost of an elaborate structure is given by Kāshi as 200 kopaki tomān, and a note on the money unit *kapakī* (*sic*) is added on p. 91, n.5, close to the description above.

19. Bagheri, 'A newly found letter of Al-Kāshī', pp. 243–44 (the word for astronomer here: P.II, is from the root of '*hay'a*', configuration; the word *mostakhrej*: P.II, is another uncommon term, which is translated in the published translation above as 'calculator'. The number of teaching places is given in that translation as 12 for the 20 in the original.
20. Kheirandish, 'An early tradition in practical geometry', pp. 79–144, a detailed study of the theoretical, practical, Arabic and Persian traditions of *A'māl al-handasa* (*Geometrical Constructions*), of Abu'l-Wafā' Buzjāni (d. ca. 378–79/998).
21. Kheirandish, 'An early tradition in practical geometry', includes the full text of the postscript signed 'Kubanāni Yazdi' and a section on his letters and writings (pp. 107–13).
22. Kheirandish, 'An early tradition in practical geometry', includes references to the encyclopaedia articles on this figure: Younes Karāmati, 'Abū Isḥāq al-Kūbunānī', pp. 68–71, and Vahid Qanbarinaniz, 'Abu Eshāq Kuhbanāni Kermāni (in Persian in collaboration with Khorshid Qanbarinaniz, 2009). The latter's main author kindly shared with me the manuscripts of Kubanāni's letters.
23. Kheirandish, 'An early tradition in practical geometry', includes a discussion of the relation between the two texts under discussion, and their transcriptions on pp. 117–19.
24. Kheirandish, 'An early tradition in practical geometry', discusses the relation between theoretical and practical aspects of geometry in various parts of the chapter; the important question of that relation is discussed from other angles by Gülru Necipoğlu, 'Ornamental geometries: A Persian compendium at the intersection of the visual arts and mathematical sciences', pp. 11–78, and Jan P. Hogendijk, 'Mathematical classification of the contents of an anonymous Persian compendium on decorative patterns', pp. 145–61.
25. Jan P. Hogendijk, 'Ancient and modern secrets of Isfahan', p. 121.
26. Hāfez Esfahāni, *Natijat al-dowla*, ed. Taqi Binesh, pp. 11–22 (autograph copy: p. 18).
27. Mohebbi, 'Hāfeẓ Eṣfahāni', p. 510.
28. Ibid., pp. 510–11.
29. Majd al-Din Mohammad al-Hoseyni Majdi, active 16th century, *Zinat al-majāles*, p. 772, gives the name of the clock maker simply as Mohammad Mokhtare' and includes a few lines about its mechanical model, position, function and context. Hasan Narāqi, *Tārikh-e ejtmā'i-ye Kāshān*, p. 92 reproduces the passage, including a key phrase missing in the edition, as noted by Charles Melville, 'A mechanical clock in Kashan in the early 17th century', n. 13, (kindly shared with me prior to publication). The phrase itself is relayed by Melville as 'in his day [i.e. about a century later] the mechanism was defective'; the author's words there may also be read as 'in our day, that craft (*san'at*) [i.e. clock making] has become deficient', especially in the context of the next sentence, which refers to 'an illiterate (*ommi*)

figure called 'Ināyat, with an [inferior] construction (*sākhta*), [still] not unworthy of watching'. On the latter character and his construction, see Melville's important essay, 'A mechanical clock in Kashan'.

30. Mohebbi, 'Ḥāfeẓ Eṣfahāni', p. 510 (mentions only the dates of Soltan Bayezid II).
31. Binesh, editor's Introduction, in Hāfez Esfahāni, *Natijat al-dowla*, pp. xiv–xxi, esp. pp. xv–xvii. He also names the various cities within greater Persia where Esfahani worked, from 'Marv, Balkh, Sarakhs and Qum to Yazd, Kashan, Herat and Qandahar'.
32. Cf. Khvāndamir, *Habib al-seyar*, vol. IV, pp. 94–98.
33. Binesh, Introduction, pp. xiv, xx; he appears (p. xv) to equate Soltan-Ahmad with the author's patron concerning the clock and the Khaqan-e Sa'id with the Persian ruler (p. xvii) rather than the Ottoman sultan. Cf. Mohammad Rezā Nurbakhsh, 'Sā'at-e mekāniki dar Iran', pp. 400, 401, citing *Natijat al-dowla*, p. 80. Binesh, p. xx, apparently misunderstands the phrase *'āqebat(-e) mahmud ... zāhir nemishod* (*Natijat*, p. 16) to refer to Soltan-Mahmud (Güregen).
34. Hāfez Esfahāni, *Natijat al-dowla*, p. 7. He also notes earlier successes, such as his first contribution in 882/1477 and the invention of the 'Esfahani key' in 889/1484 (p. 8).
35. Binesh, Introduction, pp. xvii, xx – recording that Hafez Mohammad was in Hesār Shādmān when he heard the news.
36. See Khvāndamir, *Habib al-seyar*, vol. IV, pp. 312–13. Binesh has confused Amir Khosrowshāh with a certain Amir Khosrow, son-in-law of the sayyed, Amir Gheyās al-Din Mohammad. The date 928/1522 is actually the death of Amir Khān, who had murdered Gheyās al-Din, see *Habib al-seyar*, vol. IV, pp. 584, 593–94. The information above has been usefully provided by Professor Charles Melville.
37. Hāfez Esfahāni, *Natijat al-dowla*, has the title "*hazrat padshah*" used interchangeably for the Iranian King (ed. p. 14), and the Ottoman sultan Bāyezid II (App. IV): on pp. 15–16, the author also relates that he was not given the job at first, because he was not a Khorasani and the prestige for being successful should not go to an 'Eraqi, i.e. from western Iran. It is not implied, contrary to the secondary sources noted above, that 'Ali-Shir was the author's patron.
38. Hāfez Esfahāni, *Natijat al-dowla*, p. 8.
39. Binesh, Introduction, p. xv, refers to Gheyās al-Din Mansur Dashtaki as the figure to whom the text is dedicated, though Hāfez Esfahāni himself (p. 13) refers to him as Gheyas al-Dowla wa'l-Donya wa'l-Din Mansur. For Gheyās al-Din Mansur Shirāzi, see Khvāndamir, *Habib al-seyar*, vol. IV, pp. 603–4 and his death in 948/1541 in Hasan Rumlu, *Ahsan al-tavārikh*, pp. 1282–84, where his abortive commission to restore Nasir al-Din Tusi's observatory in Maragha for Shāh Esmā'il is noted. On Mansur Dashtaki, see also Kheirandish, *The Arabic Version of Euclid's Optics*, vol. I, pp. li and lix; Stephen P. Blake, *Time in Early Modern Islam*, pp. 119–20, and nn. 43–44.
40. Blake, *Time in Early Modern Islam*, p. 51, also mentions three clocks by Hafez Esfahani in Herat, Samarqand and Kashan without specific documentation or substantiation.
41. Relevant examples may be found in Nurbakhsh, 'Sā'at-i mekānīkī', pp. 395–408, and 'Iran's early encounter with three medieval European inventions', pp. 549–58; Melville, 'A mechanical clock in Kashan', includes cases in Yazd, Isfahan and

Kashan, significantly distinguishing between different kinds of clocks of the time and their estimated dates: in the case of Kashan, he refers to an endowment deed from 1473, citing an earlier 'inventor of the *vaqt-o sa'at* … evidently a water clock (clepsydra) … testify[ing] ... to a tradition of such devices in Kashan … which might have inspired Hafiz … [Isfahani]'s mechanical (weight driven) version'.

42. I gratefully acknowledge the timely assistance of Professor Charles Melville and Dr Younes Karamati regarding the interpretation of this problematic text, as well as other helpful suggestions: Professor Melville's useful consultation of the relevant primary and secondary sources beyond his capacity as a volume editor, and Dr Karamati's insightful contributions, from his critical distinction between the dating of Esfahāni's construction of the clock, and composition of his *Natijat al-dowla*, to his confirmation of their likely date ranges as detailed in this chapter.
43. There, reference is to the 'hazrat pādshāh-e mabrur ilderem Bāyezid', which must be a mistake on the part of the author or copyist, as it would date back to the much earlier Bayezid I yildirim, 'the thunderbolt' (r. 750–805/1389–1402).
44. Hāfez Esfahāni, *Natijat*, pp. 12–13.
45. Kheirandish, 'The '*Manāẓir*' tradition through Persian sources', p. 130 and n. 23.
46. Elaheh Kheirandish, 'Books on mathematical and mixed-mathematical sciences', n. 42.
47. İhsan Fazlıoğlu, 'Mīram Čelebī: Maḥmūd ibn Quṭb al-Dīn Muḥammad ibn Muḥammad ibn Mūsā Qāḍīzāde', pp. 788–89.
48. Fazlıoğlu, 'Mīram Čelebī', pp. 788–89, adds that 'Mīram Čelebī's father, the scholar Quṭb al-Dīn Muḥammad … came with his grandfather ʿAlī Qūshjī to Istanbul', where the soon deceased Qotb al-Din had married the mother of Miram. Boris A. Rosenfeld and Ekmeleddin Ihsanoglu, *Mathematicians, Astronomers, and other Scholars*, no. 940, p. 316, introduces Miram Çelebi as the 'grandson' not great grandson of the same two figures above, the 'grandson of (Qāḍīzāde) al-Rūmī (no. 808)' (from his son) and of al-Qūshjī (no. 845) (from his daughter)'. The primary source, Tashköprüzāde's *al-Shaqā'eq al-no'māniyya*, pp. 327–28, whose author is mentioned as being 'among the many students of Mīram Čelebī' in Fazlıoğlu's encyclopedia article cited above, has an entry on that figure (no. 252) as well as Qotb al-Din Mohammad (no. 521), where the death date given for both as 931/1524–25 as well as their name sequences make a father–son relationship problematic. The same primary source includes under Qushji (no. 128) a line to the effect that the maternal grandson of Qushji (son of his daughter) was named Qotb al-Din.
49. One of the three manuscript copies of this text in Istanbul (Ayasofia 2414: 1r–37v) was kindly sent to me by İhsan Fazlıoğlu, who attributes the text to Miram Čelebi. The works and list of manuscripts of that author in Rosenfeld and Ihsanoglu, *Mathematicians, Astronomers, and other Scholars*, pp. 316–17, no. 940, excludes the above text and its manuscripts. The cover of the Arabic treatise, entitled *Resāla fi Qows qozah wa'l-hāla (Treatise on Rainbow and Halo)*, carries the name Qādizāda Rumi, penciled next to as 'li (by) Miram Çelebi', while the form 'Mohammad ebn Mohammad ebn Qādizāda al-Rumi' appears inside the text (fol. 2r): the latter form would be closer to the name of Qādizāda Rumi's grandson, assumed to be Qotb al-Din Mohammad ebn Mohammad … Still, it may be safe to consider the text's author as being, not the grandson of Qādizāda, reported to have

died young according to Tashköprüzāde, *al-Shaqā'eq* (*'māta fi shabāb'*), but Miram Çelebi. For the family's details, see the previous note. The self-reference of 'needy' (*faqir*) in this text is exactly the same form used in the Persian anonymous treatise. That Kamāl al-Din Fāresi (d. 718/1318) expanded optics to include rainbows and halos is noted in Sabra, *Optics of Ibn al-Haytham*, vol. II, pp. lxxii–lxxiii.

50. Elaheh Kheirandish, 'Books on mathematical and mixed-mathematical sciences'; Anonymous, *Resālat al-manāzeri men qebali al-hekmati*, Part III, 4.
51. The Arabic colophon contains the name 'Sa'dollāh ibn 'Isā' as the copyist; it is possible to read, though unlikely, that the anonymous author completed, not transcribed, the treatise in the year 919/1513 'while hunting with Selim … [I]'.
52. Kheirandish, 'The mixed mathematical sciences', p. 86; also, Elaheh Kheirandish, 'Qusṭā ibn Lūqā al-Ba'labakkī', pp. 948–49.
53. David A. King, 'Some remarks on Islamic scientific manuscripts and instruments', p. 115.

Bibliography:

Anon., *Resāla fi sabab ru'yat al-ashyā' wa bayān al-madhāheb fihi wa bayān ru'yat al-ashyā fi'l-marāyā al-masnū'a (Treatise on the Cause of the Vision of Objects and the Explanation of Traditions [on Vision] and the Vision of Objects in Constructed Mirrors),* in Fehmi Edhem Karatay, *Topkapı Sarayı Müzesi kütüphanesi Arapça Yazmalar Kataloğu* (Istanbul, 1961), p. 321.

Anon., *Resālat al-manāzeri men qebali al-hekmati (Treatise on Optics Pertaining to Philosophi{cal Subjects})*, [Arabic?]: Part III, 4.

Bagheri, Mohammad, ed., *Nāma-hā-ye Gheyās al-Din Jamshid Kāshāni beh pedarash* (Tehran, 1996); English trans., 'A newly found letter of Al-Kāshī on scientific life in Samarqand', *Historia Mathematica* 24 (1997), pp. 241–56.

Blake, Stephen P., *Time in Early Modern Islam: Calendar, Ceremony, and Chronology in the Safavid, Mughal and Ottoman Empires* (Cambridge: Cambridge University Press, 2013).

Derāyati, Mostafā, *Fehrestvāra-ye dastnevesht-hā-ye Irān (Dinā)*, vol. 3 (Tehran: Ketābkhāna, Muza va markaz-e asnād-e majles-e shurā-ye eslāmi, 1389/2010).

Ebn al-Heytham, *Ketāb al-manāzer*, Books I–III: On direct vision; Books IV–V: On reflection, and images seen by reflection, ed. Abdelhamid I. Sabra, 2 vols (Kuwait: The National Council for Culture, Arts and Letters, 1983–2002).

Esfāhani, Mohammad Hāfez, *Natijat al-dowla,* in *Seh resāla dar ekhterā'āt-e san'ati: sā'at, āsiyā, dastgāh-e rugan kashi natijat al-dowla, ta'lif-e Mohammad Hāfez Esfahāni*, ed. Taqi Binesh (Tehran: Enteshārāt-e Bonyād-e farhang-e Irān, 1350/1971).

Fāresi, Kamāl al-Din, *Tanqih al-manāzer li-dhowi al-ebsār wa'l-basā'er*, 2 vols (Hyderabad: Dā'irat al-Ma'ārif al-'Uthmānīya, 1347–48/1928–30).

— *Tanqih al-manāzer li-dhowi al-ebsār wa'l-basā'er*, part I, ed. M. Hejāzi and M. Mokhtār (Cairo: al-Hay'at al-Mesriya al-'Āmma l'il-Ketāb, 1404/1984).

Fazlıoğlu, İhsan, 'Mīram Čelebī: Maḥmūd ibn Quṭb al-Dīn Muḥammad ibn Muḥammad ibn Mūsā Qāḍīzāde', in *The Biographical Encyclopedia of Astronomers*, ed. Thomas Hockey et al. (New York: Springer Reference, 2007), pp. 788–89.

Hartner, Willy, 'When and how did the impetus of science in Islam come to an end?', in *Introduction to the History of Science: Source Book*, compiled by A.I. Sabra (Cambridge, Massachusetts, 1966), pp. 99–120.

Hogendijk, Jan P., 'Ancient and modern secrets of Isfahan', *Nieuw Archief voor Wiskunde* 2 (2008), p. 121.

— 'Mathematical classification of the contents of an anonymous Persian compendium on decorative patterns', in *The Arts of Ornamental Geometry: A Persian Compendium on Similar and Complementary Interlocking Figures*. Supplements to *Muqarnas*, vol. 13 (Leiden: Brill, 2017), pp. 145–61.

Karāmati, Younes, 'Abū Isḥāq al-Kūbunānī', in *Encyclopaedia Islamica*, ed. Wilferd Madelung and Farhad Daftary (London: Brill, 2009), pp. 155–58, in association with the Institute of Islamic Studies (translated by Farzin Negahbān).

Kennedy, E.S., 'A letter of Jamshīd al-Kāshī to his father: Scientific research and personalities at a fifteenth-century court', *Orientalia* 29 (1960), pp. 191–213.

Kheirandish, Elaheh, *The Arabic Version of Euclid's Optics: Kitāb Uqlīdis fī Ikhtilāf al-manāẓir*, ed. and trans. with Historical Introduction and Commentary, 2 vols. *Sources in the History of Mathematics and Physical Sciences*, no. 16 (New York: Springer-Verlag, 1999).

— 'Qusṭā ibn Lūqā al-Baʿlabakkī', in *The Biographical Encyclopedia of Astronomers (BEA)*, ed. Thomas Hockey et al. (New York: Springer Reference, 2007), pp. 948–49.

— 'Windows into early science', in *Sciences, Crafts, and the Production of Knowledge: Iran and Eastern Islamic Lands (ca. 184–1153 AH/800–1740 CE)*, ed. Carol Bier, Elaheh Kheirandish and Najma al-Din Yousefi. Special Issue of *Journal of the International Society for Iranian Studies* 41, no. 4 (2008), pp. 66–74.

— 'Footprints of "experiment" in early Arabic optics', in *Evidence and Interpretation in Studies on Early Science and Medicine: Essays in Honor of John E. Murdoch*, ed. Edith Dudley Sylla and William R. Newman. Special Issue of *Early Science and Medicine* 14, nos. 1–3 (2009), pp. 79–104.

— 'Optics', in *Encyclopaedia Iranica*, online at www.iranicaonline.org/articles/optics (30 December 2010) [accessed 7 April 2019].

— 'A quartet of Persian scientific traditions: Geometry, astronomy, mechanics, optics', unpublished lecture, *Persian Culture as A World Culture*, Centre for Iranian Studies at SOAS and the Soudavar Memorial Foundation, 4 November 2011.

— 'An early science quartet: Geometry, astronomy, mechanics and optics, ca. 1000 CE', 20 min., co-produced and co-narrated by Maera Siddiqi, as an extension of a 3-minute version to Harvard Film Archives' 'Documentary Shorts' in 2011, https://vimeo.com/51476052 [accessed 25 March 2019].

— 'The mixed mathematical sciences: Optics and mechanics in the Islamic Middle Ages', *The Cambridge History of Science*, vol. 2, *Medieval Science*, ed. David C. Lindberg and Michael H. Shank (Cambridge: Cambridge University Press, 2013), pp. 84–108.

— 'Light and dark: The checkered history of early optics', in *God is the Light of the Heavens and the Earth: Light in Islamic Art and Culture*, ed. Jonathan Bloom and Sheila Blair (New Haven: Yale University Press, 2015), pp. 61–85.

— 'An early tradition in practical geometry: The telling lines of unique Arabic and Persian sources', in *The Art of Ornamental Geometry: A Persian Compendium on Similar and Complementary Interlocking Figures*. Supplements to *Muqarnas*, vol. 13 (2017), pp. 79–144.

— 'Books on mathematical and mixed-mathematical sciences: Arithmetic, geometry, optics and mechanics', in *Treasures of Knowledge: An Inventory of the Ottoman Palace Library Commissioned by Sultan Bayezid II from his Librarian 'Atufi* (Leiden: Brill, forthcoming).

Khvāndamir, Gheyās al-Din, *Habib al-seyar fi tārikh afrād-e bashar*, ed. Jalāl Homā'i and Mohammad Dabir-Seyāqi, 4 vols (Tehran: Khayyām, 1333/1954).

King, David A., 'Some remarks on Islamic scientific manuscripts and instruments and past, present, and future research', in *The Significance of Islamic Manuscripts: Proceedings of Inaugural Conference of Al-Furqan Islamic Heritage Foundation*, ed. John Cooper (London: Al-Furqan Islamic Heritage Foundation, 1992), pp. 115–43.

Majdi, Majd al-Din Mohammad al-Hoseyni, *Zinat al-majāles* (Tehran: Ketābkhāna-ye Sanā'i, 1342/1963).

Melville, Charles, 'A mechanical clock in Kashan in the early 17th century', in *Studia Litteraria Universitatis Iagellonicae Cracoviensis* Special Issue. Volume in Honour of Professor Anna Krasnowolska (2019), pp. 135-41.

Mohebbi, Parviz, 'Ḥafeẓ Eṣfahāni', *Encyclopaedia Iranica*, vol. XI, fasc. 5 (2002), pp. 510–11; online at www.iranicaonline.org/articles/hafez-esfahani [accessed 25 March 2019].

Narāqi, Hasan, *Tārikh-e ejtmā'i-ye Kāshān* (Tehran: Mo'assasa-ye motāle'āt va tahqiqāt-e ejtemā'i, Enteshārāt 42, 1345/1966).

Necipoğlu, Gülru, 'Ornamental geometries: A Persian compendium at the intersection of the visual arts and mathematical sciences', in *The Arts of Ornamental Geometry: A Persian Compendium on Similar and Complementary Interlocking Figures*. Supplements to *Muqarnas*, vol. 13 (Leiden: Brill, 2017), pp. 11–78.

Nurbakhsh, Mohammad Rezā, 'Sā'at-i mekāniki dar Irān', *Ayandeh* 13, no. 6–7 (1366/1987), pp. 395–408.

— (Nourbakhsh), 'Iran's early encounter with three medieval European inventions (875–1153/1479–1740)', Special Issue, ed. Carol Bier, Elaheh Kheirandish and Najm al-Din Yousefi, *Iranian Studies* 41, no. 4 (2008), pp. 549–58.

Qanbarinaniz, Vahid, 'Abu Eshāq Kuhbanāni Kermāni, reyāzidān va monajjem-e bozorg-e qarn-e nohom-e hejri', *'Olum va fonun, ketāb-e māh* 122 (1388/2009), pp. 68–71 (in Persian, in collaboration with Khorshid Qanbarinaniz).

Rashed, Roshdi, 'Kamāl al-Dīn Al-Fārisī (d. Tabriz [?], Iran, 1320)', *Dictionary of Scientific Biography (DSB)* 7 (1973), pp. 212–19.

Rosenfeld, Boris A. and Ekmeleddin Ihsanoglu, *Mathematicians, Astronomers, and other Scholars of Islamic Civilization and their Works (7th–19th c.)* (Istanbul: Research Center for Islamic History, Art and Culture: IRCICA, 2003).

Rumlu, Hasan Beg, *Ahsan al-tavārikh*, ed. 'A. Navā'i, 3 vols (Tehran: Enteshārāt-e asātir, 1384/2005).

Sabra, A.I., 'The appropriation and subsequent naturalization of Greek science in medieval Islam: A preliminary statement', *History of Science* 25, no. 3 (1987), pp. 223–43.

— *The Optics of Ibn al-Haytham*, Books I–III: *On direct vision*, translated with Introduction and Commentary, 2 vols. Studies of the Warburg Institute series, ed. J.B. Trapp (London: Warburg Institute, 1989).

— 'The Commentary that saved the text: The hazardous journey of Ibn al-Haytham's Arabic Optics', *Early Science and Medicine* 12 (2007), pp. 117–33.

Saunders, J.J., 'The problem of Islamic decadence', *Journal of World History* 7 (1968), pp. 701–20.

Sayılı, Aydın, *Ghiath al-Dīn al-Kāshī's Letter on Ulugh Bey and the Scientific Activity in Samarqand*; Persian text, English and Turkish translation (Ankara, 1960).

— *The Observatory in Islam and its Place in the General History of the Observatory* (Ankara, Türk Tarih Kurumu Basımevi, 1960; 2nd edn, 1988).

Tabātabā'i, Mohit, 'Navādir-e Samarqand', *Āmuzesh va Parvaresh* 10, no. 3 (Tehran: Vezārat-i farhang, 1319/1940), pp. 9–16 and p. 57 (Persian text).

Tashköprüzāde, A., *al-Shaqā'eq al-no'māniyya fi 'olamā' al-dowlat al-'othmāniyya*, ed. Ahmed Subhi Furat (Istanbul: Üniversitesi, Edebiyal Falailtesi Yayinlare, 1985).

Varjāvand, Parviz, *Kāvesh-e rasadkhāna-ye Marāgha* (Tehran: Amir Kabir, 1366/1987).

Index:

Page numbers in italics refer to illustrations; 'n' after a page number indicates the endnote number.

A

B

C

H

L

N

P

Q

R

S